MEMORY!

HOW TO REMEMBER ANYTHING

Paul Mellor

∞INFINITY
PUBLISHING

Copyright © 2011 by Paul Mellor

ISBN 978-0-7414-6844-4 Paperback
ISBN 978-0-7414-9298-2 eBook

Printed in the United States of America

Published October 2012

∞

INFINITY PUBLISHING
1094 New DeHaven Street, Suite 100
West Conshohocken, PA 19428-2713
Toll-free (877) BUY BOOK
Local Phone (610) 941-9999
Fax (610) 941-9959
Info@buybooksontheweb.com
www.buybooksontheweb.com

To Max and Ben

Christmas Eve babies who are babies no more.
May you continue to exercise your mind.
It will take you wherever you want to go.

Acknowledgements

I thank my parents, Don and Helen Mellor, who instilled in me the love of learning and the importance of memory. My dad can still recall his high school locker combination. My mom can still rattle off the 50 states in alphabetical order in less than 60 seconds. Impressive indeed, but what's more impressive about these WWII veterans is their zest for life, their positive attitude, and their wonderful sense of humor. I hope my brain is just as healthy when I'm in my 90's.

I thank my teachers from grade school to college, who reminded me to study up. I thank *Toastmasters International*, an organization that helped me speak up.

I owe a big thank you to Janet Frick, who developed the layout of this book. She was always pleasant, cheerful, and patient with my many changes, as she was with my first book.

A huge thank you goes to Sherry Marcini, who is beauty and brilliant in every way. I thank you for your assistance in editing, artwork, and counsel. From cover to cover, your presence is felt on every page. I appreciate you immensely, and for your professional approach on this project that you spent months working on.

I thank Lawrence Stutts, Caroline Baltzell, Kaity Baltzell, and Malorie Matos for your valuable input in helping me write this important book.

I thank Tony Dottino, founder of the *USA Memory Championship*, who has helped spread the importance of memory training throughout the country.

I thank the hundreds of associations and corporations who have contacted me to speak on Memory. Oh, how I love what I do.

Table of Contents

Chapter 5

Chapter 6

Chapter 7

Chapter 8

Chapter 9

Chapter 10

Introduction

E very day millions of people pace. While looking down at the floor or up at the ceiling, they walk and wonder. They ask themselves any one of many questions ...

"Did I turn the iron off?"

"Did I turn the security system on?"

"Where did I put my glasses down?"

"Where's the checkbook going to turn up?"

"Where were my keys left?"

"What I told him, was it right?"

They rack their brain looking for that misplaced file, scratch their head trying to recall the name, and believe they've lost their mind when they can't remember where they parked.

If I could only remember. That's a statement millions of people say. Yet, the solution is so close it's frustrating. It's something that slipped their mind, something they can't put a finger on, and something that winds up on the tip of their tongue. Are you one of these people, or don't you remember?

As one who teaches memory skills throughout the United States, I'm amazed at the raised hands I see after I ask, "Who thinks they have a bad memory?" Many of those hands are young. They're from people who are well educated, yet frustrated thinking they're losing their mind. They can't recall names, could never speak without notes, and often lose track of their parked cars. Nothing wrong with taking the bus, I say. Of course, there's pressure remembering when to get off.

From Atlanta to Anchorage, from Hartford to Honolulu, and from Miami to Minneapolis, I've witnessed a lot of raised hands from people who struggle with their memory. If there were only a magic pill that would eliminate forgetfulness. Oh, what the demand would be.

Pharmaceutical companies are trying. They're rushing to develop a product that would lick our memory deficiencies; a pill helping us find our way through life. No doubt, the line would stretch longer than those waiting to purchase the latest *iPhone.*

There are products on the market claiming to improve memory. Whether it's an herb or energy booster, every drugstore has something that states they can bolster the brain with the words *improves memory* printed somewhere on the packaging.

If the products worked, would we still need to hide our spare key? Would we still call our neighbor, "*What's-his-name*"? Would statements such as "*I know it's here somewhere*" be a thing of the past? Unfortunately, those comments will probably never go out of style and there will always be a *What's-his-name* living on every block.

I believe we don't need pills to remember. I believe everyone with a healthy brain can improve their memory tenfold. I believe that because I've seen it. It's happened to me. It can happen to you.

I once believed people were born with either a good memory or a bad memory. Hey, some people just had it. However, for the ones who hadn't, it gave them a legitimate excuse when telling their teacher they had forgotten their homework. I never used that excuse. I had a dog, instead.

In school, the word *memory* was never one of my teacher's favorite words. "Don't memorize it," she would say. "I want you to know it." I think her belief was that trying to memorize information puts the mind in a trance. Perhaps she thought, the needed information entered our head only during test time. Then, it would fade into a distant memory never to come back again. Perhaps she thought, it was a shortcut to learning and we would be cheating ourselves if we memorized it instead of knowing it.

If *memorization* and *shortcuts* were so bad, why did my teacher apply them? I've long left Eden Park Elementary School, but I can recall her teaching the music scale by saying, "*Every Good Boy Does Fine.*"

I also recall when she taught us the names of the five Great Lakes. Think *HOMES* and you'll remember. I did and it worked. It was *Erie* how *Superior* my mind would be. My teacher helped me remember the information by making me understand the information. I could grasp it.

It wasn't until I joined the *Richmond Toastmasters Club* that I became interested in learning about Memory. *Toastmasters*, a world-wide organization founded in 1924, helps people develop and polish their communication skills. *Toastmasters* was a big part of my life. I enjoyed writing, rehearsing, and giving speeches. I gave speeches on a wide range of topics, but never had a genuine passion for any of the subject matter.

However, on December 31st, 1994, while others were anticipating their passion at the stroke of midnight, I was meeting mine. It was on a shelf at the Bon Air Library in Richmond, Virginia.

I found *The Memory Book*, by Harry Lorayne and Jerry Lucas. I remembered my mother had checked the book out from her library years earlier while I was living in Cranston, Rhode Island. She's a voracious reader and *The Memory Book* was in the middle of one of her stacks. I flipped through it, but never spent time reading it. However, on that last day in '94 I brought the book home. This time I read it.

I found a topic that can help everyone; one that could certainly help me. Everything we do involves memory. By learning to strengthen it we become more powerful, more productive, and more persuasive.

I believe memory is the most important topic there is, yet often overlooked. Who wouldn't want to improve their memory? I learned the same techniques for remembering numbers or names can be used for beating absent-mindedness, giving speeches without notes, helping one recall Bible verses, and remembering playing cards. It can help in every aspect of your life.

Yes, I have a genuine passion for this topic, and learned that trying to remember doesn't have to be difficult. It can be fun. The best part is the answers to our memory problems are all in our head.

Chapter 1

The Basics

Learning From Our Dictionary

L ook up the word *patriot* in a dictionary. You'll find it in less than 30 seconds.

Dictionaries are organized, with each entry listed in alphabetical order. It makes no difference if you were holding a pocket-sized edition, or flipping through the big one at the downtown library, you would find it easily.

As long as you know how to spell the word, you'd locate it promptly. It also wouldn't matter if you were asked to look up the word *pumpernickel* or *hemisphere* or *fondue* or *trumpet*, you'd turn to it quickly.

How much time would it take finding those same words in a different book? Instead of a dictionary, this book lists words in no particular order, has no table of contents, index, or glossary, making your task more difficult. You wouldn't know where to look. You'd flip to this page and that page searching for the word in question.

The only way to find the word is to start at the beginning. You'd have to read the first page, the second page, the third page, and so on, until Presto! You found it! It's similar to walking into another room of our home, not remembering why we entered. So what do we do? We go back to where we started, hoping to get back on track. Dictionaries are always on track.

I am grateful to Noah Webster. That big book of his is always at arm's length when I'm in my office. With the help of Mr. Webster, I am a freak of nature. Give me a word and I will locate it in seconds from his 1600-page tome.

If Webster's words were thrown into the book haphazardly, it would be a book seldom used. If *thunder* were next to *cantaloupe* and *jungle* were next to *yodel*, who would have time to hunt for those words? There's no order. We know the words are in there, but not even a SWAT team could get them out.

Our minds can be like that. We struggle to think of the actor who won the *Academy Award* a few years earlier. "I know his name, but I can't think of it now." Sound familiar?

Noah Webster spent 27 years compiling his dictionary, with words strategically placed in a way we could instantly find them. *Thunder, cantaloupe, jungle,* and *yodel,* you say? No problem. They're on pages 1494, 215, 776, and 1661, respectively.

It may have seemed laborious putting those words in order, but look at the benefits. Any word needed could be found immediately. To find a word, one didn't need to memorize the pages, but simply the 26 letters of the alphabet. It's a system that works. A system is what memory training is all about.

If memory were like trying to memorize a 1600-page volume, with words in no particular order, it would be mind-numbing. Instead, we're going to develop a system similar to Noah Webster's. It's easy to learn, yet won't take 27 years to develop. To get started, we must highlight one of Mr. Webster's words. In my dictionary it's on page 51. The word is *anchor.*

Know Your Anchors

According to *Webster's,* the word *anchor* means anything that gives or seems to give stability or security; to keep from drifting.

I became aware of the importance of anchors as a young boy. My grandfather, Chester Phillips, often took my sister and me fishing off the Massachusetts coast, near Plymouth. If he had neglected the anchor, I may be speaking Portuguese now.

There were a lot of anchors on those fishing expeditions. The obvious one was the apparatus tied to a rope that plunged to the ocean floor. That anchor kept the boat in place. The seat was another type of anchor. It gave me the stability to keep me in place. The fishhook was an anchor. It kept the worm in place. The lighthouse was an anchor. It led us back to port.

The world is full of anchors. To the pilot, it's the runway. To the hunter, it's the scope. To the coffee drinker, it's the mug. It's the starting point keeping us on course.

When we're interrupted during a conversation, our mind searches for an anchor when we ask, "What was the last thing I was talking about?" When we misplace out keys, our mind looks to an anchor as we retrace our steps and ask, "Where was I?" When we drive on country roads, not sure to take the turn, our anchor is the red barn, or better yet, the GPS.

Sadly, many people have lost their anchors. Those who suffer from Alzheimer's have not only lost their keys, they may not know what the key is for. For some, a remote control is just a stick with buttons, a bar of soap is just something that smells, and a loved one may be just a stranger in the room.

Human beings need anchors to function. Without anchors, the simplest question is virtually impossible to answer. Here are a few:

Guess which number I'm thinking of?
Guess which movie I watched last night?
Can we meet in Texas?

If you guessed *817* you answered the first question correctly. If not, don't feel badly. The only anchor provided was that it was a number. A question using a better anchor would have been, "Which number am I thinking of between 816 and 818?"

For the second question, if you had guessed *ET*, fix yourself some popcorn. You're correct, but how would you have known? It would have helped if someone provided an anchor by saying, "It's the letter right after *d*, and the one immediately before *u*."

Can we meet in Texas? Yes I'd love to, but where? Which county, which city, which corner? Give me an anchor.

There have been a few times, before the use of cell phones, I had planned to meet someone at a location, but each time waited several minutes until we located one another. Whether it was my buddy in a restaurant parking lot, my parents outside a bus station, or my cousin at a ballpark, several minutes had elapsed because we hadn't settled on a specific spot, and therefore couldn't find one another.

Since those occasions, I've learned to give exact locations to meet someone. Anchors have kept me straight.

Knowing my anchors, I can count to one hundred in less than 60 seconds. If I talk really, really fast I can do it in half that time, but I would need to go in the order of 1, 2, 3, 4, 5, 6, 7, 8, 9, 10, 11…98, 99, 100. If I started at 35, then went to 8 and then to 11 and then to 73, I would be unsure of myself if 23 or 62 were mentioned. I would have to rely a lot on my memory. I would need a very, very good memory to recall all those numbers without repeating or omitting the others.

I don't like to rely on my memory. I prefer to develop strong anchors to take the pressure off remembering. That's why in Mr. Webster's dictionary, I turn to page 86. It's there I find the word *association*.

Association Do's

It's Christmas morning when your teenager opens the gift box with the car keys. Stand back and grab your angel; not him, the one on top of the tree. Johnny is going bonkers. The power of association has an amazing grip on people. Did anyone tell your son he only got keys? Who said he's getting a car? His association juices got the better of him.

Your boss just phoned. She wants to see you in the morning. Why is your head spinning after learning about the call?

It's your surgeon's first day on the job. Your surgeon's first day? Why are your first thoughts to phone your priest?

Everything we do links with association. A mop is an association with cleaning. A pencil is an association with writing, a chair with sitting, an oven with baking, a tub with bathing, a doorbell with alerting, and the Division of Motor Vehicles with … waiting.

It's a never ending list how much association comes into play, and how fast we react to it. For instance, a woman with a baby is sitting next to you on a cross country flight. With that in mind, you associate irritability, fussing, and crying. Then, you wonder what the baby will do.

To build a better memory we must harness the power of association. Try memorizing the following lists:

List #1

Egg, eggshell, Shell gasoline, Gasoline Alley, alley cat, catfish, fishbowl, bowling ball, ball of fire, firetruck.

List #2

Firetruck, bowling ball, egg, alley cat, Gasoline Alley, eggshell, ball of fire, fishbowl, Shell gasoline, catfish.

Can you tell the difference between the lists? List #1 flowed. It rolled off our tongue. When we got to *egg* we automatically shifted to *eggshell*. Once we got to *eggshell* we pulled into *Shell gasoline*. From *Shell gasoline*, we didn't think about *eggshell* anymore. Instead, our mind went to *Gasoline Alley*. It was easy because we associated one word into another.

When we got to *fishbowl* our mind leaped to *bowling ball*. If we got interrupted during the reciting of this list, we'd stop and search for our anchor, by asking, "Where was I?" Psst, bowling ball. "Oh, that reminds me, the next words are *ball of fire*."

It would have taken much longer to memorize this list without anchors and associations. Each one of those words, beginning with *egg*, was an anchor at one time. After *egg* was an anchor, *eggshell* took its place. With the power of association, that reminded us the next word was *Shell gasoline*. Then, *Gasoline Alley* was an anchor, which by association reminded us that *alley cat* were the next words.

Anchors are the starting point. We would wander without them.

Using the power of anchors and association, recall the series of words, beginning with the anchor *egg*, _____, _____, _____, *alley cat*, _____, _____, *bowling ball*, _____, *firetruck*.

The retracing of our steps, after we forgot why we walked into another room of our home, is the anchor which helps us remember. Also, the comment, "Where was I?", asked after being interrupted, is the question that leads us to the anchor. It helps us get back on track with the conversation.

In List #2, the words were not in an order we could grasp. It was difficult to recall *bowling ball* came after *firetruck*, or *Shell gasoline* came after *fishbowl*. We would need a supercharged memory to recite those words in order.

Unfortunately, life is more like List #2, than #1. We have lists to remember, tasks to perform, and topics to address that don't flow as easily as A, B, C. Therefore, *anchor* and *association* need a little more assistance. With the inclusion of *exaggeration* we can make any list flow effortlessly.

Exaggeration Alert

The cow jumped over the moon. London Bridge is falling down. My Bonnie lies over the ocean. (Hey Bonnie, I told you not to walk over London Bridge).

Let's not forget about Humpty Dumpty on a brick wall, the little old woman who lived in a shoe, and that bough that's about to break.

No wonder kids are running away from home. Do we really think our child is going to drift into a pleasant sleep after listening to those bedtime stories?

Those classic nursery rhymes have one thing in common: they're exaggerated stories that stay with us generation after generation. If

Humpty Dumpy didn't fall, if the bough didn't break, and if the old woman lived in a convalescent home, who would remember?

Exaggeration doesn't just live in story books. It is found on the front pages of our newspapers and on the evening news. It's the fire on Main Street, the murder on Elm, and the day the circus came to town. It's the story that's different, out of the norm, and one that catches our attention.

There are many people, myself included, still keeping the newspaper of September 12, 2001. Spectacular events, happy or sad, remain fixed in our memories. Dates, not only September 11, 2001, but also November 22, 1963, and December 7, 1941, will always and should be remembered.

In my seminars, I ask attendees what they were doing on that November day in 1963. Many people remember. I hear, "I was taking a spelling test." "I was watching my mother iron a shirt." "I was reading my law book in class." "I was in a diner in downtown Indianapolis." "I was talking to my friend, Ellen." They recite their actions with conviction and with no hesitation.

One Texas gentleman I asked knew exactly where he was on November 22, 1963. He and his 5th grade class were standing on a curb in downtown Dallas, Texas. He remembers waving to the President of the United States. Shortly after returning to school, he learned what the rest of America knew.

Those who remember the Kennedy assassination apply anchors and association. I was somewhat surprised when one senior citizen couldn't recall what he was doing on November 22, 1963. "No idea," he said. "Are you sure?" I asked, finishing the sentence with "JFK." "Oh, now I remember," he replied. "I was walking down the hallway. I was holding a cup of coffee …"

When I mentioned *JFK* it anchored his memory to that tragic event. He was able to associate that horror to what he was doing when he heard the news. He couldn't recall what he was doing the day before or after that November day, but when the President was assassinated, he remembered. That was the anchor.

It's not only tragedy taking hold of our memory, but other extraordinary events, as well. We vividly remember the day we got married, the game winning hit, finishing a marathon, and the birth of our child (shot par that day).

Why can we recall, with such clarity, events that happened so long ago, but not events that happened yesterday or the day before? The mundane just doesn't cut it. We tend to recall the bizarre, unusual, and extraordinary event much easier than the routine.

It's very difficult, if not impossible, to visualize two things at the same time. We're able to think of things very quickly, but unless the images are connected, it's unusual to pull off this feat.

In your "mind's eye" visualize your *mattress*, your *sink*, a *police car*, a *basketball*, an *elephant*, and a *trampoline*.

Did your mind move from one image to the next? If so, it probably zipped at top speed. You visualized those images quickly, but "saw" them one at a time. There is no correlation with any of those six objects. Therefore, there is no association, and we desperately need that *A* word to remember.

Here's another memory test. Visualize a *fish* and a *hook*. Imagine a *clown* and a *balloon*. Now, picture an *umbrella* and *rain*. This section is easier to recall, because there's an association. We can picture the fish attached to the hook, we can mentally see the clown holding colorful balloons, and we can catch sight of the rain pounding the umbrella.

If the words were rearranged, we would have to create an association using exaggeration. For instance, try to memorize the order now: *umbrella, balloon, fish, clown, rain,* and *hook*.

The anchor is the *umbrella*; that's the starting point. The next word is *balloon*, which we have to connect to the anchor. Since there is no im-

9

mediate association between the two, we'll utilize exaggeration to bring the words together.

The image is exaggerated when we put the *umbrella* into the *balloon's* world or vice versa. For instance, imagine *balloons*, with some escaping through an opening, under an *umbrella*. That's weird.

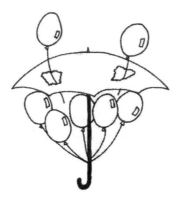

Other images include: *balloons* stuck to an *umbrella*; opening an *umbrella* with hundreds of *balloons* flying out; an *umbrella* popping *balloons*; an *umbrella* inside a huge *balloon*; or a hot air *balloon* shaped like an *umbrella*.

From *umbrella* we associate *balloon*. *Balloon* is now the anchor. That's what we know. Next, an association must be made to remember *fish*. Using exaggeration, we can mentally see a *balloon* catching a fish. Or, we can mentally see *fish* stuck in *balloons*.

The anchor moves to *fish*. The next word is *clown*. Imagine a *clown* eaten by a *fish* or a *clown* with a *fish* head.

Now, the *clown* takes over the anchor. Note we're not bringing the other words into play. We're not thinking about *umbrella*, *balloon*, or *fish* again. We'll think of them only if called upon. Instead, we're linking only two words at a time.

Clown to *rain*. Imagine *clowns* dancing in the *rain*. Visualize *rain* puddles of *clowns* or it's *raining clowns*.

The anchor moves to *rain*. *Rain* to *hook*. Imagine it's raining *hooks*. This will keep the kids from going to school.

Yes, the images are strange. Yes, there will probably never be a time when you have to remember an umbrella held by balloons. However, life comes at you fast, and you have to be fast to be able to remember lists and tasks and speeches and names and a lot of everything else.

Mentally seeing exaggerated images is effective brain training. The remaining pages go into specifics, but it's imperative to acquire this memory principal of success: the use of exaggeration is paramount. I am not exaggerating.

Visual Cues

It's easier to remember words, such as *hot dog*, *police car*, *mattress*, and *balloon* than the words *vital*, *totally*, *gripe*, and *exact*. Visuals are memorable. They have texture, shape, and color.

Rarely do you see empty red, double-decker buses on the streets of New York or short lines for Chicago's boat tours. People pay money to experience the sights.

Sights are memorable. Words are not. For instance, take the word *giraffe*. Don't visualize the tall, dark orange, brown and white animal with the 18-inch tongue leaning over to pluck green leaves off a tree. Instead, visualize the letter *i* between the letters *g* and *r*. Can you do that?

How powerful is your mind? It's more powerful than the computer sitting on your desk, or the one held in your hand. Ask the computer to conjure up a picture of a *giraffe* and the wait begins. First, you have to turn the machine on; second, you have to let it warm up; third, you have to log in; fourth, you have to type *giraffe*; and fifth, you have to wait. How long did it take your brain to see the African animal? It's no contest. The brain wins.

Seeing the image in our "mind's eye" helps us retain the information. We can visualize the Golden Gate Bridge or the golden fields of Kansas. We can picture our grandparent's home, the corner store, and a ballet dancer on stage. We can taste the lemon, smell the bread, and cringe when the fingernails approach the chalkboard. Our memories are in pictures and we develop them each day.

The following exercise helps you narrow an image from vague and fuzzy, to one that is crystal clear.

Vague Image	*Clearer Image*
nutrition	apple
wood	rocking chair
transportation	taxi
pottery	clay pot
fluffy	pillow
height	ladder

Continue with the remaining list:

bounce	_____
bright	_____
hurry	_____
slow	_____
wake-up call	_____

Once you come up with an image, it's easier to connect it to something you already know.

So far, with remembering each list, we never attempted to remember more than two things at the same time. Remember? We went from *egg* to *eggshell* to *Shell gasoline*. When we got to *gasoline* we automatically recalled *Gasoline Alley*, without holding onto the previous words.

We remembered *umbrella* held by *balloons*. Then, we remembered *balloons* connected to the *fish*. From *fish* we mentally saw the *clown*.

Just like reciting our *ABC's* or counting to 100, we never need to connect more than two items at the same time. A trained mind is like a dictionary with anchors along the way, attaching new information to what we already know.

Chapter 2

The Anchors

Loci Method

L ocation, location, location. That's something any realtor says is most important. Memory experts say the same. One anchor system, known as Loci, has been utilized for ages and is still in use today when we utter the phrase, "in the first place."

Long before the tape recorder, fax machine, telephone, and computer, information had to be remembered. The ancient Romans could memorize lengthy speeches by mentally associating parts of their speech with objects in their home.

For example, the first part of their speech would be associated with their door; the second part with a table; the third part with a vase or column or statue. By going in order, orators didn't need notes, because they were able to make exaggerated associations with each object.

This method is not only effective with speeches, but also with tasks and lists.

To construct a Loci Method of your own, write down ten objects in one room of your home. Choose these items while you're away from the room you're going to use. This way, you're able to focus while visualizing them in their particular location. These items will act as anchors helping you recall information.

Choose items that are stationary, instead of items that will be moved or discarded, such as the rolled up napkin on the counter or the newspaper on the table. Be specific with each object. For instance, focus on the handle of the refrigerator, not the entire appliance; the cooking rack instead of the entire oven; or the rotating plate instead of the microwave itself.

Other possible objects include, *trash can, flowerpot, dishwasher, wall painting, faucet, blender,* and *toaster.*

To get started, begin in the kitchen.

Object # 1 _____   Object # 6 _____

Object # 2 _____   Object # 7 _____

Object # 3 _____   Object # 8 _____

Object # 4 _____   Object # 9 _____

Object # 5 _____   Object #10 _____

After you finish writing these anchors, turn your eyes from the words and visualize each object. The end result is being able to mentally see each item, in order, quickly. Practice until you can visualize your anchors in less than ten seconds. It's imperative you know your anchors.

Once your anchors are in place, you can retain any list of items by associating what you want remembered with that anchor.

Let's attempt to memorize these ten objects: *paintbrush, flowers, hat, newspaper, marshmallows, parachute, penguin, horseshoe, frog,* and *trombone.*

Visualize the first object in your kitchen, and associate it with the first object from our list (*paintbrush*). Exaggerate the image by enlarging the *paintbrush* and dumping gallons of paint on your first anchor. See it in your "mind's eye." Afterward, visualize your next anchor and associate that object with the next object on the list (*flowers*).

If your anchor is *faucet*, imagine the *flowers* spewing out of the faucet. The exaggeration, coupled with the action of the *flowers* exiting the spout, is an image that's memorable. It's too mundane if our visual were watering the *flowers* from the sink.

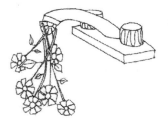

There should be no confusion if an item on your list is also one of your anchors. For instance, if you wanted to remember *flowers*, and *flowers* was one of your anchors, then just imagine your lovely *flowers* attacked by another set of *flowers*.

Moving to the next Loci we come to the *dishwasher*. We look inside and what do we see? Of course, it's a huge hat.

After *dishwasher* our next anchor may be the *candle* on the counter. If so, then visualize *candle* with the next object to be remembered (*newspaper*).

Associate the remaining six objects to each one of your anchors. Make sure you visualize those objects colliding with each anchor. Use a lot of action and make it ridiculous. It's the ridiculous that helps us remember.

When you need to remember your list, just look to your anchor and your image will show up in living color.

Once you have your ten anchors, write down ten more from another room. Focus on fixed objects, such as *lamp, fireplace, bureau,* or *ceiling fan.* It won't take long before you have 50 or more anchors. Don't despair if you have a small home with few objects. If you have only a refrigerator you already have ten objects. You have the *butter,* the *mustard jar, ice cream carton, head of lettuce, frozen dinner, Dr. Pepper, Chinese take-out, pizza slice, spoiled milk,* and the empty *ice tray* that you keep forgetting to fill.

Some of my anchors are on my college campus, my childhood home, and homes of people I know. Any object can be an anchor, as long as they can be organized in your mind. Even if you rearrange your furniture or restock your refrigerator, you'll still be able to recall your anchors. Periodically, mentally revisit those anchors beginning … *in the first place.*

When you want to remember a different list, you won't be confused by what you had originally placed there. Your memory will naturally kick in, as long as you use the techniques of exaggeration.

The Loci Method works because it anchors your memory, not allowing it to drift, since you know where to look.

When remembering a list, most people try to stack the information. They try to remember too many things at once. A trained memory is like a dictionary or efficient filing system. Once you have preset anchors, you can attach anything you need remembered to that anchor.

Body Anchor Method

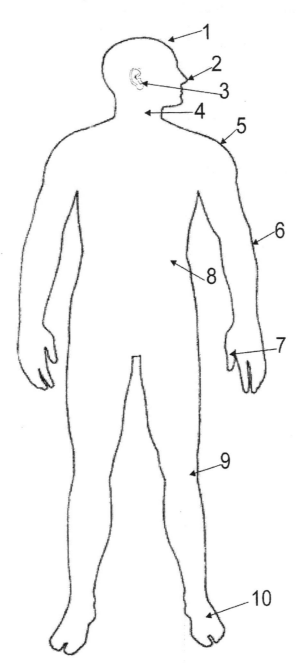

This system works well, because you're always with half of what you need to remember. It follows you wherever you go. It makes no difference if you're at the gym, in the pool, at work, on the couch, or on a plane. The Body Anchor Method is a memory aid you can't get rid of. Unless you have an out of body experience.

1 represents your *head*

2 represents your *nose*

3 represents your *ear*

4 represents your *neck*

5 represents your *shoulder*

6 represents your *elbow*

7 represents your *thumb*

8 represents your *waist*

9 represents your *knee*

#10 represents your *foot*

Associate what you need to remember with each body part.

Let's try it. Here's our list…

(1)   Plant <u>flowers</u>
(2)   Order <u>tickets</u>
(3)   Buy <u>birthday</u> card
(4)   Set <u>dental</u> appointment
(5)   Buy <u>peanuts</u>
(6)   Drop off <u>shirts</u> at cleaners
(7)   Get <u>oil</u> changed in car
(8)   Return library <u>book</u>
(9)   Call <u>plumber</u>
(10)   Make <u>bank</u> deposit

To remember the list, associate each numbered body part with a task in a very ridiculous manner. Focus and visualize:

~ *Flowers* drooping over your *head.*

~ *Tickets* flying out of your *nose.*

~ Birthday *cards* hanging from your *ears.*

~ *Teeth* sticking into your *neck.*

~ *Peanuts* spinning around your *shoulder.*

~ *Shirts* wrapped around your *elbow.*

~ *Oil* dripping from your *thumb.* Although that could happen, a better image may be using your *thumb,* instead of the dipstick, to check the oil.

~ *Books* hanging from your *waist.*

~ *Plunger* swinging from your *knee.*

~ *Piggy bank* spinning on your *foot.*

A constant companion with these associations was action. Did you notice? The objects weren't just lounging around, they were doing something. They were hanging, dripping, or swinging. They were flying or sticking or wrapping. With action we remember.

We experience action at concerts. The performers don't stand still, they move, dance, and jump. The stage moves too, with its flashing lights and neon signs. All that movement makes the experience memorable. Our minds notice when objects move.

In the early days, Las Vegas casinos lured customers with its flashing lights and neon signs, too. Today, they've taken it a step further. They've added towering fountains that seem to dance in front of your eyes. They have volcanic explosions where you can feel the heat. They showcase pirate ships that tilt and rock while buccaneers swing on ropes high above.

Action gets people's attention.

We see action at sporting events, especially with the movement of a ball. After a game, ask the third baseman how many times the ball went to him. He'll know exactly. "It was seven. The first was a slow roller, the second was hit to my left, the third was…" He remembers because he did something. He moved. He leaned forward. He threw. Ask the right fielder how many times the ball was hit to the third baseman and he won't remember. Why? He was not involved. Unlike the third baseman, it meant nothing to him.

The same is true when we drive. If we're not behind the wheel making turns and stepping on the gas, the likelihood of us remembering the way to Grandma's house is slim. We weren't active. We looked out the window, watched the cows, thought about the big project on Monday, and paid no attention to the red car that cut us off on Highway 62. The driver not only remembers the incident, but can take you back to the spot three months later.

Adding a dose of action to every link creates memorable images.

The Body Anchor Method is useful when you're having a conversation and you don't want to interrupt, yet you want to remember what to say. As a reminder, take the key word of your statement or question and link it to a body part.

For instance, when your friend tells you about her daughter's cooking class, this may remind you of the new cookbook you saw at the store. Rather than interrupting her, simply associate a cookbook covering your head. Once your friend finishes her story, you'll go to your anchors to retrieve the information.

When your son bounces in from school, excited about telling you he's the team's new pitcher, you may not want to cut short his enthusiasm. Instead, when you associate a trash bag wrapped around your waist or elbow, you'll be reminded to tell him to "pitch the trash."

Sometimes there are things you do want to remember that you do not want to discuss. For instance, when your friend mentions she's taking her phone to get repaired, you're reminded about the repair needed on your son's bike. Rather than reaching for a pencil to jot the thought down, or rudely stopping her in mid sentence with, "Hey, remind me …," use your body anchor. Associate your thumb caught in the bike's spoke. If you anticipate grimacing, you can always associate the bike riding over your friend's phone. Each method you're reminded.

A salesman told me how he used the Body Anchor Method to sell a car. Early in the conversation, he recalled the prospect saying he had a tee time later that day. The salesman associated *golf clubs* with one of his anchors which reminded him to direct the customer to the larger make car with the bigger trunk. "Mr. Jones, look how easily your clubs can fit in here."

It's happened to every person who has ever had a conversation. Sooner or later we're going to think, *I forgot what I was going to say.* The Body Anchor Method prevents that, but you have to act quickly. As soon as you think of what to say, without wanting to interrupt the speaker, mentally throw your key word on a body part. Who *nose*, from *ear* on out, this method may be all you *knee-d*. Anything less would be a total *waist*. Go *a-head* and try it.

Number/Shape Method

Numbers are boring. They sit and do nothing. They're not colorful, playful, or memorable. The Number/Shape Method changes that. The shape of the number takes on an object, thus making it memorable.

1 is shaped like a *rocket*.

2 is shaped like a *swan*.

3 is shaped like a *pitchfork*.

4 is similar to a *sailboat*.

5 looks like a *saxophone*.

6 resembles a *golf club*.

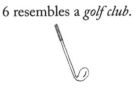

7 is shaped like a *diving board*.

8 represents a *snowman*.

9 looks like a *flagpole*.

10 is a *bat* and *ball*.

If you notice an object other than what's listed, make that your choice. For instance, the number *1* resembles a *pencil*, *2* resembles a *coat hanger*, and *3* looks like an *unfinished heart* on its side. With a little imagination, the number *4* looks like a *roof*, *5* looks like a *fishhook*, and number *6* resembles a *cherry*. The number *7* looks like a *cane*, *8* looks like a *racetrack*, *9* looks like a *bent needle*, and *10* looks like an ice fisherman's *pole* placed beside the *opening in a lake*.

Decide which object works best for you. This is your list. Each number will have one specific picture. It will be your anchor to associate new information with what you need to remember.

Remembering The Bill of Rights

To remember the Bill of Rights, the first 10 Amendments of the U.S. Constitution, associate the main idea with each one of your anchors. Here's an example:

1 = rocket The 1st Amendment represents freedom of speech. To remember, link what we know (*rocket*) to what we're trying to know (*freedom of speech*). Imagine a public speaker, standing atop a rocket, lifted off to space. Rocket means 1. Speaker means *freedom of speech*. By linking them, it strengthens our memory.

2 = swan The 2nd Amendment is about the right to keep and bear arms. Imagine a *swan* with huge *arms*. The *arms* are waving a huge *gun*. The image is absurd and ridiculous, but memorable.

3 = pitchfork The 3rd Amendment states that no soldier shall, in time of peace, be quartered in any house without the consent of the owner. To remember, associate *pitchfork* to the key word in that amendment, (*quarter*). Now, imagine *quarters* spinning on a *pitchfork*.

4 = sailboat The 4th Amendment is about unreasonable searches and seizures. Visualize a *sailboat* with thousands of *flashlights* guiding its path. It's ridiculous, but it works. Having the sailboat searched isn't bizarre enough.

5 = saxophone The 5ᵗʰ Amendment provides that no person can be forced to be a witness against him or herself. Taking the fifth means we don't talk. Visualize a *tongue* being used to clog a *saxophone*.

6 = golf club The 6ᵗʰ Amendment represents the right to a speedy and public trial by an impartial jury. Associate *jury* to *golf club* and it sticks in our mind, especially if a jury box is speeding on the fairway.

7 = diving board The 7ᵗʰ Amendment is about the preservation of trial by jury. Imagine a *diving board* preserved in a glass jar. Another image could be a *diving board* used as a *preservative* on your bread. By remembering the key word *preserved*, we can easily remember the 7ᵗʰ Amendment.

8 = snowman The 8ᵗʰ Amendment is about unnecessary cruel and unusual punishment. People shall not be allowed to be tortured or be imposed with excessive bail or fines. Imagine setting fire to a *snowman*. That's cruel. Another visual is pitching bales of hay at a snowman. *Bale* reminds us of excessive *bails* or fines. Although the spelling is different, *bales* and *bails* are pronounced the same, and that makes it memorable.

9 = flagpole The 9ᵗʰ Amendment states that "the enumeration in the Constitution, of certain rights, shall not be construed to deny or disparage others retained by the people." In other words, it states any rights that weren't specifically listed would not be forfeited. This includes raising a family, marrying, and moving from place to place. Once we understand what this amendment states, associate the key word *List*, on a *flagpole* to remind us of this important amendment.

10 = bat and **ball** The 10ᵗʰ Amendment recognizes that states are allowed to do many things at the local level. For instance, traffic laws and child custody laws are all in the domain of the states. The key word is *state*. Picturing a *state* is difficult, but picturing a *steak* isn't. The word *steak* is similar to *state*. Visualizing hitting a *ball* with a *steak*, instead of a *bat*, reminds us the state plays an important role in the 10ᵗʰ Amendment.

We've just learned the Bill of Rights and all we did was link two items ten times.

Number/Rhyme Method

The Number/Rhyme Method is another method used for remembering information. Choosing a word that rhymes with a number makes it memorable.

1 = *bun, gun, run, sun*

2 = *shoe, glue, zoo*

3 = *tree, sea, key*

4 = *door, floor, boar*

5 = *hive, dive, chive*

6 = *bricks, sticks, kicks*

7 = *Kevin, heaven*

8 = *gate, bait*

9 = *sign, pine, wine, dine*

10 = *hen, pen, men*

Choose only one word for each number. For instance, if you chose *Sun* for 1, picture a place when you were under the sun. Was it at the beach? Which beach? Were you in the water or sun bathing? Each number picture should take you to a specific place where you saw this object. For example:

2 = *shoe*   Visualize a particular shoe, in a particular place.

3 = *tree*   Mentally see a tree.

4 = *door*   Which door are you referring to? Go to it.

5 = *hive*   Imagine a huge beehive.

6 = *bricks*   Which bricks? Are they a part of your house, chimney, walkway, or stacked behind your garage?

7 = *Kevin*   Do you know someone named *Kevin*? If not, here's your chance. Another image is *heaven*. Visualizing clouds may be better than picturing *Heaven's Gate*, since *gate* represents number 8.

8 = *gate*   Visualize a particular railroad gate.

9 = *sign*   Is it a *yield, stop*, or *right of way* sign? Choose.

10 = *pen*   Get one in your head. That's your visual for number 10.

Going to the store to shop? Associate each item needed to each anchor. Here's your list: (1) *ice cream*, (2) *bread*, (3) *toothpaste*, (4) *English muffins*, (5) *milk*, (6) *baking powder*, (7) *yogurt*, (8) *corn*, (9) *onions*, and (10) *spaghetti*.

Visualize seeing the *sun* inside an *ice cream cone*.

Associate *bread* stuffed into your *shoes*.

In your "mind's eye," visualize *toothpaste* covering the *tree*. And while you're at it, associate *English muffins* spinning on your *doorknob*.

Five represents *hive*. Imagine dumping *milk* over all those bees.

Imagine *baking powder* covering the *bricks*, and remember to see *yogurt* spilled over your friend, *Kevin*.

Ears of *corn*, instead of a *gate*, are coming down at the railroad crossing. Try to see that. After you do, look at the stop *sign* made of *onions*. That's sweet.

For number 10, associate *spaghetti* wrapped around a *pen*.

This system won't keep you walking back and forth the entire grocery store. For example, once you reach for the bread, and then notice the *English muffins*, you'll remember to grab them, even though it's farther down your list.

The next day, if we have to remember another list, the previous list will fade from our memory. The action-oriented image helps us remember. To prove it, as you're reading these pages, imagine squirting ketchup over this page. Now, look away for a moment, and then come back to the next paragraph.

As you're reading these words, imagine highlighting the entire paragraph with a yellow marker. Go ahead and do it. I know this goes against everything you've stood for. You've never been one to write in books, but do it with this one. Take a yellow highlighter and cover these words.

Okay, snap out of it. When you were reading about highlighting the page, were you still looking at the ketchup stain? Fortunately, our brain keeps us straight. It's difficult to imagine two separate bizarre images at the same time.

Keep the Number/Rhyme Method simple by associating each number to one particular place. Seeing it in your "mind's eye" will make it memorable.

Alphabet Anchor Method

This system enables you to recall up to 26 items. Since the objective is to create a picture, the *sound* of the letter will represent a visual image. For example, *elephant* and *envelope* begin with the letter *E*, but are pronounced *L-ephant* and *N-velope*. Once you pronounce the letter, you're on the way to pronouncing the word.

A	=	Ape	ape in cage
B	=	Bee	bees buzzing around your face
C	=	Sea	sea with high waves
D	=	Deed	notarized deed of trust
E	=	Eel	eel swimming
F	=	Effort	effort from weight lifter
G	=	Genie	genie in bottle
H	=	H-Bomb	mushroom cloud from bomb
I	=	Eye	eyeball
J	=	Blue Jay	blue jay on bird feeder
K	=	Cake	birthday cake with candles
L	=	Elephant	elephant at zoo
M	=	Emcee	emcee with microphone
N	=	Envelope	dropped into mailbox
O	=	Odor	skunk getting ready to spray
P	=	Pea	green peas on plate
Q	=	Cue	pool table with a cue stick
R	=	Arch	Gateway Arch in St. Louis
S	=	S-Curve	switchback curves on road
T	=	Tee	hitting golf ball off tee
U	=	Unicycle	riding unicycle
V	=	Venus	stars and galaxies in sky
W	=	W.C. Fields	cigar smoke from W.C. Fields
X	=	X-ray	X-ray at doctor's office
Y	=	YMCA	stationary bike at gym
Z	=	Zebras	zebras running

Attach what you want remembered to each item.

Do you want to remember to return a library book, send letters, and sharpen pencils? Then associate book to ape. See the ape throwing millions of books around the cage.

Letters to *Bee*. See bees carrying letters from flower to flower. *Pencils* to *Sea*. See millions of pencils floating in the sea, or a giant wave of pencils is about to crash upon you. Get the point?

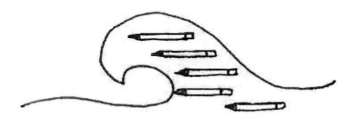

Use the alphabet peg to remember this list:

A - paper weight

B - motorbike

C - cigar

D - wrestling

E - trumpet

F - tollbooth

G - poster

H - cell phone

I - Niagara Falls

J - paint

K - music box

L - toy box

M - wedding cake

N - calendar

O - sunrise

P - blanket

Q - lamp

R - calculator

S - chicken

T - kettle

U - moon

V - microphone

W - telescope

X - tree limb

Y - snowball

Z - mustache

This system is perfect for locating your car at the mall. Can't remember you parked in *K*? You will when you associate your car parked underneath a cake (K-ake). By associating your car with the cake, you'll be reminded of where you parked when you ask yourself, *where's my car? Oh yeah, cake. I parked in K.*

Phonetic Alphabet Method

The phonetic alphabet has been around for centuries, and is the best way for remembering numbers. It's a system that codes numbers to letters to form a word.

In the English language, there are ten consonant sounds. Coincidently, ten is also the number of digits (0-9).

Since numbers are difficult to remember, they will be replaced with words. Those words will help us remember any number.

To start, we must know which letters correspond to which number.

0 = *s/z*, and *soft c*. You'll notice your teeth, tongue, and lips are in the same position when you utter the words <u>S</u>ay, <u>Z</u>oo, and i<u>C</u>e. As a reminder ...<u>Z</u>er<u>O</u> ends with O.

1 = *t/d*. These two letters produce the same sound. Notice the position of your tongue when you begin to say the words <u>T</u>ea and <u>D</u>ew. As a reminder ...the letters *t/d* stand on 1 leg.

2 = *n*. There's no sound like the *N*. Words such as <u>N</u>o, <u>N</u>ew, and k<u>N</u>ee begin with your tongue pressed to the roof of your mouth. As a reminder ...the letter *n* stands on 2 legs.

3 = *m*. Your lips are together when you begin to say <u>M</u>a, <u>M</u>ow, and <u>M</u>e. As a reminder ...the letter *m* stands on 3 legs.

4 = *r*. Note the position of your lips and tongue when you pronounce <u>R</u>ye, <u>R</u>ay, and <u>R</u>ah. As a reminder ...the number fou<u>R</u> ends with *r*.

5 = *L*. The words <u>L</u>ay, <u>L</u>ow, and <u>L</u>aw produce the same sound. Your tongue touches the roof of your mouth. As a reminder ... Roman numeral 50 is *L*.

6 = *ch/sh/j*, and *soft g*. Words, such as <u>CH</u>ew, <u>SH</u>oe, <u>J</u>oy, and <u>G</u>ee all start with your lips puckered. As a reminder ...mirror image of 6 resembles *j*.

35

7 = *k/q, hard c* and *g*. The *KA* sound equals the number 7. Words, such as <u>K</u>ey, <u>Q</u>ue, <u>C</u>ard, and <u>G</u>o begin with the same sound. As a reminder ...an upside down 7 is seen in the letter *K*.

8 = *f/v/ph*. Lips are close together when you utter the letters *f/v/ph*, such as i<u>**F**</u>, <u>**V**</u>ie, and <u>**PH**</u>onetic. As a reminder ...the cursive *f* resembles an 8.

9 = *p/b*. The popping sounds of <u>P</u>ea, <u>P</u>a, <u>B</u>ee, and <u>B</u>oo equals the number 9. As a reminder ...a mirror image of *P* resembles 9.

A recap of the Phonetic Alphabet:

0 = s/z/soft c

1 = t/d

2 = n

3 = m

4 = r

5 = L

6 = ch/sh/j/soft g

7 = k/q/hard c and g

8 = f/v/ph

9 = p/b

The Rules

Like everything in life, there are rules to follow. Here are a dozen to stay on course for remembering numbers:

- Ten digits are replaced by ten consonant sounds to make words.

- The vowels *a, e, i, o, u,* as well as *y, w,* and *h* are not coded to any letter. They're used as fillers.

- The letters *th,* when together, have no value, such as *th*ou, *th*ey, and *th*e. The *th* sound is slightly different than the *t* and *d* sound.

- You do not have to be a good speller. It's the sound that matters. Therefore, the word *k***ni***fe* translates to 2 and 8, because the letter *k* is silent.

- The letter *x* equals the number 70. *X* is pronounced *e**KS***, because *k* equals 7 and *s* equals 0.

- Double letters count as one. **Su*mm*er** codes to 034, not 0334. **But-ter** is 914, not 9114. However, the word *accent* is 7021, because it's pronounced aK-CeNT.

- *tion* equals 62, as in opera(**shun**).

- *tch* equals 6 because it's a quick *ch* sound, such as i*tch*, ha***tch***, wa***tch***, and wi***tch***.

- *dg* equals 6, as in fu***dg***e, ju***dg***e, and e***dg***e.

- *ck* equals 7, not 77. Words, such as wha***ck***, hi***ck***, and ho***ck***ey have the *ak* sound. A hard *k* represents the number 7.

- **T***ough* equals 18, because it's pronounced ***tuf***. **R***ough* is 48, because it's pronounced ***ruf***. **D***ough* is 1, because it's pronounced ***d***oe. Only the *d* sound is heard.

- Learn this system. It will change your life.

100 Anchors

1- hooD	26 - NaCHo	51 - waLLeT	76 - CouCH
2 - hoNey	27 - NeCK	52 - LioN	77 - CaKe
3 - haM	28 - kNiFe	53 - LiMe	78 - CoFFee
4 - oaR	29 - kNoB	54 - LawyeR	79 - CaP
5 - wheeL	30 - MouSe	55 - LiLy	80 - VaSe
6 - SHoe	31 - MuD	56 - LeaSH	81 - FeeT
7 - Key	32 - MoNey	57 - LoG	82 - PHoNe
8 - iVy	33 - MuMMy	58 - LeaF	83 - FoaM
9 - hooP	34 - haMMeR	59 - LiP	84 - FiRe
10 - DaiSy	35 - MaiL	60 - CHeeSe	85 - FiLe
11 - ToaD	36 - MatCH	61 - SHeD	86 - FiSH
12 - TiN	37 - haMMoCK	62 - CHaiN	87 - FiG
13 - DiMe	38 - MoVie	63 - JaM	88 - FiFe
14 - DooR	39 - MaP	64 - CHeRRy	89 - FBi
15 - TaiL	40 - RoSe	65 - JaiL	90 - BuS
16 - DiSH	41 - RoaD	66 - JuDGe	91 - BaT
17 - DeCK	42 - RaiN	67 - SHaKe	92 - PiaNo
18 - TV	43 - RaM	68 - CHeF	93 - BoMb
19 - TuB	44 - ReaR	69 - SHiP	94 - BeaR
20 - NoSe	45 - RaiL	70 - KeyS	95 - PiLLow
21 - wiNDow	46 - RoaCH	71 - KiTe	96 - PeaCH
22 - oNioN	47 - RoCK	72 - waGoN	97 - BiKe
23 - gNoMe	48 - RooF	73 - GuM	98 - BeehiVe
24 - wieNeR	49 - RoPe	74 - CaR	99 - PiPe
25 - NaiL	50 - LaSSo	75 - eaGLe	100 - ouThouSeS

Learn these anchors. Practice by reviewing them in tens. Note the words from numbers 10-19 begin with either the letter *t* or *d*. Words from 20-29 have the letter *n* as the beginning consonant. Words from 30-39 all have the *m* sound.

Pay attention to the capitalized letter in bold. These are the letters that code to a number. Although some of these words begin with a vowel, the vowels have no value.

For each number, visualize where you've seen this object. Make that object your anchor. For instance, for 92 imagine a particular piano you have seen. Do this with each number.

For number 5 imagine a specific wheel, whether it's the wheel from television's *Wheel of Fortune* or a bicycle wheel. If it's the latter, don't confuse this with the bike for number 97.

Personalize these objects. Find the best word that works for you. These are your anchors. For example, here are words you could choose for 70-79.

70 - **g**a**s**, **k**ey**s**, **k**i**ss**
71 - **c**a**t**, **c**oa**t**, **k**i**t**e
72 - wag**o**n, g**un**, **c**a**n**
73 - **c**o**mb** (*b* is silent), g**un**, **G**ua**m**
74 - **c**a**r**, **c**o**r**e, **ch**oi**r** (pronounced **k**wi**r**e)
75 - **g**a**l**, ea**g**le, **c**oi**l**
76 - **c**a**sh**, **c**ou**ch**, **q**ui**ch**e
77 - **c**a**k**e, **k**i**ck**, **qua**k**e
78 - **c**o**ff**ee, **c**ou**gh**, **c**a**v**e
79 - **c**a**p**e, **c**u**p**, **c**u**b**e

It may seem like a daunting task to memorize 100 objects for 100 numbers, but you'll be able to accomplish this easily. There are plenty of moments to practice. When you're on the highway, glance at license plate numbers and convert numbers to your anchor word.

Look at your digital clock and code the last two numbers to an object. For numbers 00-09, you'll be able to mentally see a *seesaw, seed, sun, swim, soar, sail, switch, sock, safe,* and *soap,* respectively.

Anytime you need to recall a list of items, or recall a number from 1-100, associate that object with what you want remembered.

Here are some examples:

You want to remember your car gets *37*mpg. Visualize your car swinging on a *hammock.*

You want to remember the *Disney Channel* is channel *48.* Imagine *Disney* characters dancing atop your *roof.*

You want to remember Joe DiMaggio's *56*-game hitting streak. Imagine the Yankee Clipper hitting the ball with a *leash.*

Image Chris Evert playing Martina Navratilova with a *vase* and you'll know they competed against each other *80* times.

Can't recall where to set the thermostat? You will when you associate it with a *chef's* hat (68).

When you learn the phonetic alphabet like the "back of your hand," your memory will vastly improve. Once you grasp Chapter 3 (page 41), your memory will soar.

Chapter 3

How to Remember Numbers

The process begins in the beginning. Shortly after our parents name us, we're numbered. Through the years, we sort through all sorts of numbers.

We carry a social security number, locker number, grade point average number, uniform number, telephone number, credit card number, house number, license number, and an IQ number, which would be very low if we had to remember all these numbers.

Everywhere we turn numbers are numbing us. Until now...

Numbers come at us from different directions. However, when analyzed, you realize there are only ten of them.

0 1 2 3 4 5 6 7 8 9

Ten digits. That's it! By themselves they're not so hard to remember. However, when they're strung together and rearranged, numbers are downright difficult to deal with.

Numbers clog our mind because they create no memorable picture. All they do is get in our way causing us to forget.

Utilizing the Phonetic Alphabet, (see pages 35-37), changes any boring, humdrum number into a colorful, electrifying object or phrase. It has no boundaries. Your memory power will soar once you learn this approach. In fact, after I mastered this system, I chose to speak professionally on *Memory Skills*.

Learning this method takes effort, but achieving anything of importance takes time. Becoming skilled with the phonetic alphabet is similar to learning a foreign language, but easier. With a foreign language, there are multiple words, phrases, and accents you need to master. With the phonetic alphabet, you have to know only the letter codes for each of the ten individual numbers.

Here's a review.

0 = s/z/soft c
1 = t/d
2 = n
3 = m
4 = r
5 = L
6 = ch/sh/j/soft g
7 = k/q/hard c and g
8 = f/v/ph
9 = p/b

Examples

The number 12 is coded to *t/d* for the 1; and *n* for the 2. By placing vowels around these two consonant letters, the following words are created: **tuna, tune, teen, tan, ton, tone, tin, den, dine, done, twine, twin,** and **tiny.**

Some of these words produce more visuals and movement than others. For instance, a *tuna* can swim, it can be caught in a fishing line, and it can produce a scent. Open a can of tuna and your cat will be at your feet in seconds.

If we wanted to remember the Dallas Cowboys won Super Bowl XII, the number for 12, we can imagine a cowboy *tuna* throwing a football.

Visualize a *tuna* in a voting booth and you'll remember the 12th Amendment is about the process for electing the President and Vice President.

Imagine a *tuna*, dressed in long *tails*, delivering the State of the Union Address, and you'll always be reminded that Zachary *Taylor* was the 12th President.

To remember the cholesterol count of a slice of cheese pizza is 12mg, imagine a *tuna* eating pizza.

Mentally see a *tuna* hitchhiking, because it has *no car*, and you'll know <u>No</u>rth <u>Car</u>olina was the 12th state to join the union.

Oh, what joy it would be to see a *tuna* drumming under the Christmas tree. It would also stick in your mind what your true love gave you on the 12th day of Christmas.

Imagine a *tuna* drinking wine and you're reminded that Highway 12 cuts through wine country in Northern California.

I have nothing against the number 12. It's never caused me any harm, but I would rather do away with it. A tuna is more fun to be with than plain old 12. I've fished for tuna, I've eaten tuna, and I've seen tuna on the *National Geographic Channel*. I can remember *tuna* a lot easier than the number 12, only because there's life in it.

The phonetic alphabet can add life to any number. Here's another example using the number 21. With 2 coding to *n*, and 1 coding to either *t/d*, we get the following words: **net, knead, need, nod, neat, nude, window, went, want,** and **knot**.

Window is a good choice because it opens and closes. It is an object that produces action.

Visualize former astronaut John Glenn using a *window* to put out candles on his birthday cake. That bizarre image also tells us he was born in 1921. Taking it a step further, we can "see" him dumping wet **paint** on the cake. Wet **paint** translates to **1921**.

The birthday cake is the anchor reminding us it's his birthday we want remembered.

Imagine an *artist* painting all the *windows* in the White House and you'll remember that Chester A. *Arthur* was the 21st President.

Imagine a *window* that's *ill*, and you'll be reminded that *Illinois* is the 21st state.

To remember an egg is about 212mg of cholesterol, visualize a giant egg wearing a collar (a word similar to *cholesterol*) attached to an *antenna* (212).

Note the ingredients in that picture. Visualization: egg, collar, and antenna. Action: spinning. Exaggeration and Association: collar around egg connected to an antenna.

Antenna isn't the only option for 212. The word *Indian* can also be used, as well as the words, ***not now***; ***want honey***; and *undone*.

When I moved to Richmond, Virginia, I opened a checking account at *Crestar Bank*. While others were struggling to remember their PIN number, I simply looked at the big, red sign in front which read *Crestar*. My PIN number was 7401; the first four consonant sounds in *Crestar*. (Don't bother, the bank is no longer around).

We live in a world of letters and numbers. We've been schooled in reading letters, but not numbers. A quick glance at the following letters … C A R D I N A L S … and you have them memorized. You didn't remember the *C* and then memorize the *A*, and then tried to remember the *R*. Instead, you were able to take all those letters and remember them, because you read them as one.

You can do the same with numbers. With a little practice, you'll be able to see the numbers … 7 4 1 2 5 0 … as easily and quickly as you read C A R D I N A L S.

Anytime you need to remember a number, change it into a word and link it to what you want remembered. The phonetic alphabet will help with remembering historical dates, measurements, codes, and more.

Visualize sitting in the back seat of a plane flying over Mount *McKinley*, and you'll know William *McKinley* served as President from 18**97**-19**01** (**b**a**ck** **s**ea**t**).

Imagine Neil Armstrong pulling *wagons* on the *choppy* moon, and you'll know the first moon landing was **7-20-69**.

Visualize placing a phone call to a Vegas casino, and you'll know the area code to Sin City is **702** (*casino*).

Mentally see a *toboggan* passing through airport security, and you'll always remember **1972** was the first year it became mandatory to screen passengers and luggage at U.S. airports.

Imagine a double-decker bus in the *outfield*, and you'll know the two-story bus was invented in **1851**.

When you imagine a huge *dog bon*e wedged at the door of the New York Stock Exchange, you'll know it was **1792** when the trading first began.

Visualize taking a *chisel* to Seattle's Space Needle, and you'll be reminded the structure's height is **605** feet.

Imagine a *roach* crawling down the nose of the Statue of Liberty, and you'll remember the length of Lady Liberty's nose is **4 feet, 6 inches**.

Imagine Charles Lindbergh *landing* in Paris, and you'll know the date he touched down from his trans-Atlantic flight was **5-21-27**. Plus, the first three consonant sounds in Lindburgh are 5-21.

The average person could never memorize over 60 numbers of Pi. You can, but then, you're not average.

3.14159265358979323846264338327950288419716939937510058 20974944592307...

MY TURTLE plays the PIANO in a CHILLY MALL with a HEAVY PACK. People PAY MONEY for this. I'M VERY excited! However, GINGER, my MOM, is FUMING he PLAYS ON, especially since he has a FEVER. Get him a TOPCOAT, a CHEAP MOP, and BUY HIM a COLD CELL PHONE so he can get a SUBWAY CAR out of there. Oh BROTHER, HELP. NOW, I'M SICK.

The uses of the phonetic alphabet are endless, as long as your imagination is.

Beginning on page 235 to 301 is a directory for you. Each single, double, triple, and quadruple number is coded into a word or phrase. The work is done for you. Only the bold letters correspond to the numbers. When you need to remember a number, locate it in the directory, and link it with what you want to remember.

Chapter 4

How to Speak Without Notes

It has been said the brain is a wondrous thing. It starts working the moment we are born, but has a tendency to stop the moment we stand to speak in public.

That statement was probably delivered with notes.

There's nothing wrong with speaking with notes. It shows we care about our message and about the people who are present to listen. Nothing is worse than listening to a speaker who doesn't care about his message. Seeing a speaker with notes tells us, hey, at least the guy's trying.

Effort aside, it tells us something else. Does the speaker realize we're in the room? He hasn't brought his head up since he stood behind the lectern 30 minutes ago. Watching the top of a speaker's head has a direct correlation to the inside of our head. We start daydreaming. *Jamie's soccer practice is tomorrow... must wash uniform tonight; chicken in freezer ... must take out tomorrow; proposal due on Friday ... must look for new job on Monday.*

A speaker who is glued to his notes may lose his audience, but he does help them organize their lives. Daydreaming will do that for you. We don't want our audience to daydream. Dream yes, they can accomplish goals you help to inspire. Dream yes, they can overcome any obstacle. Dream yes, they can succeed.

Whether we want to inspire, motivate, inform, or humor the audience, our goal is to connect with them. Notes get in the way.

Can you imagine how ineffective comedians David Letterman, Jay Leno, or Ellen DeGeneres would be if they used notes? Granted, they may lean toward cue cards, but the words aren't held in their hands. Their hands remain free to gesture. Watch George Carlin's four-minute monologue, *I'm a Modern Man* on *YouTube* and decide for yourself if he would have been as effective had he clutched 3x5 note cards.

Yes, Martin Luther King and John F. Kennedy succeeded by using notes, as did that fella in Gettysburg, but most likely, their stage was a bit bigger than the one we'll stand on.

Our stage may be a hotel ballroom, a high school auditorium, or the office break room off Main Street. We want a clear pathway to our audience, void of lecterns and note cards that get in the way of our message.

There's pressure in delivering a speech without notes, but there are rewards when speaking without them. You're one speaker who maintained eye contact, spoke confidently, and gestured without fumbling for printed words.

Giving a speech is no different than sitting down at *Starbucks* with our best buddy. We talk, don't we? We communicate our thoughts freely, openly, and easily. We're not pulling sheets of paper out from our breast pocket with the words, "Thank you for having me here today." When we discuss one topic, it reminds us to talk about another.

Conversations advance because of reminders; attaching new information to what we already know. The following exchange between Bob and Judy is an example.

Bob: "Hi Judy, how's George?"

Judy: "He's great. He got a new job downtown."

Bob: "Which reminds me, I went downtown to the concert last night."

Judy: "Which reminds me, my son wants concert tickets for Christmas."

Bob: "Which reminds me, for Christmas we're cutting down a tree."

Judy: "Which reminds me, a tree blocked the road to Mount Vernon."

Bob: "Which reminds me, how's Martha?"

Notes are the *Which reminds me's* in public speaking. When we finish with one topic, we glance down to see what we talk about next. Memorizing a speech word for word is not what we want. We want to be able to communicate a message.

For instance, if we tell three people, on three occasions, about our week-long vacation to New York City, our story will not be told exactly the same to each person. Yet, the message will be the same.

We'll talk about our experience of riding on a subway, standing on the observation deck of the Empire State Building, attending a Knicks game, and skating at Rockefeller Center. We don't need notes for that. We've experienced it and we remember. However, what we may need notes for is recalling the order we visited them, as well as the sights and sounds we heard along the way. Note cards keep us on track.

Usually, when note cards are used, only key words are printed reminding the speaker what to talk about next. The word *Subway* will automatically trigger his mind to talk about his journey beneath New York's streets. He'll talk about the mad rush to find a seat, how others were holding onto poles, and how some were holding onto others.

The next word on the note card will read *Empire State Building.* This reminds the speaker to talk about the long line waiting to get to the top, feeling the wind once he reached the top, and the view of all those yellow cars below. One thought will remind him of another. But what happens after he finishes talking about the Empire State Building? He must pivot to another NYC adventure and remember.

Good thing he has notes, because his next card reads *Knicks.* In his mind he's saying, *Oh, which reminds me.* "We went to Madison Square Garden and watched the Knicks beat the Cavs. It was fun. During the game …"

From *Knicks* the next card may read *Skating;* a reminder to talk about the adventure on ice.

If he could only remember without using notes, his stage presence would be stronger. He'd be free to gesture and his eyes would be on the audience. He can still accomplish this and use notes. The best part is, the notes will never be seen by the audience.

It's almost impossible to think of two things at the same time. We can think of things very, very quickly, but it's difficult for our mind to see two images at once. Try it for yourself. Can you think of an *igloo* and a *telephone* at the same time? How about thinking of a *moose* and a *letter opener*? Try thinking of a *ping pong table* and the *Chesapeake Bay Bridge–Tunnel*.

Linking

If you're like most people, your mind moved from one image to the next at rapid speed, but the images were not combined.

Let's take the four subjects in the earlier speech - *Subway, Empire State Building, Knicks*, and *Skating* - and commit them to memory. To do this, we must remember that premise about how we make conversation; we attach new information to what we already know.

The first part is *Subway*. After we discuss this we have to talk about the *Empire State Building*. By attaching new information (*Empire State Building)* to what we already know (*Subway*) we are able to remember. However, a subway and a building don't go together. I've never witnessed a building board a subway. I've also never seen a subway ride an elevator to the top floor.

Each time I've passed through New York City subway turnstiles, nothing unusual has happened. It's been relatively mundane. Yes, I've been crammed with the masses and the subway car does rock, but the lights have never gone out and the windows have never broken. Plus, the people have kept to themselves.

However, if I saw the President of the United States, the Pope, or a 16-foot alligator on the train, I would remember. It's out of the ordinary; it's different; it doesn't happen every day.

The keys to remembering two things at the same time is to create unusual images that are combined into one.

To remember *Subway* and *Empire State Building* one image needs to be made. Standing behind the solid yellow line and seeing the Empire State Building come down the track is an experience long remembered. I didn't expect it. I anticipated a subway. Boarding a building is bizarre, crazy, and foolish. It's also memorable. It's that exaggeration that helps us lock in the information.

If you want to speak without notes, create one of these crazy pictures. Don't worry, you're not going to laugh out loud. Instead, you're going to smoothly move from your *Subway* story to your *Empire State Building* experience.

After we talk about the *Empire State Building* we move to the *New York Knicks*. Applying the same principal, we associate new information (*Knicks*) to what we already know (*Empire State Building*). Notice we're not including *Subway*. We stepped out of that subway car when we started speaking about the Empire State Building. The subway is long gone.

Crazy, bizarre, ridiculous, that's the connection we want to make between *Empire State Building* and *Knicks* basketball. We want to put the building where the ball goes or put the ball where the building goes. For instance, imagine dropping thousands of *basketballs* off the *Empire State Building*. Can you mentally see them speeding through the air like tiny oranges falling to the ground? Why do we throw thousands of basketballs, instead of just one? The volume enables us to embed that image into our mind. If it were only one, we may not see it. With thousands, they're everywhere.

Another image could be mentally seeing the *Empire State Building* playing *basketball*. The referee may call "foul," but spectators call it memorable.

From *Knicks* basketball we speak about *ice skating*. We remember the order because we're connecting new information (*Skating*) to what we already know (*Knicks*). And what do we do with the Empire State Building? It's back on the corner of 5th and West 34th where it belongs.

Bouncing a basketball outside a skating rink is not memorable. We want to mentally see an image that's totally ridiculous. It's the ridiculous that we remember. Remember?

Imagine ice skates on a basketball. A crowd would gather for that. The basketballs are skating on the rink.

It takes a split second for our mind to see that image. The more bizarre and action oriented the visual, the more it becomes cemented in our memory.

Can you remember the list? The first word was *Subway,* and that reminds us of _____ and that reminds us of _____. That reminds us of _____.

Did you mentally see the Empire State Building on the subway track? Then, did you "see" the Empire State Building playing basketball? From basketballs, did you visualize the balls skating on ice? One image kicks into another.

We can confidently give this speech because we've added color and pizzazz to our brain. Instead of physically seeing the words on note cards, we're mentally seeing the images we created. We can do this with any speech we give.

In rehearsal, read the speech from a piece of paper. Then, place the paper down and attempt to recite it from memory. If you stumble, go back to the paper and see where you can link the last word you're able to memorize to the next word. Start at the beginning and keep practicing.

Fight your way to the end of your speech even if you do forget. You won't have the luxury of walking back to your kitchen table to glance at your notes during your big speech. Afterward, begin the speech again. If you find yourself stuck, pause, slow down, repeat what you said, and somehow get through your talk. This is rehearsal, so now's the time to throw yourself into the fire, if only the simulator.

If you're giving a speech without notes, you must have an exit strategy. That doesn't mean you yell, "*FIRE!*" or consider a fainting spell, but it means you have to comfortably know what to do if, God forbid, you do forget. For instance, while reciting the "Gettysburg Address," you don't want to be standing on stage in front of 200 people and say, "*Four score and seven ... bear with me for a moment.*"

If you got to *"Four score and seven years ago,"* and forgot, you can counter with, *Yes, Abraham Lincoln was on his way to giving an inspirational speech...*

If you're unable to recall the word or sentence you need, pause and ask a question about what you just said. Speaking on education? Ask, "How much time do you read to your children?" Speaking about fitness? Ask, "What are some of your fitness goals?" Speaking about the budget? Ask, "Wouldn't you agree we have to cut expenditures?" This extra pause may be the time you need to get back on track.

Do you know how many stage actors forget their lines? More than we know, I'm sure. They may not remember, but somehow, they get through it. That's why they're called actors. The audience doesn't have a clue.

Singers and musicians can't get away with it so easily. Deep into the 2008 *American Idol* competition, artist Brooke White forgot her lyrics. She stopped and started over. Judge Paula Abdul wasn't so sympathetic, stating as a performer you just can't do that, and if you have to, ad lib.

Speakers have it easier. We can slow the pace, speed the pace, ask for a glass of water, and ask for the heat to be turned down. We can stand still, sit on a stool, walk about, or kneel. We can ad lib. Piano players, and those who play the harp, can never get away with all that. If a musician can't remember the tune, everyone in the audience will think that didn't sound right. If a speaker doesn't remember the speech, the audience may not be aware of it.

Whether it's Vegas, or Branson, or down at the neighborhood bar, singers have to get it right. There's only one way to sing "The Impossible Dream." Motivational speakers have hundreds of ways to deliver it.

Be authentic. The audience doesn't want you to be someone else. They're not looking for a speaker who looks and sounds like Elvis. They came to hear you. You have an advantage. You know the words you're going to say, while the audience doesn't. If you do forget, just go down a different road, preferably one that doesn't come to a dead end. Try to avoid looking frazzled and out of sync, and say something. We ad lib with our friends, don't we?

Using Acronyms

An effective method many speakers use for remembering a speech is applying acronyms. No matter what your topic, pull out a key word and draft your speech using the letters from that word.

If your speech is about growing roses, then make *ROSES* the basis of your talk. *R* can represent *Rain*. We need rain to make them grow. *O* stands for *Oxygen*. They need to breathe and they need light. *S* could stand for *Soil*, *E* for *Environment*, and *S* for *Sweet* smelling. Since you're already familiar with your topic, you can easily glide from one segment to another.

In your opening remarks, state the key word to the audience. Not only does this help you to remember the speech, but it keeps the audience on track, as well. They now become participants. They know after you speak about the first *R*, you're going to mention an *O* next. The beauty of this system is if you forget, you can ask, "What do you think the *O* stands for in growing roses?" You may hear *Oasis* or *Observation* or *Organic*. This question and answer period allows you to start thinking really hard about what your *O* stands for. And, perhaps they may give you a better answer than the one you planned to use.

Giving a talk about Education? If so, use *TEACH*. *T* stands for *Time* management, *E* stands for *Effort*, *A* for *Achieve*, *C* for *Clarity*, and *H* for *Habit* or *Handwriting* or *Humor* or *Honors*.

Are you motivating your sales staff? If so, use *SALES*. *S* stands for *Service*. *A* stands for *Accountability*, *L* equals *Leadership*, *E* for *Engage*, and *S* for *Smile*. Each word automatically reminds you what your message is about. For instance, being *Engaged* means conversing with the prospect, asking open-ended questions, showing you care, and you're available to assist. You'll know to share examples and systems relating to that key word. Plus, your acronym method creates a memorable device for your salespeople to remember for the entire day. Using acronyms is an easy to follow system not only helping the speaker to remember, but also the listener.

When drafting your speech, make sure a dictionary or thesaurus is nearby. The latter is a great, outstanding, wonderful, terrific, splendid, majestic, and impressive tool. Use it.

Senator and statesman Daniel Webster (1782-1852) said, "If all my talents and powers were to be taken from me by some inscrutable providence, and I had my choice of keeping but one, I would unhesitatingly ask to be allowed to keep the Power of Speaking, for through it, I would quickly recover all the rest."

There is a power to speaking. And, a power to speak without notes.

Chapter 5

How to Remember Names

It's your parents first nightmare; a time they could have avoided months before, instead of putting it off until the last minute. They could have easily consulted family, friends, and even professional help from the numerous books they browsed through the past nine months. Instead they waited, thinking this day would never come.

Now, as they hold you, adore you, and kiss you, their fears are becoming more evident. After gently placing you in your warm crib, they look frantically at each other asking the question they should have answered a long time ago; an answer that will be carried with you forever.

"What are we going to name it?"

They have to name you something. Names are important. There's a lot of pressure naming a child. For the first few weeks, it may seem strange identifying this newborn by their name. Before long, you'll realize there couldn't have been a better choice.

No matter which name is chosen, it will be the right one. Your child will put that name on all their books and papers, write it when buying a home, and give it when looking for a job. The name will represent who they are and they'll carry it wherever they go. It will be the first thing they say when they meet someone. It will be the first thing they look for after they're quoted in the newspaper, and nine times out of ten, it will be the first thing they write to check if their pen has any more ink.

In today's fiercely competitive world, the edge goes to the person with the best memory. It's that simple. Since we're all in the people business, it pays to remember names.

You're Very Special

Outside the Kodak Theatre, in the hours leading up to the *Academy Awards* ceremony, hundreds of people wait patiently hoping to catch a glimpse of their favorite stars. The moment these celebrities step out of their limos, fans are calling their names. Why are they able to remember their names so easily? They don't know these people. They never invited them to their homes. They don't share an office cubicle with them. They remember their names because they are interested in them.

To remember someone's name we must be interested in the person who owns it. You may think it's easy to recall a celebrity's name because we see them in our living rooms. Whereas the folks we meet on a daily basis will never grace magazine covers or be seen on television and movie screens. Still, it should be easier to remember these people, because we've spoken to them and they've spoken to us.

We shook their hand, exchanged business cards, and sat next to them. We remember them because their son plays ball with our kid, they live in our neighborhood, attend our church, and know some of the same people we know. That's why we remember them. We share a common bond.

The more interested we are in the people we meet, the more likely we'll remember that person's name. Each person we come into contact with today is different than the person we may meet tomorrow. Each has a special quality and uniqueness. The people we meet are experts. They know about subjects we don't. They might be practiced in pottery, music, photography, dog training, American history, or woodworking. They're talented, unique, and have a lot to offer. Yes, every person we meet knows something we don't.

Treat each person as the most important person in the world, because they are. They're taking time out of their life to be with you, when they could be talking or doing business with someone else. See each person as an individual and act interested.

Whether you're a school teacher talking to a student, a shop owner meeting a customer, or a salesperson talking to a client, focus your attention on that person and show an interest. You may want to visualize this person is your mother's cousin or best friend, or the person you're meeting is about to give you a check for $100,000. It's difficult to forget her now.

Whether you're speaking to the checkout person at the grocery store or the person you're introduced to at the meeting, show a genuine interest in what they're saying. Remember, you're in the people business each day of your life. You can't get along without them. They're the ones who sell you paint at the hardware store, the ones you call to order a pizza, and the ones we trust when we send our children to school. Actually, they're just like us. They work hard, are loved by others, and want to live happily ever after.

Showing an interest in everyone we meet is the first step for remembering their name. That interest will compound as others will be interested in you.

FOCUS, FOCUS, FOCUS

Think back when you first learned to drive. You were focused on the job at hand, making certain mirrors were in the correct position, your seat belt was securely fastened, and turn signals came on at every turn. You never considered talking on the phone or turning on the radio. By concentrating on the road, you eliminated distractions. However, after a few weeks you might have added a few. You were able to put cream in your coffee, munch on french fries, and call your friend about the bad drivers hogging your lane.

Our concentration level might have slipped since our first day on the road. The same holds true when meeting people. After meeting one, then another and then another, our concentration level subsides. We begin thinking about other things. At the party we may be thinking about the tray full of shrimp, instead of the person standing in front of us. The chandelier in the center of the room may appear more sparkling than the people below it.

If you want to make a good first impression, it's important to concentrate. If not, the person you're with may not give you a second chance.

Usually, when we're meeting someone for the first time, we're not in familiar territory of our home or backyard. Instead, we're sitting in a hotel meeting room, shopping in aisle three, or strolling on a city sidewalk. There are distractions all around us. Couple that with trying to remember a name and the pressure is on to concentrate.

Focus on the individual when you're ready to introduce yourself. Avoid thinking about the next person you're going to meet. Concentrate. You get only one chance to make this first impression. Take advantage of it.

One of the first words spoken when meeting someone is our name. That's why it's called an *introduction*. Unfortunately, it's usually the first word forgotten when given by the other person. The name escaped us. It went over our heads and out the window. Thirty minutes into our conversation we're still wondering, *Whom am I speaking with?* The embarrassment is too overwhelming to reintroduce ourselves. We weren't concentrating.

Concentrating on remembering a name can take place hours before you meet someone. Driving to a business meeting where you know you're going to meet new people, concentrate not only on the road, but on the people you're going to encounter. Anticipate meeting these people and remind yourself to focus on the names when they are given.

At work, when you're on your way to the Accounting Office, concentrate on the people you know you're going to see. Remember? There are four people in the department. There's Barbara, Judy, Henry, and Lynn. By going over the names in your mind, you won't be caught off guard when you bump into them.

So far, we know we're going to be interested in the person and we're going to concentrate when the name is given. We're two steps ahead of the game before we even come into contact with anyone.

Eyes on You

When it comes to spectators, you can't beat tennis fans. They look to the left. They look to the right. They look to the left. They look to the right. Not all tennis fans appear to be in disagreeing form, they just keep their eye on the ball. If you look right when you should be looking left, you're going to miss all the action. The same applies to remembering names.

Keeping your eye on the ball, or person, keeps you in the game. It's virtually impossible to remember someone's name if you're not looking at the person who's providing it. If, after being introduced, you hear a comment about how nice your shoes are, don't count on that person remembering you. They were looking at your feet, instead of your face.

Watch people meet and notice where they're looking when the name is given. They're looking up, they're looking down, they're looking at the light fixture, the salt shaker, the tie on the person standing across the room. Often the eyes don't lock with the other person they're speaking to, and therefore, neither does the name. The next time you make a purchase, make note if the clerk is more interested in your face or President Grant's.

Looking people in the eye shows you're confident about yourself and you care about the person before you. It's essential for remembering a name.

If you arrive at a party and the host/hostess wants to introduce you to everyone, you're in deep trouble. You've now lost control of the situation. More often than not, the host already has low expectations of your ability for recall. That's why during the introductions, he'll rapid fire the names to you as quickly as a mud puddle finds your five-year-old's new shoes. He feels it's his obligation. When it's all over, the only name you remember is your own.

You may encounter another host who shouts, "Hey everybody, this is Josh. Say hi to Josh." This system does work. Hours later, your memory is as sharp as ever when you whisper to your host, "Tell everybody I'm leaving."

If you plan to go to the party, take it upon yourself to make the introductions. Concentrate on one person at a time. Look each person in the eye, make a comment or two, and then move to the next person. One person, one name, nothing complicated. Focusing on an individual by looking at their face will greatly enhance your ability for recalling the name.

For the rest of our lives, we'll always have a clear and vivid picture of our own mother. Why? She kept telling us, "Look at me when I'm talking to you." There's a lesson in that. If you want to be remembered and want to remember others, look the person in the eye and give the person a big smile. Who can forget a friendly face?

Listen Up Everybody

In the rotunda of the Virginia State Capitol in Richmond, stands the most famous statue of George Washington. Sculpted by French-man, Jean Houdon in 1785, the figure is life-like. No wonder. It is the only statue Washington posed for. When visitors approach the statue they are in awe. Their full attention is directed at Washington. They look at him, walk around him, and study the magnificent detail of our first Commander in Chief. When people walk away from the rotunda there's no doubt whom they just met.

However, imagine what would happen if Washington, all of a sudden, came to life. As we're gazing up at him, Washington begins to move his arms and legs, bends forward and speaks. If so, what would we do? We may ponder what the President thinks of us and if he likes what we're wearing. We may be thinking of something clever or witty to say to see if we can make old George laugh. When Washington stood still we thought about him. However, when he comes to life, we start thinking about ourselves, and therefore, we fail to listen.

The problem we face when meeting people is they're not statues. As we study them, guess what? They're studying us! We want to make a positive impression by saying something intelligent and of value. In doing so, we're not listening when the name is announced because we're engrossed in ourselves. How can we remember a name if we don't hear it?

Many people who don't hear the name don't bother getting it right. If it were *Judy, Jenny,* or *Janet,* who cares? I'll never see her again, and if

I do I'll just say, "Hi" and leave it at that. However, months later when you do see her, you may wish you had listened more closely to her name when it was first given. It doesn't have to be difficult to listen. It's not as if you have to memorize their social security number or their favorite verse. It's only a name.

Listen closely for the name. Lean slightly forward, pay attention, and you'll make that person feel like a million dollars. For instance, if you're unsure if the name is *Marie* or *Maria*, ask. There's nothing wrong with saying, "Did you say your name is Maria?" People won't be offended, they'll be flattered. They'll remember you because you're the only person who took the time to want to remember their name.

If the name you hear is unusual, don't hesitate to ask about the origin of it. "Is that a Russian name? I've never heard that name before. Tell me about it. Is it a family name?" People enjoy talking about their name. Remember, they've owned it for years and they're proud of it. They take it with them wherever they go. They may give you suggestions to remember it. For instance, "It's Mollisee; rhymes with policy." "It's Losee; like a low C." "It's Bumberger; like a bad hamburger."

How is your name memorable? If you haven't already, think of ways to make your name meaningful to others. The time you take to do this will be greatly appreciated by those you meet.

The names *John, Mary,* and *Michael* aren't the most popular names. More people are named *Mac, Buddy, Friend, Hey,* or *Chief,* especially by those who have poor listening skills. If you haven't heard the name, the odds are not in your favor you'll remember it. There's a reason why we have two ears and one mouth. By taking the time to listen for the name you're taking the time to learn it.

Guaranteed Return Policy

Potatoes can be very hot to the touch, especially those that have been cooking for 60 minutes. I learned this when I reached into the oven to pull one out. When I grabbed hold of it, I got rid of it immediately. It's a lesson I've long remembered. Names are like hot potatoes. When you're handed a name, get rid of it immediately. Throw it back where it came from. You'll remember the name when you repeat it to the person who gave it to you.

Make your first reply the name you just heard. It will reinforce the name. "Hi, my name is Jerry, what's your name?" "Jerry, hi. My name is Sam." It's one thing to hear the name; it's another to say it. Allow the name to sink into your head and then let it roll off your tongue. Getting into the habit of repeating the name enhances our ability to remember. Before long it will be natural for you to repeat the name. Everyone you meet, throw their name right back. "Cindy, how are you?" "Chuck, glad to see you." "Rita, thanks for stopping by."

By saying the name at the beginning of the conversation, it takes pressure off our mind than if we had to remember the name at the end of the conversation. It's much easier to remember it's Jack we're speaking with when we say "Jack, nice to see you," versus "Nice to see you ... um, Jay? Jim? John?" By the time we say "Nice to see you," we've already forgotten the name because we're thinking about what we're going to say.

Continue to use the name during the conversation, but be careful not to overdo it. Try saying the name at least three times during the conversation. "Jeff, you're in an interesting business. What would you say, Jeff, is your biggest challenge?" "I look forward to seeing you again Jeff. Have a great night."

Repeat the name to yourself several times, but don't lose track with what is being said. Knowing the name of your jumpmaster is one thing; not knowing how to deploy the parachute is another. If you're standing with new acquaintances, quickly go over their names in your mind.

Look at the person to your right and say to yourself, "Al, Al, Al." Now, the person across from you, "Steve, Steve, his name is Steve." It only takes an instant to repeat the names. This exercise will help you secure those names into your mind.

Jot the name down if an opportunity presents itself. Many times at meetings a guest will introduce himself. Take advantage of the moment by writing the name on a piece of paper. Trace the name and circle it. Draw an arrow in the direction where the person is sitting and quietly repeat the name. Again, it takes only an instant to do this. You're not writing a mathematical equation or listing the lakes in Minnesota. You're writing a name. That's it. It's easy and simple, yet powerful and pleasing when you present it to the person at the end of the meeting.

Repetition, whether saying it, thinking it, or writing it bolsters our memory. When someone tells you their name, pretend they're saying, "Repeat after me."

Thanks for Noticing

Whoever said, "No two snowflakes are exactly alike," didn't spend last winter in Buffalo. I could have sworn I spotted two that looked identical. If I were asked which one was responsible for closing schools, I'd have a difficult time identifying them in the police line-up. "I think the second from the right is the one, but then the third from the left looks familiar too."

People, on the other hand, are nothing like snow, even though some may act like flakes.

We are different and rare in every way. An exhibit at *Disney World* flashes a sign that is forever changing. It shows the number of the billions and billions of people in the world. Fortunately, names aren't included. So many people, each with two eyes, a nose, and a mouth, yet they all look differently. Our job is to study the faces we meet and find something that's distinguishable.

Look closely at the eyes. Are they small, large, close together, or far apart? What color are they? Are they blue, brown, or green? What about the eyebrows? Are they thin, bushy, or one straight line? Choose one hundred people off the street and you'll find one hundred different looking eyes and eyebrows.

Study the face some more. Look at the forehead. Is it wrinkled or smooth? Is it large or small? See any freckles? Drop down to the nose and what do you see? Is it pug, narrow, or wide? Is it crooked or straight? Look at the chin. Is it cleft or prominent in any way? Does the jaw protrude? Any dimples? Are the lips thin, full, or about average? How do the teeth look? Are they straight? Is there a gap in the middle? What about high cheek bones? What color is the hair? Is it curly, straight, or balding? Are the ears large or small? After studying all these features it's no wonder why people look differently.

Watch the evening news and study faces of the reporters. Ask yourself, what feature stands out on this person? What do you notice first about their faces? Study the people in commercials and shows. How are they different? Look at photos in the newspaper and study the faces. Study people at the mall. Make mental notes of lips and lobes, chins and cheeks, and brows and bangs.

If you're unable to find one outstanding feature, don't fret. By taking the time to study the face, you're farther along than most people who don't even look at the face and can't remember the name. Get into the habit of studying every face you see. Therefore, it will become second nature when you see a prominent feature.

Get the Picture

Our parents didn't know any better. It's not their fault. They gave us names such as *James, Mary Ann, Susan, Barbara, Peter, Tiffany, Martha, William, Ken, David,* and *Carol*. It might have meant something to them, but for the rest of us it means nothing. What's a *Susan*? What's a *Daniel*? How can I remember the name *Deborah*? I don't even know what it is.

Our parents didn't know that. If they wanted our names to be truly memorable they would have given us names such as *Bookshelf, Radioknob, Keyboard,* or *Frozenyogurt.* These names mean something. "Your name is *Curtainrod?* Hey, I know what that is. I have one of those. By the way, whatever happened to *Dipstick?*"

Most names don't have any significant meaning and they're difficult to remember. In order to retain information for a long time, we have to associate that new information to something we already know.

We're more apt to remember a guy named *Barsoap* than we are a guy named *Phil.* Why? We've seen it, bought it, and used it. We can relate to this guy's name because we know what a bar of soap is. When we see him we think of soap. However, when we see Phil there's a struggle to remember his name because it doesn't remind us of anything. Unless your name is *Phil,* you know someone with the name *Phil,* or you wished your name was *Phil,* it may be hard to remember his name. Therefore, the key to remembering names is to make them meaningful. Visuals accomplish that.

Names, which we had trouble remembering because they had no meaning, will come alive. They're no longer going to lay dormant. They're going to get up and walk and if we can make them run, so be it. These names are going to be enlarged. They're going to fly. They're going to be involved. Every name we hear will be significant, spectacular, and memorable. John Doe won't be any ordinary person. He'll be unforgettable because we'll make him memorable.

Boring, lazy, humdrum names will be exchanged for vibrant, energetic, and exciting names. Let's take the name *Steve.* What word sounds like *Steve* that's meaningful? It must be a name that's tangible and useful. How about *Stove* or *Sleeve?* We know his name isn't *Stove,* but we know what a stove is.

We're associating what we know and are familiar with (*Stove*) to something unfamiliar (*Steve*). By linking the two it's difficult to break them apart. The consonant letters in *STeVe* are *STV*. By placing vowels in and around those letters we come up with *Stove*. *Sleeve* is also similar, because we're keeping the letters *S* and *V*.

Another example is the name *Jim*. What's a *Jim*? I don't know, but I know what a *Gym* is. By associating *Gym* to *Jim* we can't go wrong. We come out with the same sound. We also come out looking smart because we remembered his name. Of course, we needn't tell him how we remembered.

How about the name *Brenda*? Taking the consonants and throwing out the vowels we get *BRND*. What word do you see? *Brand* is one word but it's hard to picture. We want a word that we can visualize and understand. The word *Bread* comes close. The letters *BRD* jump out. *Blender* is another word. We now get the letters *BND* which is similar to *BreNDa*. If we picture a *Blender* on *Brenda*, we'll remember her name. We won't mistakenly call her *Blender*, even though we may crave a strawberry milkshake when we see her.

The name *Evelyn* is similar to *Violin*. *Cheryl* with *Shovel*. The sounds are comparable. *Beverly* to *Beverage*. *Ray* to *sunRAYS* and *Bruce* to *Bruise*. The examples listed are just that. You may come up with better images. The bottom line is, you have to remember the name. As long as you remember the name it doesn't matter what you think of. The only goal is to remember the name and recall it easily.

Once we have an image of the name, connect it to the outstanding feature on the person. If Cheryl's outstanding feature is her long hair, visualize *Shovels* instead of hair coming down her face and shoulders. It's an image not soon to be forgotten.

The more bizarre and ridiculous the picture, the more likely you'll remember the name.

If you meet *Nick* and notice his nose, mentally see a razor (representing *Nick*) replacing his nose. Each *Nick* you meet will be associated with *Razor*.

Each association will mean one specific name. For instance, don't be confused you'll call *Blanche* by the name *Avalanche* when you see her. You won't. The association will remind you of the name. Once you get to know Blanche, the image of the *avalanche* will melt and you'll see her as *Blanche*. Again, we're attaching new information to something we already know.

Visualize *Dollar Bills* when you meet someone named *Bill*. Seeing hundreds of dollar *Bills* flying around *Bill's* nose creates a more vivid picture than seeing just one. If it's only one we may miss it, but several spinning around his nose is memorable. Weeks later when we run into *Bill*, he's already reminding us of his name. You can take that to the bank.

The more we drown him in *bills*, the easier it will be to recall his name. However, start on the face. He may change his tie, his shirt, and jacket, but that face is going to be with him no matter where he goes or what he does.

Practice with the associations provided at the end of this section, or create your own. With a little effort, you'll have standard pictures for every person you meet. Meeting people will begin to take on a new adventure. Everyone has a name and because of that, a picture. Our job is to get that picture into focus each time.

I Can Relate to That

Of the four *Beatles*, Paul McCartney is the one I recall the most. I always felt connected to him. It's a bond similar to what my sister feels toward Jackie Kennedy, my mother to Helen of Troy, and my best friend to Lawrence of Arabia.

Many of us may have difficulty remembering names, but that isn't the case when meeting people who share our name. "Your name is Percy? Hey, that's my name too."

Does the person you're meeting share a name with anyone you know or know of? If so, use your imagination and link the two together. Imagine the two as best friends or roommates.

Meeting a *Donald*? If so, imagine he lives a floor below *Donald Trump* or was Trump's college roommate.

Meeting a *Fred*? Pretend his grandfather was the brains behind the Fred Flintstone character. The image immediately creates an "Oh, Wow." It's those "Oh Wow's" that help us remember.

Meeting a *Jennifer*? Imagine she's best friends with Jennifer Lopez. Perhaps she'll get you a backstage pass.

It takes a split second to see those images, but it's that split second that helps us remember.

Dynamic Duos

What's the name of Frank's wife? Who is Jay married to? Our new neighbors are Sheila and what's-his-name.

It's one thing trying to remember a name, it's another when you have to remember two of them. However, many times we'll know the name of one, but not the other. It's no surprise. We work with Cindy, bowl with Larry, and Jason mows our lawn. Howard is our accountant, Sal is our mail carrier, and Wendy teaches our daughter how to play the piano. It would be nice to remember the names of the people they live with.

If you remember one, it's easy to remember the other by using visuals and association techniques.

Ryan and Shelly are engaged; Tina's young son is David; Mitchell and his little sister, Tracy live next door; and Tyler and Sophie are a great couple. How do we remember all that?

At first glance, the name *Ryan* creates no visual. However, when you say the name s-l-o-w-l-y, a picture evolves. The name *Ryan* becomes *RYE-in.*

Imagine a *Shell* sandwich on *Rye* and you'll remember *Ryan* is married to *Shelly*.

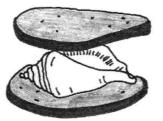

If there's *Mayo* on a *Shell*, you'll know he is married to *Michelle* (Ma-Shell), instead.

The name *Tina* isn't memorable until you realize there's a *Tea* or *Tee* in her name. The name *David* doesn't mean much either, but it does when you remove the vowels; *DVD*.

Spin a *DVD* atop a *Tee* and that's an image that sticks. It also sticks in Tina's mind that you remember her son's name.

Mentally *Trace* over a catcher's *Mitt* and you'll know the two kids next door are *Tracy* and *Mitchell*.

Visualize sewing a tie, and you'll always remember *TIE-ler* (Tyler) and *SEW-phie* (Sophie) go together. Concerned about remembering the next *Sophie* you meet who's married to Tom Pierson, not Tyler? That hazard is avoided when you incorporate their last name into the association. Imagine *Tomatoes Sewn* onto your *Pierced* ears.

It makes no difference what the last name is, there's always something memorable to come out of it.

Meaningful Last Names

Every last name has meaning. If not, it will rhyme or sound like something that is meaningful. No matter how long or hard to pronounce, breaking it down into syllables helps us see pictures.

Color Me Beautiful

There are colorful last names, such as *Green, Redford, Goldberg, Silverstein, Pinkston, White, Blackman, Copperfield, Browning, Blue,* and *Gray.* Think of the people you know with a color in their name. You'll come up with quite a few. Visualize dumping paint on their head. Their name will tell you which color to use. It will be an image that will have a lasting impression, but not on them. The more paint the better.

Once you apply the coat, you won't have any trouble knowing if it were on Mr. *Greenberg, Greenwell, Greenwood, Greenfield,* or *Greenbaum,* or plain old Mr. *Green.* Mentally seeing the green paint will remind you it's Mr. Greenfield. Depending on which *Green,* you can go a step further and visualize him painting the field green, the well green, the wood green, or the bomb green, without having it blow up in your face.

We all come in many shapes and sizes. Some of us come in different colors. So, be ready with your paintbrush when one comes your way.

The Right Place

It would be simpler to remember a name if it also told us where they lived. Many names do. We can imagine Joe, the football great, lived in Montana, or Kirstie, the actress, slept in the Alley. Since they don't we have to imagine they do. The people we meet come from many places. They come from *Rivers, Holmes,* and *Waters.* They live in *Meadows* and *Fields* and *Woods.*

Browse through the newspaper or phone directory and you'll find names with places, such as *Hall, Ward, London, Jordan, Starr, Moon, Houseman, Parish, Lane, Lancaster, Barnes,* and *Barnhill.*

Some of the names might be deceiving. You may not see a place, but if you look closely you can see the *Bar* in *Barton,* the *Car* in *Carlton,* and the *Town* in *Townsend.* Look a little closer and there's a *Trailer* right in front of you when you're introduced to Miss *Traylor* and the *Grave* in Mr. *Gravely.*

Go to the kitchen and you'll meet a lot of people. There's Mr. *Stover,* Mrs. *Stewart,* and Dr. *Rangely.* Look over there and you'll see Mr. *Sinkler,* Mr. *Spooner,* and Mrs. *Washburn.* It's not *being* in the right place at the right time that matters, but *seeing* the right place at the right time.

The Job Line

Many last names are working hard putting in long hours each day. Be on the lookout for these names, such as *Taylor, Miller, Weaver, Shoemaker, Barber, Mason, Hunter, Parker, Butcher, Farmer, Marshall, Letterman, Bishop, King, Chancellor, Foreman,* and the *Blacksmith,* who we prefer to call *Smith.* These names are begging you to remember them, because they're all doing something. They're alive and active.

Visualize throwing knives at Mrs. *Carver,* bricks at Mr. *Brickman,* and nails at Mr. *Carpenter.* You'll never mistake Ms. *Cooke* with Ms. *Baker,* by associating a chef's hat on the former and flour on the latter. Occupational names are working when you may think they're not. There's a *Cop* in *Koppel*, a *Bailiff* in *Bailey*, and a shortstop in *Glover*.

Take a look in the backyard and you'll see the workings of Mrs. *Gardner* and Mrs. *Douglass*. Could they be planting Mr. *Rose* or Mr. *Bush*? There are numerous employed names in the workforce. Although it may take a little effort to find them, they're working hard each day to be remembered.

Hello In There

It would be easy to remember a person's name if they were called *Handcuffs*, *Guitarstrings*, or *Peneraser*. Those names are simple to recall because they're all things. We've seen handcuffs, played with guitar strings, and used pen erasers. We can visualize those objects. At first glance, most last names aren't things, but with a sharp eye and imagination, you'll find them.

Brockington is a name that may appear strange. What's a *Brockington*? I've never seen one of those. Therefore, it's hard to remember because it's a new word. But wait, let's break it down and find words within that name we are familiar with. We see a *Rock*, a *King*, and a *Ton*. There's also the word *Rocking*. The word *Brock* is similar to the word *Broccoli*. With a little imagination, we can picture a king lifting broccoli that weighs a ton.

We've now taken a name, which at first didn't mean anything, and made it memorable.

Most everyone is carrying something. There's a *Harp* in *Harper*, *Staples* in *Stapleton*, and a *Key* in *Keaton*. There's a *Full Lip* in *Phillips*, a *Meltdown* in *Melton*, and a *Mart* in *Martin*.

There's the *Goodman* family who feels well, the *Kaufman* family who can never shake their cold, and the *Pleasants* who are always doing fine. There are the *Nuckols* and *Nichols*, the *Branches* and *Buckmans*, the *Coles* and *Chapmans*. Things are everywhere. No matter whom you meet, whether it's late at *Knight*, middle of the *Davis*, or at high *Noonan*, you'll find something memorable about a name.

The Wild Kingdom

The *SPCA* is understaffed. They have no control over the thousands of animals running through city streets, walking on country roads, or shopping in neighborhood stores. Perhaps you're one of these roaming creatures. If so, you're not alone. There are many names that are animalistic and they could be living in your community.

Keep your eyes open for *Byrd*, *Cowens*, *Hawkins*, *Lyons*, *Salmon*, *Henderson*, *Robins*, *Fox*, *Lambert*, *Wrenn*, *Deerfield*, *Fowler*, *Swanson*, or *Morgan*, who's usually atop the horse. Don't overlook Mr. *Finley*, Mrs. *Barker*, Professor *Doggett*, and Rev. *Catlett*, either.

Be careful not to be tickled by Mrs. *Featherstone*, scratched by Mr. *Clauson*, or be chicken of Mrs. *Cox*. Take good care of yourself by not smoking *Camels* with Mr. *Humphrey*, pigging out with Mr. *Hamilton*, and monkeying around with Miss *Gibbons*. If you do, the *Hunts* will track you down, while the *Carter's* will cart you away. So watch out! It's a jungle out there.

The Grocery List

Associate products to people who have brand names. Visualize wrapping Mr. *Reynolds* up, heating Mrs. *Campbell*, or camping with the *Coleman's*. Don't hesitate to drive Mr. *Ford*, grab a bite with Miss *McDonald*, or wipe down with Mr. *Scott*. Sit down for tea with Mrs. *Lipton*, dunk donuts with Mr. *Duncan*, and munch out with Mrs. *Graham*. Careful now, names can fill you up.

A Simple Breakdown

Any last name, no matter how unusual it may be, can be broken down to something memorable. Think *Blacksmith hammer* when you meet a *Smith*, *Smyth*, or *Schmidt*. Don't worry about being confused. You'll know which name it is because you've already listened carefully for it, looked the person directly in the face, and repeated the name.

Names that end with *Witz*, think *Wits* and visualize a huge brain. Names that end with *Son* tell you whose son it is. Is it Joseph's son, Peter's son, or Albert's son? Think *Beer Stein* when introduced to names that end with *Stein*. Visualize *Men* with names that end with *Man*. Some of them might be mighty like Mr. *Strongman* or weak like Mr. *Holloman*. Put skies on people whose last name end with *Ski* and put *Buns* on people whose last name end with *Berg*. If you know someone with the same name, associate that person to your new friend.

Everywhere you look and everyone you meet has a name doing something. Who are you going to meet today?

In the following exercise, pick out common word(s) from each name. Say the name slowly and record as many words as you hear.

Rozelli _____

Massenburg _____

Giannotti _____

Gustafson _____

Hauser _____

Abernathy _____

Marandino _____

Rembecki _____

Saunderlin _____

Schaefer _____

Skoracky _____

Taliaferro _____

Tonetti _____

Voelcker _____

Cheverton _____

(See page 100 for suggestions)

Feeling of Belonging

We all belong to something. We may work in the computer room with five other people, wear the same uniform as twelve others on the basketball team, or be one of ten on the Board of Directors. No matter whom you meet, they can be associated with a group.

The method for remembering groups is fun. It always works, whether it's the three people who work at the cleaners, the young family of four who live down the street, or the members of the Lakeside Baton Club.

MADD, NOW, and NATO

Mothers Against Drunk Driving, National Organization for Women, and the *North Atlantic Treaty Organization*. Acronyms help us remember.

Ask most people if they know the names of the nine Supreme Court Justices and the answer will be "No." They may know one or two, but all of them are too many to recall. Without acronyms it would be hard to remember.

To remember the justices who were in office at the beginning of 2011, we could repeat the names over and over; *Roberts, Alito, Ginsburg, Sotomayor, Kennedy, Breyer, Thomas, Kagan*, and *Scalia*. But who wants to do that? It takes too much effort. It's better to form an acronym; taking the first letter of each last name to form a word or phrase.

K BAGS SKRT. Using our imagination, we can visual that **Kay bags** a **skirt**. She's doing this as she's speaking to the justices.

KGB'S STARK. Yes, the KGB is a stark contrast from the United States Supreme Court.

KK, STABS, GR. KicK, STABS, and *GRab*, and you're off to court.

There are many other combinations that will jumpstart your memory for remembering, whether it's the Justices or any other group. Rearrange the letters to come up with a memorable acronym.

Drafting the Letters

Another method used for remembering a group is called Acrostic. The first letter of the names you want remembered form a meaningful sentence. Here's one example to recall the Justices:

The Supreme (K)ourt's Rulings, By Great Statesmen, Are (K)aring.

It's Story Time

If statements aren't exciting we can make up a story.

The *Cagey* (Kagan) *Robber* (Roberts), a doubting *Thomas* (Thomas) with *a Lead Toe* (Alito), *Scaled* (Scalia) the Supreme Court building full of *Briar* (Breyer). Then, drank a bottle of *Gin* (Ginsburg), as well as the *Mayor's Soda* (Sotomayor) right out of the *Can* (Kennedy).

By placing the Supreme Court building into the picture, it reminds us the names are for the Supreme Court Justices. We need that anchor (Supreme Court) placed into the story.

Every few years Justices come and go, but remembering them will always be fun and easy.

Come up with an acronym, acrostic, or story for the following groups:

Rose Bowl Grand Marshals (2004-2011)
J. Williams, M. Mouse, O'Connor, Lucas,
Lagasse, Leachman, Sullenberger, and Deen

Moon Walkers
Aldrin, Armstrong, Shepard, Conrad, Bean, Mitchell,
Scott, Irwin, Young, Duke, Cernan, and Schmitt

National Teachers of the Year (2004-2011)
Mellor, Kamras, Oliver, Peterson, Geisen,
Mullen, Wessling, and Shearer

No matter which group, no matter how many, there are methods for remembering.

What's My Line?

In the 1950's and 60's, "*What's My Line?*" was one of television's most popular game shows. A panel of four people asked *Yes* or *No* questions to guess a contestant's occupation.

Today, many of us are still playing the game. We may know the person's name, but aren't sure where they work or vice versa. This can be especially embarrassing after we ask, "How are the trucks running?" and then learn the station where he works is the radio, not the fire.

Knowing what people do for a living reinforces our ability to remember them. It also demonstrates that we're taking an interest. The key with placing people with the right job is making the correct association.

Here is a partial list of President Obama's 2011 Cabinet, and suggestions for remembering them:

Robert Gates / Department of Defense. Closed *gates* are keeping the enemy from *robbing* us.

Eric Holder / Department of Justice. *Just hold* on, you might have made an *error*.

Kenneth Salazar / Department of Interior. A *salamander*, living in a *can*, is an *interior* designer.

Gary Locke / Department of Commerce. *Lock* up the *garage* in the *Commerce* building.

Hilda Solis / Department of Labor. Go up the *hill* and *console* the woman in *labor*.

Thomas Vilsack / Department of Agriculture. The *village ransacked* the *tomatoes*. A friendly version is the *village* used a huge *sack* to gather *tomatoes* for the farmer.

Ray LaHood / Department of Transportation. A *ray* of light hits the *hood*, and now it's time to go.

Arne Duncan / Department of Education. Why *aren't* the students wearing *dunce* caps?

No matter whom you meet, and what they do, you can associate their name to their occupation.

In the examples below, associate the name to the job by linking them in a very bizarre and unusual way. If the name has no meaning, change it slightly to form a memorable picture.

Mr. Montgomery, an accountant.

_____

_____

_____

Mr. Perkins, a telephone installer.

_____

_____

_____

Mrs. Drummond, a physical therapist.

_____

_____

_____

Mr. Ferguson, a postman.

_____

_____

_____

Ms. Wilton, a pharmacist.

_____

_____

_____

Mr. Appleton, a golf pro.

_____

_____

_____

Mrs. Rodriquez, an architect.

_____

_____

_____

Miss Sullivan, an attorney.

_____

_____

_____

It PAY$ to Remember Names

The ability to remember a name and recall it easily gives you an instant advantage. No matter what your profession, you'll be stronger and more influential because of your memory proficiency.

As a banker it demonstrates courtesy. As a lawyer it demonstrates confidence. As a librarian it demonstrates compassion. Because we remember the name, the teller exhibits competence, the attorney displays persuasiveness, and the librarian gets the overdue fine.

A restaurant stays busier, an organization becomes more productive, and a sales force hits quotas when its owners, leaders, and salespeople take the effort to remember names.

Nothing makes you more powerful, more persuasive, and more popular than remembering a name and recalling it easily. Whether you're a politician campaigning for a vote, a manager looking for a result, or a store owner looking for repeat business, a strong memory is essential.

We all come into this world owning nothing, except a name. Through the years we protect it, correct others who mispronounce it, and feel a slight resentment if someone forgets it. By remembering a person's name, it makes that person feel good, and makes them want to know us.

There's no better sound than the sound of our own name.

Names & Associations

Aaron	**Iron**	Ann	**Raggedy Ann**
Abigail	**Abdomen**	Annette	**A Net**
Adam	**Adam's Apple**	Anthony	**Ant**
Adele	**Farmer in the Dell**	Antoinette	**A Twin Net**
Adrienne	**Aid (Red Cross)**	April	**Showers**
Agnes	**Agony**	Archie	**Gateway Arch**
Al	**Ale**	Arnold	**Arm**
Alan	**Allen Wrench**	Art	**Artist**
Alex	**Axle**	Arthur	**Author**
Alexandria	**Licks Hand**	Ashley	**Ashtray**
Alice	**in Wonderland**	Audrey	**Audio**
Alfred	**Hitchcock**	Augustus	**Gust of Wind**
Alfreda	**Alfredo**	Avis	**Rent a Car**
Alisha	**Leash**	Barbara	**Barbed Wire**
Alma	**Alma Mater**	Barry	**Berry**
Alonzo	**A Loner**	Bart	**Bartender**
Alton	**Altar**	Beatrice	**Bee**
Alvita	**Cheese**	Becky	**Beak**
Amanda	**A Man**	Bella	**Bell**
Amy	**Aim-e**	Ben	**Bench**
Andre	**Hand Dry**	Benjamin	**Franklin**
Andrew	**Hand Drew**	Bess	**Boss**
Andy	**Griffith**	Beth	**Bath**
Angel	**Halo**	Betsy	**Ross**
Anita	**Knee**	Betty	**Betting**

Bernard	**Burrr! Nod**	Cameron	**Camera**
Bernice	**Burning**	Carl	**Curl**
Bertha	**Birthday**	Carman	**Car Man**
Beulah	**Beautiful**	Carol	**Car Oil**
Beverly	**Beverage**	Caroline	**Caroling**
Bill	**Dollar Bill**	Carrie	**Carry**
Billy	**Goat**	Carson	**Cars**
Blair	**Bear**	Carter	**Cart**
Blanche	**Avalanche**	Cathy	**Cat**
Bob	**Kabob**	Cecil	**Seal**
Bonita	**Bow and Arrow**	Chad	**Chaps**
Bonnie	**Bonnet**	Charles	**Prince**
Boyd	**Boy**	Charlie	**Horse**
Brad	**Braid**	Charlotte	**Spiderweb**
Brandi	**Brandy**	Cheryl	**Shovel**
Brandon	**Branded**	Chip	**Potato Chips**
Brenda	**Blender**	Chris	**Cross**
Brent	**Bent**	Christy	**Crusty**
Brett	**Barrette**	Chuck	**Throw**
Brian	**Brain**	Cindy	**Cinder**
Bridget	**Bridge**	Claire	**Eclair**
Brittany	**Brick**	Clarence	**Clarinet**
Bruce	**Bruise**	Clark	**Clock**
Buck	**Buck Teeth**	Claudine	**Claw**
Bud	**Bud**	Clay	**Clay**
Byron	**Red Baron**	Clem	**Climb**
Calvin	**Call In**	Cleo	**Cello**

Clete	**Football Cleats**		Dean	**College Dean**
Cliff	**Cliff**		Debbie	**Dobber**
Clint	**Eastwood**		Dee	**Letter D**
Cody	**Morse Code**		Deidre	**Deed**
Colin	**Colon (:)**		Della	**Deli**
Colleen	**Column**		Delores	**Dealer (cards)**
Connie	**Con Man**		Denise	**Niece**
Constance	**Constable**		Dennis	**Dent**
Cornelius	**Corn**		Derek	**Oil Derrick**
Cory	**Apple Core**		Dexter	**Decks**
Courtney	**Court**		Diana	**Princess**
Craig	**Creek**		Dick	**Duck**
Crystal	**Crystal Bowl**		Dion	**D Flashing On**
Curt	**Curtain**		Demetri	**Me a Tree**
Cynthia	**Cinders**		Dolan	**Dole Pineapple**
Cyrus	**Citrus**		Dolly	**Dolly**
Daisy	**Daisy**		Dominic	**Domino**
Dale	**Doll**		Donald	**Trump**
Dan	**Dandelion**		Donna	**Dinner**
Dana	**Great Dane**		Doris	**Door**
Daniel	**Boone**		Dorothy	**Wizard of Oz**
Darla	**Dollar**		Doreen	**Door in Rain**
Darlene	**Darling**		Dot	**Polka**
Darren	**Deer**		Douglas	**Digging for Glass**
Darryl	**Barrell**		Drew	**Draw**
David	**DVD**		Duane	**Drain**
Dawn	**Rising Sun**		Dudley	**Milk Duds**

Duke	**Dock**	Estelle	**Stall**
Dustin	**Dusty**	Ester	**Letter S**
Dwight	**Light**	Ethel	**Ether**
Earl	**Hurl**	Eugene	**Huge Jeans**
Ed	**Mister Ed**	Eva	**Evening**
Edie	**Eat**	Evelyn	**Violin**
Edgar	**Cigar**	Everett	**Mount Everest**
Edith	**Bunker**	Faye	**Hay**
Edna	**Bed**	Faith	**Prayer**
Eileen	**I Lean**	Felecia	**Felt a Leash**
Elaine	**Lane**	Felix	**The Cat**
Eleanor	**Elephant**	Ferguson	**Fur**
Elise	**Lease**	Florence	**Floor**
Elizabeth	**Lizard**	Floyd	**Flood**
Ellen	**Lion**	Forrest	**Forest**
Elliott	**Idiot**	Foster	**Fist**
Elmo	**Eskimo**	Frank	**Hot Dog**
Elsie	**Cow**	Frasier	**Fraser Fir**
Emile	**Meal**	Fred	**Flintstone**
Emily	**Letter M**	Freda	**Fried**
Emma	**M & M's**	Gail	**Wind**
Emmett	**Mitt**	Garland	**Judy**
Eric	**Rock**	Garrison	**Carry Son**
Ericka	**Rocker**	Gary	**Garlic**
Erin	**Errand**	Gavin	**Gavel**
Ernie	**Urn**	Gene	**Jeans**
Ervin	**Curved Van**	Genevieve	**Generous**

Geoff	**Chef**	Helen	**Hell (devil)**
George	**Washington**	Henry	**Hen**
Gerry	**Cherry**	Herb	**Herb**
Gertrude	**Girdle**	Herman	**Hermit Crab**
Giles	**Gel**	Hershel	**Hershey Bar**
Gill	**Fish Gill**	Hilda	**Hill**
Ginger	**Ginger Snaps**	Hillary	**Clinton**
Gladys	**Glad Trash Bag**	Holly	**Holly (Christmas)**
Glenn	**Glue**	Homer	**Home Run**
Gloria	**Glory (flag)**	Hope	**Hop**
Gordon	**Accordion**	Horace	**Whole Rice**
Grace	**Grease**	Howard	**HOW! (Indian)**
Grady	**Grate**	Hugh	**Hoe**
Graham	**Cracker**	Hubert	**Sherbert**
Greg	**Egg**	Ian	**Eel**
Guy	**Big Guy**	Ida	**Eye Drops**
Gwen	**Gown**	Ingrid	**Grid**
Hal	**Hail**	Iola	**Eye**
Hank	**Honk**	Irene	**Running Eyes**
Harley	**Harley Davidson**	Iris	**Flower**
Harold	**How Old?**	Irvin	**Curved Van**
Harrison	**Hairy Son**	Isaac	**Eye Sacks**
Harry	**Hairy**	Isabelle	**Icy Bell**
Harvey	**Carve**	Israel	**Rail**
Hattie	**Hat**	Ivan	**Eye on Van**
Hazel	**Hazy**	Jack	**Tire Jack**
Heath	**Heart**	Jackie	**Jacket**

Jacob	**Hiccup**	Joyce	**Joist**
Jake	**Shake**	Juanita	**Wound Up**
James	**Jam**	Jud	**Shed**
Jamie	**J for Me**	Judith	**Jewish**
Jane	**Chain**	Judy	**Chewed Tee**
Janet	**Janitor**	Julia	**Julia Child**
Janice	**Janitor on Ice**	Julie	**Jewelry**
Janine	**Chin**	Julius	**Caesar**
Jason	**Chase Son**	June	**June Bug**
Jay	**Letter J**	Justin	**Juice**
Jean	**Jeans**	Karl	**Collar**
Jeff	**Chef**	Karen	**Car**
Jennifer	**Gin**	Kate	**Kite**
Jerome	**Go Home**	Kathleen	**Cat Lean**
Jerry	**Cherry**	Kathy	**Cat**
Jessica	**Chest**	Katie	**K Tie**
Jill	**Chill**	Kay	**Letter K**
Jim	**Gym**	Keith	**Key**
Joan	**Phone**	Kelly	**Kelly Green**
Jody	**Shoddy**	Kelvin	**Kettle**
Joe	**Sloppy Joe**	Ken	**Can**
Joel	**Jewel**	Kendall	**Candle**
Joey	**Kangaroo**	Kermit	**the Frog**
John	**Portajohn**	Kerry	**Carry**
Joseph	**Show Stuff**	Kevin	**Cave In**
Joshua	**Shower**	Kim	**Comb**
Joy	**Joy Stick**	Kirby	**Curb**

Kirk	**Keg**	Lloyd	**Loud Music**
Kristen	**Christmas**	Lois	**Lois Lane**
Kristy	**Crusty**	Lonnie	**Loan**
Kurt	**Curtain**	Lorenzo	**Lawman**
Kyle	**Coil**	Lorraine	**Rain**
Lance	**Lancer**	Lou	**Loop**
Larry	**Lard**	Louise	**Sneeze**
LaToya	**Toy**	Lowell	**Low Well**
Laurie	**Truck (UK)**	LuAnn	**Love Hand**
Laverne	**Lavatory**	Lucille	**Loose Wheel**
Lawrence	**Rinse**	Lucy	**I Love Lucy**
Leah	**Hawaiian Lei**	Luke	**Luke Warm**
Lee	**Leech**	Lydia	**Lid**
Lenora	**Ignore Her**	Lyle	**Aisle**
Leon	**Lion**	Lynn	**Linen**
Leonard	**Leopard**	Lynnette	**Hair Net**
Leroy	**Lawyer**	Mabel	**Table**
Leslie	**Less Sign (<)**	Madeline	**Mad Lion**
Lester	**List Her**	Mae	**West**
Letitia	**La T-shirt**	Maggie	**Magazine**
Lewis	**Boo Us**	Malcolm	**Milk**
Lila	**Lie Down**	Marcia	**Marshmallow**
Lillian	**Lily**	Margaret	**Margarine**
Lincoln	**Abe**	Maria	**Sound of Music**
Linda	**Lint**	Marie	**Marry Me**
Lindsay	**Lint in Suds**	Marilyn	**Monroe**
Lisa	**Pizza**	Marion	**Mirror**

Mark	**Marksmith**	Montgomery	**Mountain of Gum**
Martha	**Washington**	Mort	**Mutt**
Martin	**Mart**	Morton	**Morton Salt**
Marvin	**Marvelous**	Muriel	**Mural**
Mary	**Had a Lamb**	Myron	**My Run**
Mason	**Mason Jar**	Nancy	**Nun**
Matthew	**Mat**	Naomi	**Name Me**
Maureen	**Listerine**	Natalie	**Gnat**
Max	**Ax**	Natasha	**No Touch**
Maya	**Migraine**	Nathan	**Gnat**
Meg	**Mug**	Neil	**Kneel**
Mel	**Melt**	Murray	**in a Hurry**
Melanie	**Melt a Knee**	Morley	**More! More!**
Melissa	**Molasses**	Nelson	**Nails**
Merna	**Mourner**	Newton	**Fig Newton**
Michael	**Muscle**	Nicholas	**Nickel**
Michelle	**Shell**	Nick	**Razor Nick**
Mickey	**Mouse**	Nicole	**Coal**
Mike	**Microphone**	Nora	**Norway**
Mildred	**Mildew**	Norma	**Normal (98.6)**
Miles	**Smiles**	Olivia	**Olive**
Minnie	**Mini Skirt**	Oral	**Mouth**
Mitch	**Mitt**	Ordell	**Order Form**
Missy	**Messy**	Orlando	**Disney World**
Mona	**Moan**	Orville	**Oar**
Monica	**Harmonica**	Oscar	**the Grouch**
Monte	**Mountain**	Otis	**Oats**

Owen	**Oh Win**	Ray	**Sunshine**
Paige	**Page**	Reba	**Rub**
Pamela	**Pan**	Rebecca	**Rub Back**
Patricia	**Pat on Head**	Reggie	**Ridge**
Patty	**Hamburger**	Regina	**Raging Bull**
Paul	**Pole**	Reid	**Reading**
Pearl	**Pearl**	Renee	**Running**
Peggy	**Miss Piggy**	Richard	**Rich Man**
Penelope	**Pen in Envelope**	Rick	**Rickshaw**
Penny	**Penny**	Rita	**Reading**
Perry	**Pear**	Robert	**Robber**
Peter	**Peat Moss**	Robin	**Robin**
Phillip	**Full Lip**	Rodney	**Fishing Rod**
Phoebe	**Frisbee**	Roger	**Over and Out**
Phyllis	**Diller**	Roland	**Rolling**
Polly	**Want a Cracker**	Ronald	**McDonald**
Porter	**Porter**	Rose	**Rose**
Preston	**Press**	Roslyn	**Rosin**
Priscilla	**Cinderella**	Ross	**Rust**
Queen	**Queen Bee**	Roy	**Rogers**
Quincy	**Cue Stick**	Ruby	**Stone**
Quinton	**Squint**	Rudy	**Rude**
Rachel	**Reach**	Rufus	**Roof**
Ralph	**Vomit**	Russ	**Rustling Leaves**
Randle	**Candle**	Rusty	**Rusty Gate**
Randolph	**Running**	Ruth	**Tooth**
Randy	**Ran**	Ryan	**Rye Bread**

Sadie	**Sad**	Tanya	**Tan**
Samantha	**Cement**	Ted	**Toad**
Samuel	**Uncle Sam**	Teddy	**Bear**
Sandra	**Sand Dry**	Terrence	**Terrier**
Sandy	**Sandy Beach**	Terry	**Terry Cloth**
Scott	**Scotch Tape**	Thelma	**Thermos**
Sean	**Yawn**	Theodore	**Roosevelt**
Seth	**Breath**	Theresa	**Tears**
Shannon	**Shade**	Thomas	**Doubting Thomas**
Sharon	**Sharing**	Tim	**Timber**
Sherman	**Germ**	Tina	**Tiny**
Sherry	**Sherry**	Todd	**Tardy**
Shirley	**Curly**	Tom	**Tomato**
Sibrena	**Subway**	Tony	**The Tiger**
Sidney	**Kidney**	Tracy	**Trace**
Sonya	**Sun**	Travis	**Travel**
Sophia	**Sofa**	Troy	**Toy**
Stacy	**Stay!**	Truman	**Harry Truman**
Stan	**Stand**	Turner	**Apple Turnover**
Stephen	**Even**	Tyronne	**Tie**
Steve	**Stove**	Ulysses	**Grant**
Stuart	**Stew**	Ursula	**Verse**
Sue	**Sue Me!**	Valerie	**Veil**
Sylvester	**Stallone**	Vanessa	**Vanish**
Sylvia	**Silver Bowl**	Vaughan	**Horn**
Tamara	**Camera**	Vera	**Voice**
Tammy	**Tambourine**	Vernon	**Fern**

Veronica	**Venom**	Zachary	**Sack**
Vic	**Victory**	Zane	**Zany**
Victoria	**Victoria's Secret**	Zelma	**Sell More**
Vincent	**1 Cent**		
Virgil	**Fur Gel**		
Virginia	**Virginia Ham**		
Vivian	**Viva Las Vegas**		
Walker	**Walker**		
Wallace	**Wall Lace**		
Walter	**Wall**		
Wanda	**Wand**		
Warren	**War**		
Wayne	**Wine**		
Weldon	**Welder**		
Wendy	**Windy**		
Wesley	**Vest**		
Whitney	**Witty**		
Wilbur	**Wright**		
Will	**a Will**		
William	**Shakespeare**		
Wilson	**Will Sun**		
Winfred	**Win**		
Woodrow	**Wooden Row**		
Woody	**Woodpecker**		
Xavier	**X**		
Yolanda	**Yo-Yo**		
Yvonne	**Van**		

Suggestions from page 81:

Rozelli	Row, Rose, Sell, Silly
Massenburg	Mass, Burg, Messy burger
Gianotti	Letter G, Knot, Tea or Tee
Gustafson	Gust, Tough son
Hauser	House her, How sir?
Abernathy	Abs (stomach), Burr, Gnat
Marandino	Mare, Ran, Dean
Rembecki	Rim, Ram, Becky
Saunderlin	Thundering, Sauna
Schaefer	Shave fur
Skoracky	Score, Rack, Key
Taliaferro	Telephone, Tell fur, Row
Tonetti	Toe or Tow, Net, Tee
Voelcker	Vulgar, Vulture
Cheverton	Chevy ton, Shiver ton

By breaking it down to each syllable, you'll discover every name has meaning.

Chapter 6

How to Remember Appointments

Time is money. Not remembering a dental appointment, business meeting, or luncheon can cost us. If we had only remembered to write it on the calendar or put the information into our phone, everything would have been right. Unfortunately, we forgot. The upside is we still have our brain. Our brain will bail us out.

The key is to bring the day, the time, and the appointment into one visual. This is how it's accomplished using anchors of the phonetic alphabet (see pages 35-38).

Each day of the week will be coded to a number, beginning with Monday.

Monday = 1 (t/d)

Tuesday = 2 (n)

Wednesday = 3 (m)

Thursday = 4 (r)

Friday = 5 (L)

Saturday = 6 (sh/ch/j/soft g)

Sunday = 7 (k/q/hard c and g)

You need to remember a dental appointment for Thursday at 3 pm. Those are three things you need to remember.

What day?	Thursday
What time?	3 pm
What's it for?	Dental

Thursday is the 4th day of the week. Four = r. The appointment is for 3 pm. Three = m. The anchor for a combined 4 and 3 is *ram*.

The first consonant sound is the day of the week; the second sound is the time. Therefore, *ram* can only be Thursday at 3. Now, let's bring the day, time, and appointment into one ridiculous picture.

Imagine a *ram* working on your teeth. It's a talented animal, so don't worry. However, it is unusual.

As you mentally review your anchors for each day, you'll be reminded of the 3:00 dental appointment when you get to *ram*.

List the day of the week and time for the following words:

Tot _____

Wiener _____

TV _____

Dime _____

Chime _____

Wagon _____

Lily _____

For 10:00, since it's the only time with a 0 present, we can drop the 1. For example, Thursday at 10 is *rose*; Tuesday at 10 is *nose*; and Saturday at 10 is *cheese*.

What day is *keys*? How about *lasso, mouse,* and *daisy*?

For 11:00, Monday is *dotted*; Tuesday is *knotted*; Wednesday is *matted*; Thursday is *rotted*; Friday is *loaded*; Saturday is *cheated*; and Sunday is *cadet*.

For 12:00, Monday is *Titan*; Tuesday is *antenna*; Wednesday is *mitten*; Thursday is *red wine*; Friday is *Aladdin*; Saturday is *show tune*; and Sunday is *kitten*.

Think of quarters for quarter after the hour; a grapefruit half for half past the hour; and an old, vinyl 45 rpm record or a Colt 45 pistol for 45 minutes past the hour.

For specific times, see the number directory beginning on page 235.

There should be no confusion with morning or evening times. You'll know not to show up at the dental office on Monday at 8:00 *pm* when you visualize a **TV**. You'll also know the soccer banquet on Friday doesn't begin at 7:00 *am* when you visualize kicking a *log*.

Prior to settling in for the night, quickly go over the next day's anchors in your mind. When one of your objects is doing something, you'll be reminded of the appointment.

As the days pass, you won't be confused the dance recital is at 4:00 on Friday, when last week it was 1:00 on Tuesday. When you incorporate association and exaggeration with the appointment, it will override your previous image.

Practice this system without delay. There are people in your life depending on you to show up on time.

ANSWERS from previous page:

Tot = Monday 1:00
Wiener = Tuesday 4:00
TV = Monday 8:00
Dime = Monday 3:00
Chime = Saturday 3:00
Wagon = Sunday 2:00
Lily = Friday 5:00
Keys = Sunday 10:00
Lasso = Friday 10:00
Daisy = Monday 10:00
Mouse = Wednesday 10:00

Chapter 7

How to
Remember Events

E very day someone is celebrating a birthday. Today could be that special day for a friend, a relative, or co-worker. If it were, would you know?

Birthdays and anniversaries come and go. The problem is, trying to remember them is difficult because our memory comes and goes, too. September 9th, August 9th, or was it March 29th? Who remembers? Months and days run together making them difficult to tell them apart.

This chapter makes each one of your schoolmates, co-workers, cousins, kids, and anyone else's special day, memorable.

Each day of the year will have a unique meaning for you. But first, you must familiarize yourself with the phonetic alphabet (see pages 35-37).

Recap of The Phonetic Alphabet

0 = s/z/soft c
1 = t/d
2 = n
3 = m
4 = r
5 = L
6 = ch/sh/j/soft g
7 = k/q/hard c and g
8 = f/v/ph
9 = p/b

January is the 1st month, therefore every visual for January will begin with the consonant sound *t/d*. The second consonant sound represents the day of that month. For instance, the word ***denim*** can only mean January 23 (*d* codes to *1*; *n* codes to *2*; *m* codes to *3*).

February is the 2nd month; therefore each visual for that month begins with the consonant sound *n*. The next sound will be the day of that month. For instance, the word *onion* translates to February 2.

When someone tells you their birthday, visual that person cutting into a birthday cake, and imagine the object coming out. Visualizing a ***monkey*** can only mean the birthday is March 27. The first sound is the month. The second sound is the day.

If it's a wedding anniversary you want to remember, visualize the couple getting married. However, instead of exchanging rings, they exchange a ***piano*** (September, 2); an ***old shoe*** (May, 16); or a ***fish*** (August, 6).

NOTE: October is the 10th month, but each object in that month begins with a *z/s* or *soft c*, instead of a *t/d*. It's the only month with a 0 present, and therefore we don't have to recall up to four digits. For instance, October 18 translates to 018 (***stove***), instead of 1018.

The days in January will not be confused with those in November. For instance, January 14 transposes to 114, while November 4 transposes to 1104. Single digits for the 11th month include a 0.

Each date represents a visual or phrase which makes it memorable. Associate the image to the person who is celebrating the special day, and you'll hold that connection for a long time.

Do you know...

The day in 1706 Benjamin Franklin was born? If you connect *hot dog* to him, you'll know it was January 17th.

The day in 1932 actress Elizabeth Taylor was born? Think of her *yawning*, and you'll know it was February 27th.

The day in 1877 Alexander Bell uttered "Mr. Watson. Come here."? If you *fiddle* with your phone, you'll know it was August 15th.

The day in 1953 John F. Kennedy married Jacqueline Bouvier? If you imagine the couple exchanging a *button*, you'll know it was September 12th.

The day in 1973 Secretariat won the Triple Crown? If you imagine the racehorse on a *ship*, you'll know it was June 9th.

After centuries of lying dormant, the calendar has now come alive. Each day is a living, breathing organism waiting to attach itself to the event you want remembered. Get to know it and put it to work today.

January (t/d)

1 toad
2 tuna
3 tomb
4 tire
5 doll
6 dish
7 dog
8 TV
9 tub
10 dates
11 dotted
12 Titan
13 tea time
14 detour
15 title
16 hot dish
17 hot dog
18 white dove
19 hot tub
20 twins
21 tent
22 white onion
23 denim
24 diner
25 toenail
26 teenage
27 tongue
28 wet knife
29 tune-up
30 dimes
31 timid

February (n)

1 net
2 nun
3 gnome
4 wiener
5 kneel
6 nacho
7 neck
8 knife
9 knob
10 windows
11 knotted
12 antenna
13 anatomy
14 winter
15 needle
16 in touch
17 antique
18 nod off
19 no tip
20 onions
21 unwind
22 no, no, no
23 no name
24 no winner
25 new nail
26 an inch
27 yawning
28 new knife
29 onion pie

March (m)		April (r)	
1	maid	1	rat
2	money	2	rain
3	mummy	3	ram
4	hammer	4	roar
5	mail	5	rail
6	match	6	roach
7	hammock	7	rake
8	movie	8	roof
9	map	9	rope
10	mitts	10	radios
11	matted	11	rotted
12	mitten	12	red wine
13	medium	13	redeem
14	motor	14	radar
15	medal	15	rattle
16	muddy shoe	16	radish
17	medic	17	red wig
18	midwife	18	write off
19	made up	19	read up
20	moons	20	rinse
21	mint	21	rent
22	mean hen	22	reunion
23	my name	23	rename
24	minor	24	runner
25	manly	25	renewal
26	munch	26	wrench
27	monkey	27	ring
28	mean wave	28	runoff
29	mean boy	29	rainbow
30	Moms	30	rooms
31	mimed		

May (L)

1   wallet
2   lion
3   lime
4   lawyer
5   lily
6   leash
7   lock
8   leaf
9   lip
10 lettuce
11 low tide
12 Aladdin
13 yell time
14 ladder
15 ladle
16 old shoe
17 old wig
18 lead off
19 laid up
20 lines
21 walnut
22 linen
23 yell enemy
24 liner
25 lonely
26 lunch
27 lingo
28 lean off
29 line-up
30 limbs
31 helmet

June (sh/ch/j/soft g)

1   shed
2   chain
3   jam
4   cherry
5   jail
6   judge
7   shake
8   chef
9   ship
10 jets
11 cheated
12 show tune
13 huge dome
14 chowder
15 shuttle
16 huge dish
17 huge dog
18 shut off
19 chewed up
20 jeans
21 giant
22 John Wayne
23 shiny ham
24 shiner
25 channel
26 change
27 junk
28 huge Navy
29 chin-up
30 chimes

July (k/q/hard c and g)

1 coyote
2 wagon
3 gum
4 car
5 eagle
6 couch
7 cake
8 coffee
9 cape
10 goats
11 cadet
12 kitten
13 academy
14 guitar
15 cattle
16 cottage
17 aquatic
18 get off
19 giddyup
20 canes
21 candy
22 cannon
23 can ham
24 canary
25 canal
26 gun show
27 king
28 go Navy
29 canopy
30 combs
31 comedy

August (f/v/ph)

1 photo
2 phone
3 foam
4 fire
5 file
6 fish
7 fig
8 fife
9 FBI
10 fits
11 faded
12 futon
13 feed me
14 fighter
15 fiddle
16 fetish
17 fatigue
18 vote off
19 fed up
20 vans
21 faint
22 funny one
23 phone home
24 funnier
25 vinyl
26 finish
27 funky
28 funny wife
29 heavy nap
30 fumes
31 vomit

September (p/b)

1 bat
2 piano
3 bomb
4 bear
5 pillow
6 peach
7 bike
8 beehive
9 pipe
10 beets
11 potato
12 button
13 bottom
14 butter
15 paddle
16 paid wage
17 boutique
18 bit off
19 paid up
20 bones
21 paint
22 banana
23 Panama
24 pioneer
25 panel
26 bench
27 bank
28 pen wife
29 pin-up
30 poems

October (s/z/soft c)

1 sod
2 sun
3 zoom
4 soar
5 seal
6 switch
7 sock
8 sofa
9 soap
10 seeds
11 seated
12 stone
13 sodium
14 star
15 steel
16 stash
17 stick
18 stove
19 step
20 swans
21 sand
22 icy onion
23 sunny home
24 sonar
25 snail
26 snowshoe
27 sink
28 sniff
29 snap
30 swims
31 summit

November (t/d, t/d)

1 wet test
2 too, too soon
3 dates him
4 dates her
5 wet tassel
6 Dad's shoe
7 today is okay
8 date is off
9 heated soup
10 eat toads
11 toot, toot
12 hit Titan
13 dotted ham
14 dotted door
15 dotted tail
16 heated dish
17 heated deck
18 dead dove
19 dotted pie
20 Titans
21 dead end
22 heated onion
23 titanium
24 eat dinner
25 hit toenail
26 heated nacho
27 Titanic
28 diet on/off
29 heated knob
30 dead mouse

December (t/d, n)

1 twin city
2 tiny son
3 tiny sum
4 dinosaur
5 tonsil
6 tan switch
7 tiny sock
8 twin sofa
9 tunes up
10 doughnuts
11 height and weight
12 downtown
13 Tiny Tim
14 Twin Tower
15 tiny hotel
16 tiny dish
17 tan dog
18 tune TV
19 dented pie
20 eat onions
21 tenant
22 tiny onion
23 tiny gnome
24 tiny honor
25 down the Nile
26 twin notch
27 tanning
28 tan knife
29 tiny knob
30 tan moose
31 dynamite

Chapter 8

Remembering Calendars

Whoever said, "Death and Taxes are the only certainties in life," didn't own a dog. Visit a dog owner's home and the countdown begins when Fido will be asked to roll over, shake your hand, or simply sit. Dog owners relish in showing you their four-legged friend's latest trick.

Don't despair if you have no pet. With your new memory, you can be just as engaging. Your bag of tricks will have people flocking by your side asking, "Do it again, will you?" You'll be happy to oblige, especially since you won't be asked to chase down a *Frisbee*.

You know you're special because you're the only person in the room who understands anchors, association, and exaggeration. To prove your point, you're about to show everyone how you can memorize an entire calendar. When they give you a date on the calendar, you'll be able to tell them what day of the week it falls. It will also help you get invited to a few more parties.

To memorize a 365-day calendar, there are a few basics we need to know:

1. There are twelve months, beginning with January and ending with December.

2. There are seven days in each week, beginning with Monday and ending with Sunday.

3. Arithmetic. How to add.

Begin by creating visuals for each month.

January = ball drop at Times Square, representing a new year
February = snowman
March = march-ing band
April = shower
May = flowers
June = graduation cap
July = fireworks
August = ocean waves, as in a summer day at the beach
September = school bus
October = Halloween
November = turkey
December = Christmas tree

Next, we take the numbers 1 through 7, representing the seven days of the week, and transpose them to visuals. Any number system will work, whether it's phonetic, number/shape, or rhyme time. Let's use the latter.

1 = sun
2 = shoe
3 = tree
4 = door
5 = hive
6 = bricks
7 = clouds (from heaven)

As an example, let's say the first Monday of each month is as follows:

January 2; February 6; March 6; April 3; May 1; June 5; July 3; August 7; September 4; October 2; November 6; and December 4.

To remember January 2nd is the first Monday of the month, we visualize a huge *Shoe*, instead of the ball, dropping in New York's Times Square. When we see that visualization we haven't just memorized the first Monday of the month, but the other 30 days, as well.

For example, what day does January 11th fall on? If we know January 2nd is a Monday, we know seven days later, the 9th, is a Monday, too. Two days later is Wednesday the 11th.

What day falls on January 24th? By knowing that January 2nd is a Monday, we only have to do simple math to know the answer. Seven days from the 2nd is Monday the 9th. Add seven days and it's Monday the 16th. Add another seven days and it's Monday the 23rd. Add one more day. January 24th is on a Tuesday.

For February 6th visualize a *Snowman* made out of *Bricks*.

For March 6th visualize *Bricks* beating the drum of the *Marching* band.

To remember April 3rd is a Monday, simply associate a *Tree* taking a *Shower*. Once we commit that to memory, we've also remembered the other days in April.

To remember the days from May to August, visualize *Flowers* stuck in the *Sun*; a *Beehive* stuck to a *Graduation Cap*; a *fireworks* display of *Trees*, and surfers riding a *Wave* of *Clouds*.

To recall September to December, picture a *School Bus* stuffed with *Doors*; *Shoes* dropped into a *Trick or Treat Bag*; *Bricks* carving a *Turkey*; and a decorated *Door* as a *Christmas Tree*.

By remembering these 12 images, we've not only memorized the entire calendar of 365 days, but the following year and the year after that, as well. If we know the first Monday in September is the 4th, then the next year the first Monday will be on the 3rd, and the following year will be on the 2nd.

See the power of a trained memory? By memorizing 12 images, we're able to memorize over 1000 days on the calendar. However, pay attention to those leap years, as they can trip you up.

Remembering the calendar is similar to finding the word in a dictionary. It's all about mental compartments. Your friends will think you've spent months memorizing all 365 days. However, what they don't know is you've established a dozen anchors; a starting point for each month. With that starting point, you know every day of the week.

This system comes in handy in other ways, too. When you're asked if you want to go to the drive-in movie on the 7th of next month, you can reply, "Sorry Charlie, Thursday's are when I wash my hair."

Chapter 9

How to Remember
Playing Cards

*G*o *Fish* isn't just a popular card game; it's what we ask our brain to do when we try to remember information. Often it pulls the line up with nothing on the hook. Let's face it, we just plain forget.

The same is true when playing cards. Cards flash by us and we can't remember if the *3 of Clubs* or the *5 of Spades* were played. They all look the same. Think of the advantage you'd have if you could remember.

No matter what game you're playing, a powerful memory gives you an advantage and a leg up on the competition. Even if you're not holding all the cards, your mind is.

If you're not a card player, you'd be an instant hit at all the parties by demonstrating your incredible memory card trick. All it takes is learning a few simple rules, a creative imagination, and a deck of cards.

What are you waiting for? It's your move.

Linking Pictures to Pictures

So many cards, so many numbers and shapes. How can we remember them? We remember them by making each one of the 52 cards memorable, by creating one vivid image that separates it from the next.

Numbers are boring. They're just a collection of some vertical lines, horizontal lines, and loops. Since numbers are not lifelike, we'll make them so by utilizing a variation of the phonetic alphabet (see pages 35-37).

Phonetic Alphabet for Playing Cards

0 = s   reminder ... send help ... S O S
2 = n   reminder ... n stands on 2 legs
3 = m   reminder ... m stands on 3 legs
4 = r   reminder ... four ends with r
5 = L   reminder ... roman numeral 50 is L
6 = ch   reminder ... ahCHoo, ahCHoo ... I'm 6 (*sick)*
7 = c   reminder ... sail the 7 C's
8 = v   reminder ... V8 Juice
9 = b   reminder ... upside down b resembles 9

By using the phonetic alphabet, numbers are turned into words. The letters, *w, h, a, e, i, o, u,* and *y* do not transpose to any number. They are used to set up words.

For example, the *4 of Spades* does not make for a memorable image, therefore, we need to create one.

The number *4* equals an *R* sound. *Spades* begin with the letter *S*. The word **Ro**S**e** becomes the *4 of Spades*. The *R* and *S* sounds are heard.

The first sound is the number,
the second sound is the suit.

The *4 of Spades* has become memorable because it can be visualized. It's a **Ro**S**e**. You can plant it, smell it, or give it to someone you like. When you want to recall the *4 of Spades* visualize a *ROSE*. That's memorable!

Forgetful

Memorable

Diamonds

AD / Diamond
2D / Noodle
3D / Mud
4D / Rod
5D / Lid
6D / Chowder
7D / Cod
8D / Video
9D / Bed
10D / Sod
JD / Jackpot
QD / Quads
KD / Kid

Clubs

AC / Club
2C / Door Knocker
3C / Microphone
4C / Rock
5C / Lock
6C / Chick
7C / Ice Cream Cone
8C / Vacuum
9C / Bicycle
10C / Sock
JC / Jack Nicklaus
QC / Quack
KC / Kick

Hearts

NOTE: For cards 2 through 10, the words end with the letter *h*, for *hearts*.

AH / Heart
2H / Neigh
3H / Mouth
4H / Reach
5H / Leash
6H / Shiloh
7H / Cough
8H / Van Gogh
9H / Bath
10H / Sleigh
JH / Jackhammer
QH / Queen Elizabeth
KH / Khaki pants

Spades

AS / Shovel
2S / Nose
3S / Mouse
4S / Rose
5S / Lasso
6S / Cheese
7S / Case
8S / Vase
9S / Bus
10S / SeeSaw
JS / Jacks
QS / "Q"Stick
KS / Keys

The cards have now taken on a new life. Study the pictures, then close your eyes and visualize each card. For instance, the *3 of Diamonds* translates to MuD (first sound is number; second sound is suit). See in your "mind's eye" jumping into a mud puddle. The mud puddle will always represent the *3 of Diamonds*.

The pictures are memorable because they are action-oriented. The duck quacks, the dog bites, the vacuum runs, and the bike rolls. They're more memorable than the cards they replace.

For the 2C, visualize a door knocker. For the JC, visualize Jack Nicklaus swinging a golf club or simply, imagine a golf club. For the AC, imagine a caveman's club. For the QC, imagine a duck quacking, or mentally see a duck. For KC, visualize kicking a football, or just imagine a football.

For the 2N, imagine a horse. For the 4H, imagine reaching for something, such as an apple. For the 6H, imagine a rifle or cannon at the Battle of Shiloh. For the 8H, imagine the artist Van Gogh, or simply think of a van. Make certain you have one standard visual for each card. Since the visual for 3H (*mouth*) and 7H (*cough*) are similar, imagine a tissue for the latter.

For the 4D, imagine a fishing rod. For the QD, visualize working your quads at the gym, or just picture any piece of workout equipment.

Why do all the 10's begin with an S? It's the only card with a zero present. Therefore, *Sod, Sock, Seesaw,* and *Sleigh* can mean only the 10 of Diamonds, Clubs, Spades, and Hearts, respectively.

To help you associate each visual, get a deck of playing cards and write the object onto the card it represents. Therefore, when you're looking at the card, you're also looking at the object. Spend an evening studying each suit. Before the week is out, you'll automatically "see" a slice of cheese pizza when you're looking at the 6 of Spades; a jackhammer when you see a Jack of Hearts; and an ice cream cone will be dripping off the 7 of Clubs.

What's the purpose of this again?

We've taken 52 ordinary cards and associated each one with a visual. We remember in pictures. Pictures leave an impression with us. It's easier to imagine a horse sitting atop a bicycle than it is to picture the 2 of Hearts, followed by the 9 of Clubs.

I noticed a pattern with the aces.

The Aces represent the suit. Nothing complicated there.

How can I remember cards that were played?

You must go on the attack. Use a baseball bat and destroy the image of the card that's been played. For example, see yourself whacking a *Leash* (5H), a *Sleigh* (10H), a *Van* (8H), *Football* (KC), a *Rose* (4S), a *Mouse* (3S), and a fishing *Rod* (4D). When you mentally go through each card, you'll know which cards were played and which cards weren't.

Won't this confuse me when I play another game?

It could if you play back to back, so it's best to use another weapon. In the next game, visualize pouring hot coffee on the cards that were played. You could also imagine hitting each card with a hockey stick or blowing them up with a grenade.

Why so violent?

You want to win the game, don't you?

What weapons shouldn't I use?

A club, a fishing rod, and a cue stick, to name a few. All those represent certain cards. You want to use a weapon that won't confuse you with any of the 52 cards.

I REALLY LIKE THE PEOPLE I PLAY BRIDGE WITH, SO IS THERE A NON-VIOLENT METHOD TO REMEMBERING?

Yes. It's called the Link System. It's simple. Mentally place the first card into the environment of the following card and continue the pattern. Here's an example: The cards that were played are the *8 of Hearts, 5 of Clubs, King of Spades, 2 of Diamonds, 4 of Clubs,* and the *10 of Diamonds.*

Visualize a *Van* full of thousands of *Locks.* Now, imagine a giant lock and you're using it to lock up a huge *Key.* Imagine putting hundreds of keys into a plate full of *Noodles.* Now, visualize a pile of noodles, instead of *Rocks,* in your yard. Finally, imagine mowing your *Sod* with a giant rock or mowing thousands of rocks. Exaggerate the image. Make the mental images bizarre and ridiculous and you'll remember.

ISN'T THAT A LOT TO REMEMBER?

No, because we are remembering only two objects at a time. Once we get to *Rock* we are no longer thinking of *Van* or *Lock* or *Key.* One image automatically brought us to the next. As soon as a card is played, change it to a visual image and wait until the next card is put down to see the environment it's going to enter.

IT'S GOING TO TAKE SOME PRACTICE, ISN'T IT?

Yes, but here's the good part: There are only 52 cards with each represented by a visual. Devote a week to one suit. Learn the 13 pictures until you master it. Use the Link System to practice remembering the cards in random order, then move to the next suit.

HOW CAN I AMAZE MY FRIENDS AND MEMORIZE 52 CARDS IN LESS THAN FIVE MINUTES?

Mentally link each one of the 52 cards to each one of your 52 Loci (see page 17-20).

Here's an example using ten objects in your home and ten cards you want to recall in order:

Objects	Cards
Couch	2D / noodles
Television	4D / rod
Ceiling Fan	2S / nose
Lamp	QK / quack
Recliner	2H / neigh
Fireplace	AH / heart
Table	7S / case
Light Switch	9D / bed
Bookshelf	4H / reach
Plant Stand	5S / lasso

Associate *Noodles* to *Couch*. Visualize the *Couch* is covered with *Noodles*.

In your "mind's eye" imagine the next object; *Television*. Link it with the next card; 4D. Imagine hooking the *Television* with a *Fishing Rod*. See the rod bend and feel the weight as it's being tested.

Next, visualize your *Ceiling Fan* and associate it with the next card; 2S. Imagine sticking your *Nose* between the blades of the fan. That smarts, but smart you are because you'll recall what the third card is when you go back to your objects.

The next object is *Lamp*. The next card is a *Duck Quacking*. Imagine a *Duck* is sitting atop a lamp, while another duck is trying to turn the lamp on.

Continue associating each object with each playing card. Then, visualize the first place in your home. In this example, it's the couch. When you "see" the *couch*, you'll automatically see the *noodles*. Noodles equals the 2 of Diamonds.

Like dropping breadcrumbs, you'll remember each card when you go back and visualize each object of your home.

Spend time drawing up 52 additional objects in another locale. Once the list is complete, visualize each object. This way, once you memorize one deck, you can quickly memorize another by associating them with these 52 new objects. It eliminates any confusion with cards you previously memorized.

Chapter 10

101 Q & A's for Beating Absent-mindedness

Our brain is always working. Even when we sleep our brain never completely shuts down. It's active. Of course, sometimes it works at the wrong job.

We might be looking directly at our Algebra teacher, nodding to everything she says, but our brain is somewhere else. It's thinking about the upcoming party. At work, when we should be paying attention to what we're supposed to do, our brain is thinking about what we want to do, which has nothing to do with what we're doing.

Information is constantly coming at us; from our kids, our bosses, our customers, and advertisers who want us to be customers. We turn on the radio and someone is telling us about a game and who should win, or a special order that we should place, or a date and time of an upcoming show.

Driving on the highway we look at signs and stores and scenery. Our brain is moving at a pace no car could keep up with. It's no wonder why we forget. Our brain is somewhere else and it doesn't care whether we've locked the door, brought the file, or remembered our wallet. It's long down the highway doing other things while we're only there for the ride.

The following pages offer valuable systems, strategies, and solutions to save time, save money, and save face. You'll get through your day without the frustrations, the fluster, and the fumbling of finding things, losing things, and trying to remember what to do next.

101 questions and answers on battling an enemy you meet each day; A-B-S-E-N-T-M-I-N-D-E-D-N-E-S-S.

— a long word you can begin to cut into pieces, today —

1   There's a set of identical twins in my class. How can I tell them apart?

As a father of identical twin boys, Max and Ben, I learned early to tell them apart. After feeding them a bowl of spaghetti, I clean the face of only one.

Twins have been known to play tricks on parents, teachers, and dates that come to the house. "Gee Stanley, you've never treated me this well before. And another thing, when did you get so smart in Math?"

When you're dealing with twins, look for the differences instead of the similarities. Do you notice any freckles, blemishes, or outstanding facial feature, as slight as it may be, that differentiates the two?

Does Frank have a chipped tooth? Does Hank have a look of youth? Does Sandy have a twitch? Does Mandy have a stitch? Is Ray's voice high? Does Clay often sigh? Look closely and you can find something different about them.

Associate the name to the facial feature. Visualizing *phil-ing* in Phil's freckle or posting a *bill* on Bill, will help you tell them apart.

Also, as a parent, dress them differently. They're more than a set of twins, they're individuals.

#2 Sometimes I forget which door I entered the mall. How can I remember?

Architects knew what they were doing when they designed these places. So many doors, but they all look the same to me. Maybe I should continue shopping until I remember which door I came through.

Take note of the first stationary thing you see upon entering. Go ahead and touch it. I know you have no intention of buying a leather handbag, but pick it up, look inside, and smell it. The washing machines? Go over and lift the top and spin the dial. The televisions? Touch it. The lingerie? Well, that's up to you. The point is, you're getting your senses involved. You're active. You're using your sense of touch, smell, and sight.

Note the merchandise you veered from after each turn. Was it the kiosk with all the calendars? Was it the perfume counter? Was it the jewelry store with the balloons in front? Take note and you'll remember when you have to retrace your steps.

Once you're ready to leave the mall, you'll remember what you were sniffing and grabbing when you came in. But please, keep away from the mannequins.

3   I forget to turn the headlights off after driving through tunnels. Do you have any suggestion for remembering?

The highway department has asked me to make sure you're referring to *daytime* travel.

Many tunnels have signs reading, *Check Headlights* upon exiting. Those that don't have ruined many a vacation when Dad can't start the car after the family eats at the roadside picnic table. Don't blame Dad. No one reminded him to turn the lights off after driving through the tunnel 320 miles ago.

When you turn the lights on approaching a tunnel, make a game of it. Ask your daughter in the back seat, "When you see daylight shout, "Lights." If you're alone shout, "Lights On" when you're turning them on. It's just another trigger for your mind to remember.

You may also want to blast the A/C or the heater to its max. This is similar to the string tied to your finger reminding you to do something. However, if you wind up at your destination half frozen or sweating profusely, find another route on the way back without tunnels.

 # 4   I can't recall if I owe Ted $10 or $20. How should I go about paying him back?

Give Ted a $50 bill and ask for change. Then, don't say anything.

The best medicine to improve one's memory is to lend money. The worse medicine is to be on the receiving end of a cash advance.

This question should be for Ted, "How do I remind people to pay up?"

If we want to get our money back it's important that we, in a nice way, put reminders out to the owner of the extended hand. Tell the recipient it's a custom of yours to have things written on paper. In fact, let the other person write the IOU, and after you both sign it, make copies.

Have the person write your address on an envelope. A couple of days prior to the due date, put the envelope in the mail. When he sees his handwriting on the envelope, he'll know what it's for.

Communicating when and how the money is to be paid back is vital. Will he send it to you? Will you pick it up at his office or at his house? Will he make installments? When is the full amount due?

Before you dole out money, make certain all parties know when, how, and if the money will be paid back.

5   It took me three innings to find my way back to my seat. How can I remember?

Sit in most any stadium and you'll notice all sections look the same. The only difference is the view of the field. So, before you jump up and mutter, "Excuse me, excuse me," watch a couple more batters. When the batter steps out, or when the pitcher looks in, locate the tunnel taking you to the concessions. Count the number of rows you'll be passing to reach that site. You'll need that information later.

As you're about to turn down the ramp, glance upward to the section you came from. See it? It's that big, yellow sign up there reading *302*. You'll have to remember that because your boyfriend is holding the ticket stub. Which reminds me, why isn't he getting the popcorn and beer?

Pay attention when you make the turn because the food is in both directions. Armed with your peanuts, pennant, and *Pepsi* in the big plastic cup ($2 extra if you opt to get it with the home team logo) you'll be back in your seat before you miss a pitch. The reason? You had correct change, no one wanted mustard, and you took the time to make a mental dry run.

Upon entering the ballpark, additional time is saved when making mental notes of concessions and restrooms.

6   There's a special television show I want to watch next Sunday. How can I be sure to remember it?

The invention of cable television and the remote control have done more damage to our memory than we tend to admit. By the time we flip through the food, fishing, and fashion network, we've forgotten the program from where we started. Some people claim they have 100 channels. I believe they have half that, but can't recall they've gone by each channel twice.

We've noticed in the television section the special on *Whales* is coming on Sunday night at 7.

Do you know that red pen you have in the junk drawer by the sink? Go get it. Circle the listing for the program along with the other must see shows for the upcoming week.

Place the newspaper listing atop the television. I know it will go better on the coffee table or underneath the television, but put it on top. As for your remote, which is underneath the cushion of the chair, put that on top of the TV listing. This way the three most important things are connected.

If you don't plan on being near the television until the Sunday special, put the listing on something you will be near. The refrigerator will work better than the stove. We want this to be a night of big fish, not big fire.

Find a teenager to set up a digital recording device for you. That will work, too.

7 The pot roast is always burnt. How do I remember to take it out of the oven?

The best solution is a timer. They're inexpensive and come in many sizes. However, on this rare occasion when the 24-hour store is closed and your oven's clock is untrustworthy, you must depend on other means.

Once the pot roast is in the oven, look at your watch and determine what time it needs to come out. Your actions at the next hour will decide whether your family sits down to a wonderful meal or if your dog sleeps through the night soundly with a full stomach.

If you're off to watch television, bring something with you from the oven, other than the pot roast, to remind you. For instance, keeping an oven mitt on your lap could be the memory jogger that something is cooking.

If the roast is scheduled to be ready right before the news hour, visualize the lead story being a giant pot roast falling from the sky. Once the news comes on, you'll be on your way to the kitchen.

Put the mitt on if you're reading a book or magazine. Hopefully, you'll know which hand to use to turn the page.

Keep in mind, your family is behind you. Ask them to refresh your memory when the magic time arrives. As for your dog? Promise him a bone, instead.

8   How can I remember to recharge my phone?

If after every three days your friends aren't calling, it probably has nothing to do with you. When in doubt, look to the phone. Feed it some juice.

Make sure when you insert or remove the charger from the phone, the process is done on your bed. When you settle down for the night, the stretched charger cord is in your way. As the phone is charging, place the unit on the floor or nearby dresser. In the morning, bring the cord, with the phone attached, to the bed. This way, the cord is in plain sight every day reminding you to "charge up."

The key is putting the charger somewhere in your home where it prevents you from accomplishing your usual routine. For instance, placing the charger across your toothpaste, cereal bowl, or coffee maker will force you to touch it. It's that "touch" you need. Your friends will be happy, too. You're finally answering your phone.

9 The doctor says I should eat fiber, but some days I forget. How can I remember?

When it's a matter of maintaining good health, we can't afford to forget. Get in the habit of setting aside a particular time when you will eat fiber; preferably for breakfast.

As a reminder, leave the cereal box on the counter before you go to bed or tear off the box top to keep on the counter. It also would not hurt to tape a sign onto the refrigerator reading, *Have you had your fiber today?*

Mentally connect the <u>*br*</u> in <u>BR</u>eakfast with the <u>*br*</u> in <u>Br</u>an you need. Your morning is now complete.

 # 10 **After receiving directions, I still get lost. How can I remember what I'm told?**

Before you rush out of your car and ask, take a deep breath. I know you're running late, you're getting lost, and you're lashing out. So, take a minute to settle your nerves. You're a little upset. Reach into the glove compartment and get a pad and pencil. What? You say you forgot to put them in there. Oh well, you'll just have to rely on your memory.

If you're with a friend ask him to go with you. Four ears are better than two. If possible, have the person who's giving directions stand by your car; the starting point to your journey. Like the time you stood to get married, repeat back what you heard. "Okay, I turn left at Rosemont Avenue. Is that correct?" Use the word *correct* instead of *right* which might confuse you. "Then, I take my first left immediately past Windham Baptist Church, correct?"

Try to get landmarks instead of the number of lights. You may lose track when you pass the 4th, or was it the 5th, traffic light. Plus, you'll wonder if he meant those flashing lights just past his business. Seeing the bowling alley and the golden arches are easier to remember than traffic lights. It wouldn't hurt to ask, "If I've gone too far, what will I see?" This will save you from driving for miles.

Because *left* and *right* are difficult to picture, visualize a *Loaf* of bread to represent Left and a *Rose* to represent Right. When you hear "turn right onto Boxwood Boulevard," you can quickly imagine boxes of roses and you'll remember which way to turn six miles later.

11 I keep forgetting to take my umbrella. How should I remember?

It's Monday morning and you're getting ready for work. The weather report calls for showers later in the day. However, it isn't until you pull into your parking space you realize you forgot something. Not only are you dripping mad for forgetting, but soon you'll be dripping wet.

Before turning in for the night, check tomorrow's forecast. Is rain expected? If so, while it's on your mind, pull out the umbrella and hook it onto the knob of the door from which you'll be leaving. Once you try you'll stay dry.

Spend a few dollars to get extra umbrellas. Leave one at work and put another in your car. Minimize the time two of your umbrellas are in the same location. After returning from work, hook the "work umbrella" to the doorknob to take back with you the next day. Your trusted umbrella won't let you down when the rain comes.

 # 12 I left my shaving cream at the hotel. How can I prevent this?

You awoke before the sun to drive to the airport. The crying baby four rows back kept you from napping and the connecting flight out of Atlanta never showed up. Hours later you make it to Portland. Hopefully, it's the one in Oregon because that's where the meeting is. You're so tired you throw your luggage onto one bed and sleep in the other. The last thing on your mind is organizing your stuff.

Start organizing your stuff. Put your socks, underwear, and T-shirts in the drawers. Hang your clothes in the closet and put your shoes on the rack above. Rearrange all that hotel propaganda, such as the menu from *Starlights Restaurant*, the brochures of the wax museum, and the hardcover book of the *Econo Lodges* throughout North America, off to the side.

Loose change goes in the ashtray or in one of the plastic cups. Place toiletries in the corner of the sink. You'll have to slide the glass jar with the paper on top, the tiny shampoo container, and the coffee maker out of the way. Make certain the hotel key and your wallet are near your change and your wristwatch is not on the bed. Don't you feel better? You're settled in.

Upon checkout, one grab with each hand airlifts your toiletries from the corner. Gather clothes from drawers and empty out the closet. If the cord to the iron connects to the wall, leave it. It ain't yours. Put your luggage by the door, then go to the far end of the room. Walk slowly back and start scanning the room. Pick up towels in the bathroom and drop them into a corner. Find any socks in there? Look in the tub and underneath the sink. With key in hand your memorable stay is over. You didn't forget anything.

 # 13 My goal is to swim ten laps in the pool, but some days I lose count. How can I remember?

This is the case where a pad and pencil won't work. Maybe you can scratch the wall with a waterproof marker. But then, maybe the *YMCA* would cancel your membership.

When you decide to do an even number of laps, one question is already answered for you; the end of the pool where you'll finish. The pressing issue is the number of times you have to go there. Instead of doing ten laps, just think of touching one end five times. Mentally, this may also get you through the tough workout.

Once you make the turn coming back shout, "One," in the water. Don't worry, no one will hear you. The next turn coming back shout, "Twoooo." You'll save yourself from shouting, "Fivvve," because you'll be done, and because you remembered.

Not only are you promoting good health by swimming, but you could also promote each finger and thumb to each lap. Competitive swimmers would frown upon such advice, but each time you do a lap, touch the wall with a different finger and thumb. When the last is used, you're finished.

Dedicate a lap to a loved one. As you're moving effortlessly through the water, focus on a different member of your family during each lap. Say to yourself, "Bobby, this one's for you; my special grandson."

#14 I ate the most wonderful crackers at my friend's house. However, I had forgotten the brand when I went to the store. How could I have remembered?

The hors d'oeuvres were nicely placed on the silver platter. You mentioned to Barbara how good everything was, especially the crackers and dip. "Remind me to pick up some at the store," you say to her.

Hey, who do you think she is? Superwoman? She spent all day preparing this meal, polished up the silverware, and made sure all coats made it to the spare bed. Now you want her to remind you to get crackers at the store? She has enough going on.

Make your way to the kitchen and take hold of the box. Associate the *Golden Crisps* turning your teeth golden, or that you're eating Gold. Associate the *Ritz* tasting so *Right*, or that it's so Ritzy. Associate the brand into your taste buds so when you're at the store searching for that good tasting cracker, you'll remember.

If the box is empty, ask the hostess if you can tear off the box top; a reminder to get some at the store.

Trace the brand name with your finger and study the picture on the box taking note of shapes and colors. At the grocery store the box of crackers will seem to be leaning toward you when you look in that direction. You've already held the box and traced the name. All that's left is getting the dip.

15 I forgot to set my alarm clock last night. How can I remember tonight?

Why blame your memory? It's easier to lay blame on the alarm and that it didn't work. Either way, one of you needs to be adjusted, and since it's you who's reading this, here are some suggestions.

If you wear a nightcap, pajamas, or your favorite T-shirt, drape it over the alarm clock as you're getting dressed for the day. That night when you reach for your PJ's, you're going to be alarmed because that's what your hand will be on when you grab your garment. Of course, make sure the curtains are drawn as you're doing this.

Another method is to place the clock on the bed each day. This will remind you, as you settle in for the night, to set the alarm and to put it back on the nightstand.

16 How can I be sure to carry enough business cards?

It's embarrassing not to be carrying a business card when we know there are 873 of them in our desk drawer. It can also work to our advantage. Get the other person's card and promise to send yours in the mail. This gives you a good reason to add a short note and the recipient is less likely to lose the card. Also, the cards he got at the networking function are stuffed into his jacket and won't be seen until the wedding he attends two months later.

Tuck several cards into your wallet. Keep several at home, at the office, and in your car. Put some into the pockets of your suits you plan to wear.

Keep other cards in a visible place inside your wallet or purse. When you're down to your last few cards, fold one and wedge it between your car keys or slip it into your shoe. When the card pops out at the end of your day it will be your cue to stock up. Please, do it now while it's on your mind.

 # 17 I have a tendency to repeat myself. How do I remember what I've already told someone? I have a tendency to repeat myself.

You're cornered at the party and Lou is telling that same story … again. Doesn't he remember he's told you this six times? Evidently not, because here comes the part when the canoe tipped over and Helen's tuna fish sandwich came apart.

It's a good thing we don't do that, or do we? Do we tell the same story to the same person twice?

Sometimes what we have to say is so good we want to tell the story again. The problem is, the other person may not want to hear it again. To help remember what you've said, engage yourself in a true conversation. Look at the person and don't hog the speaking part. If you do, your listener will only be listening to when you come up for air in order to get his "two cents" in.

When you tell the story about visiting Wall Drug, ask questions along the way. "Frank and I went to Wall Drug. Have you been there, Beth? It's one big drugstore near Mount Rushmore with everything imaginable. We bought Suzy a pair of moccasins. And I tell you Beth, she loves them …"

Sometimes when you pose those questions, get ready, the other person may run with it for 30 minutes. Then, use your lasso, the one you got at Wall Drug, to bring her back.

Eye contact, questions, and using the listener's name will help prevent you from telling the same story. If you're still unsure, a simple statement, such as "Stop me if I've already told you this" will be much appreciated.

18 My checkbook didn't balance. How can I remember to record withdrawals?

It's amazing to see the many withdrawal receipts outside an ATM machine. And secretly, don't you want to read some of those balances to see how well people in your community are doing? I wonder how many of those transactions, represented by those floating receipts, were recorded.

One way to make sure the money is recorded is to bring the check register with you each time you make a withdrawal. However, sometimes this isn't practical. Instead, the receipt is your link so be sure to take it after each transaction.

As you're stuffing the receipt into your pocket or purse, you think you'll remember to record it later. However, the *later* is a month afterward when the call comes from the dry cleaners to remind you.

The receipt needs to be put in the same spot after each visit to the ATM; preferably a wallet or purse. Avoid mixing it with the clutter you already have in there. Take a rainy Saturday to clean it out.

The coupon for *Happy Jack Pancakes* has expired so remove it from your wallet. The pass for one free game of miniature golf should be removed, too. Remember? You got it while you were in Morehead, Minnesota. You live in South Jersey now.

Place the receipt with your dollars or wrap it around the ATM card. Each day when you record your entries, you'll always know where to find your ATM receipts. You'll be overly charged with excitement when you keep those receipts together. It's a different "overly charged" feeling you'll get from your bank.

 # 19 I'm afraid to leave my seat in a darkened theatre. How will I remember to find my way back?

The show is just about to start, but sadly, so is the urge to use the restroom. Your aim is making it to both seats in time.

Theatres aren't what they used to be. Today's typical movie house is a condominium. There are eight movies playing at 7:45. You might make it back in time for the movie but when you settle into in your seat, you'll be confused when you look up and see *Snow White*. "Isn't this supposed to be a romantic comedy? And come to think of it, who's this guy beside me?"

Before you hand the tickets to the usher, use your time wisely. Ask yourself if you need to use the restroom. Also, ask your date if she wants *Goobers* or *Raisinetes*.

As you make your way down the long corridor, note the entrance to your movie. It's #5, right beside the fire extinguisher and across from the big poster of Julia Roberts.

Before you walk down the aisle deciding where to sit, stand to the side and make that decision. "Okay, it's going to be in the middle section, 3/4's of the way up, on the left-hand side." Good choice. Now, count the rows you're walking past to get there.

The movie might be awful, but the next day Holly will tell her friends how thoughtful her date was. "... and when I said I had to use the restroom, Joey whispered, 'remember, we're eight rows from the top.'"

#20 **I'm sure my neighbor doesn't remember my name. How do I tell him without making it embarrassing?**

The greetings come each time you're raking leaves or walking to the mailbox. It's always, "Hey there." The few times you do talk you've noticed that Ned, from next door, doesn't know your name. You'd like to tell him, but how? You could lend him your power tools with your name engraved on them. At least he'd know your name. Of course, there's that chance he'd forget to return your drill.

If he's not going to say your name then you must. You can give him your name without him realizing what you're doing. It's a foolproof method when you say, "It was such a beautiful morning I said to myself, Harold Beasley, get up and take a long walk. So, I did and I feel terrific."

People want to call you by name, but their memory isn't as good as yours, so help them out.

Avoid the phrase, "You don't remember me do you?" If you haven't seen someone for a long time, don't assume they'll remember you. Wipe the uneasiness away by saying, "Janet, hi, Phil Kendall from the Little League banquet." She'll respond, "Of course, Phil, how are you?"

At every White House State Dinner there's a gentleman standing in the receiving line next to the President. His job is only getting the name of the person next in line, so he can whisper it into the President's ear.

We aren't so lucky. There are moments when we have to whisper our own name to others. When it's done right we won't have to whisper it to the same person again.

 # 21 How do I remember which page I left off in my book?

You've just read the last page and a half when it occurs to you those words were read last night. No wonder this book is taking so long to read.

If possible, finish a chapter before you put the book down, and say out loud the title of the next one. This action will help you remember when it comes time to pick up where you left off.

A bookmark would be most helpful. If you have small children, suggest they make Mommy a special bookmark. This also instills the world of reading to them and your family's love of books. Of course, your two-year-old will suggest the bookmark consist of peanut butter.

If you don't finish the chapter, read the last paragraph out loud, and emphasize the final sentence. Then, lay the bookmark horizontally across the page lining it up with the stopping point. Days later you won't have to glance up and down pages 131 and 132, because the bookmark will indicate where to begin.

#22 After leaving the mall, I can't find my car. How can I remember where I parked?

Every day parking lot malls are filled. However, many of the vehicles are never driven again because the owners have given up looking. It's one reason why city buses continue to pick up passengers outside the doors of *Macy's*.

To save on bus fare, take a moment after getting out of your car and look at the building you're soon to walk toward. What do you see? Is it the letter 'R' in *Barnes & Noble*? Is it the green awning on the Mexican restaurant? Walk directly to that landmark. As you're doing this, count the number of parking spaces, with and without cars, along the way. Once you walk that straight line to the building, you're free to go left or right to your entrance.

After your shopping spree, you'll be reminded of the landmark and where you parked. You'll also recall it was 12 car spaces away, because you became aware of your surroundings before you shopped.

 # 23 How can I remember definitions?

Vocabulary building is wonderful, only if you know what the words mean. To get a handle on it, tweak the word so they create pictures. Here are some examples.

Concede. By breaking this non-visual word into syllables, we get a very visual *con seed*, as in a con man planting seeds. To remember the definition of *concede*; to yield, or surrender, picture a con man holding up seeds as if he's surrendering.

Condone and *Condemn.* The words sound alike, but there's a mammoth difference in their meaning. It would be a bit embarrassing if you, as principal of an elementary school, told the PTA members you *"condone any student who cuts class."* The word you wanted to say was *condemn*; to disapprove of strongly, whereas *condone* means to forgive or overlook.

Creating visuals helps us remember. *Condone* sounds like *con–dough–n.* Making dough is good. *Condemn* sounds like *con–dem*, similar to *demolition.* Destroying things is bad.

Not sure what *congruent* means? You wished you had when your preteen has math homework. You might have known 20 years earlier, but now you're not too sure. You would have remembered if your teacher told you, "as they *grew, ants (con-grew-ant)* are in *agreement having identical shapes and size."*

The definition of *connoisseur* is one who is well-versed, having expert knowledge. In other words, a *con-knows-sir*, is a *sir who knows.*

And now, you're one who knows how to remember definitions.

#24 At times I forget and call my boyfriend by my old boyfriend's name. I really like this guy and don't want to jeopardize things. How can I remember?

This situation is quite common. Beginning a new relationship after a long one it's easy to blurt out, "Keith, pass the salt," when you meant to say "Antonio, pass the pepper."

The rules of thumb are to date or marry people with the same name. You can't go wrong. Calling your new guy by your old guy's name won't matter. No need to tell him you slipped when you said "Stephen," when you meant to say "Steven."

Get in the habit of calling your boyfriend "sweetie" or "honey." He'll never know you dated those same guys when you lived in West Texas three years earlier.

Don't apologize to Bruce when you begin to say your ex-husband's name. Keep your cool after you mistakenly say, "Hey, Jack." Continue the sentence with "... son Hole, Wyoming is beautiful this time of year. Let's go."

All of us, men and women, are bound to slip every now and then, so before it happens think of a recovery plan. "Sharon... (oops)... a life with you makes me so happy." Annette will be happy, too.

 # 25 How can I remember to turn the iron off?

The story goes … the husband became so annoyed at his wife's insisting she left the iron on, he decided to do something about it on their next trip. So, ten miles down the road when she said, "Harold, turn around. I know the iron is on," Harold remained calm. He steered the car to the side of the road, got out, opened the trunk and quietly handed his wife the iron. She never complained again.

If you have a large area to iron and the board remains up, it's easy to forget whether the iron was turned off. Therefore, you must make it memorable.

After ironing, loop the cord around the board and make a karate chop between the board and the outlet. Silly yes, but the action convincingly forces your mind to remember the iron is off. Don't be embarrassed, no one is watching you iron, anyway.

If the iron belongs on the shelf, then say what you're doing. "I'm putting the iron away." Also, tie a handkerchief to the handle after each use. The action of tying the knot will help you remember that it's off.

If you're still unsure whether the iron is off, get an outlet cover. Each time you iron, put the cover at the end of the ironing board or in your hand, and then plug it back in after ironing.

Have you ever thought of dry cleaning?

#26 My son claims he never received his allowance. I can't remember if I paid him. How can I be sure?

When you see Jimmy offering bribes to the *McDonald's* customers to be first in line, you'll know you've paid him too often.

If there's confusion as to whether the money was paid, remember this, you're the parent. You get the final say.

To avoid any misunderstanding, put a chart on the refrigerator showing the work needing to be done and money needing to be paid. Sign your name in ink after each payment is made. I'm not implying your kid is a rat, but a penciled "✓" could be erased by anyone. If not by him, then by that friend of his who stops over much too often.

Teach your youngster early business skills. Like any employee, have him bring his time sheet to you where you can sign it and then reward him. Keep a copy for yourself.

Set aside a time each week when the allowance is paid. Keep in mind that you ARE the payroll department, so avoid paying the money days before or when the mood strikes your kids. They might fuss and rage, but they're not going to leave you to work for the competition.

27 How do I prevent losing my keys?

If you want to avoid being laid off, become a locksmith. You'll stay busy. Faulty memories keep you working.

Keys are just waiting to be lost. They're small, always on the go, and have lots of friends looking just like them. Sometimes we think they've packed up never to return. Who knows? Maybe they've migrated south becoming one of the Florida Keys.

Keys help get us to work, help get us our mail, and play a vital role in keeping us warm when the winds start to blow outside. With all their importance, it behooves us to protect them. They need a home just like we do.

Find a place near the entrance to your door to keep your keys. Hang a key hook or put the keys in a specific corner of a drawer. Reinforce this by repeating the process 10 times. In your hand, then on the hook, in your hand, then on the hook, in your hand, then ... It will become second nature when you come through the door to automatically put the keys where they belong.

Find a place or object that identifies with the keys. For instance, you could put the _K_eys in the _K_ettle, or hook the _K_eys to the _K_alendar, or place the _K_eys inside the _K_upboard. Whichever spot you chose, make it permanent.

Be verbal if you put your keys down in an unfamiliar place. "I'm putting the keys by the plant." This prevents you from becoming absent-minded. Also, visualize keys instead of leaves dangling from the plant. Later, you'll be reminded as to what they were doing, and you'll find them quickly.

28 I'm taking a trip overseas and want to learn new words and phrases. How can I learn in a short time?

You're 55 years old. You have a master's degree and you're a corporate vice president. Yet, there are millions of 6-year olds who can speak better Japanese than you. Don't be too hard on yourself. It's not your fault. Those kids live in Tokyo. You live in Toledo.

To learn a new language, link the English word to the foreign meaning in a bizarre and imaginative way. The connection makes it memorable.

In Spanish the word *umbrella* is *el paraguas* (ehl-pah-rah-gwahs). Locking that to memory we can visualize an umbrella held up by parakeets. Hundreds of parakeets are flying inside the umbrella. The visual connection reminds you the word is *el paraguas*.

In German the word *store* is *vorrat* (fo-rrat). Visualize a store for rats and you'll know the German translation for *store*. It may also keep you away from window shopping in Berlin.

In Italian the word *morning* is *mattino* (maht-tee-no). Imagine stepping out of your bed in the morning and landing on a mat covered with tees.

Linking the two words visually speeds the process to learning a new language. Reading out loud and listening to audio tapes helps you master your new voice. Whether you ask for directions in Denmark, or a menu in Manila, you'll be ready for your trip.

29 How can I remember my dance steps?

A survey concludes couples are marrying later in life. The reason may be because they're still learning how to dance so they'll be ready for the reception. The couple with four left feet must do a couple of things right.

"Step together, step. Step together, step. Backwards, pivot, step to the side, and step together, step." Please, make up your mind.

After the dance lesson, sit with your instructor and have the steps written out. This allows your brain to soak in the information while your feet are still.

Take the dance notes home and push aside the furniture. Be careful not to throw your back out, unless it's your wife's idea to take the dance lesson. Place objects on the floor where your dance steps are to go and number them. Objects, such as telephone book, stapler, paperweight, napkin, the car from *Monopoly*, or a sock, will do.

You're ready to dance. Step on the book, then the stapler and paperweight. Pivot on the napkin and slide the car off to the right. Each step is different and memorable. You're not just taking steps, but you're moving from one destination to another. When you get to the napkin you'll recall what to do. That's when you pivot, and that's what dancing is all about. It's going from one place to another through a series of steps, some short, some backward, some to the side.

After you master these early steps find more objects around the house and place them on the floor. With each step, you'll be landing on something new and the association will help you remember. Also, practice the steps while waiting in line at the post office. No one will ever know. Soon, you'll be ready for Saturday night.

#30 How can I remember my golf strokes?

A round of golf takes less time if the guy ahead of you, in the plaid pants and sneakers, wouldn't stand by the flag counting the number of hits it took to get him there.

Perhaps you're one of those guys or gals, who after making the putt, slowly walks back to the cart unsure if a *4* or *5* goes on the scorecard. One number you are sure of is the number of golf balls it took to reach the green. "Put down an *8* for me on the lake hole."

Bring a dollar's worth of dimes with you the next time you head for the links. Put them into one pocket. After each swing, transfer one dime to the other pocket. Also, transfer a coin on the easy par 3's when you're positive you'll remember the strokes. Your 4-foot putt could turn into a 40-yard chip if there's a steep hill nearby. Then, on your final putt add another coin; 5 coins equals 5 shots.

If you run out of dimes, put *10* on your card and pick up your ball. Your partner, and those patient souls behind you, will thank you.

Why use dimes? They're small and easy to handle. They make less noise than a pocketful of quarters or silver dollars. Plus, those are the coins you always lose on the 19th hole.

31 How can I remember my wife's dress and shoe size? I often want to surprise her, but can never recall her sizes.

If you're a man you'd like this question addressed. If you're a woman you'd like the address of the questioner.

On the back of one of your business cards write the measurements of your mate. Be sure to mark out the front of the card. This is one card you don't want to hand out. It's a good idea to write your own sizes, too. Sometimes we forget if we wear a size 10 or 10 ½ shoe. Carrying a reminder card is a timesaver.

When your spouse is not in the house, go to the closet and check the sizes on dresses, blouses, and shoes. Write the number on a large sheet of paper. Draw a huge *3* and lean it against her dresses. Put the *3* on a coat hanger. Then, mark a huge *6* and put it on top of her shoes. It's an exercise taking little time, but the action of writing those numbers helps you remember. Minutes later when you throw the numbers away, you'll be surprised the numbers stay in your mind.

Use the Number/Rhyme Method to help you remember. If the shoe size is 8, associate her wearing the shoes when she's running late and 8 rhymes with *late*. A dress size 4 drapes over the door reminds you 4 rhymes with *door.*

Tuck important information of your mate's favorite color, style, and size into your wallet. Shopping will become less stressful when you walk into stores armed with all the answers. Won't she be surprised!

32   How can I remember to get my car's oil changed?

When most people hear a knock they get up. However, when it's from their car's engine they get down. To keep from feeling that way make sure your car gets its regular check-up. If you forget, your *Toyota* will let you know.

Many service stations apply a clear plastic sticker in the upper corner of the windshield indicating your car's next visit. It's a reminder you can't miss. However, if you don't want that *Grease Monkey* decal up there you'll have to find another way to remember.

If you're unsure when to bring in your vehicle, call the service station and ask when you last brought in the *Ford Mercury*. They'll give you the answer.

Setting the trip odometer to zero the day of your auto's oil change gives you an accurate reading. Once those numbers reach 4000 to 5000, you'll remember to take your car in.

Make a notation in your appointment book for three months out. Seeing the word *car* in mid February will ring a bell. You could write the number of miles, instead. All you need are the last few digits. A written *8661* written on October 15 will have a special meaning for you.

Another system to remind you to take in the car is to associate the month to the car. Think about *MARCHing* in the car, or checking the car's *Exhaust* in *August*, or changing the oil of your *Jalopy* in *July*. You'll be reminded when the new month comes.

Keeping your car running smoothly depends on a sharp mechanic and a sharp memory.

 # 33 How can I remember to bring my gym card?

It's not that you lack the motivation to work out; it's just that you can't remember where you put your gym card.

Place the gym card in the path of your morning routine. To recap, a routine is what you do without thinking. You go to the bathroom, you pour yourself a cup of coffee, you grab your gym bag, and you go to the car. Two miles later, your routine continues when you shout, "I forgot my gym card."

Place the card on your coffee maker. If your routine is a cup of joe, you'll have to touch the card to get to your coffee. Once it's in your hand, keep hold of it. Put it into your pocket or tuck it into your shoe. You've already remembered it once, so avoid looking for it a second time.

Immediately after presenting your card, put it into an envelope and place it into your gym bag. The envelope is much easier to find than searching for the small card amongst the socks and shorts. The card would appreciate it, too.

Upon exiting the gym, keep the card in your hand so you can leave it in your car. You've never forgotten your car, have you?

Purchase a hole punch machine to attach the card to your set of keys. If you're on a budget, a hammer and nail will work, as well.

If you continue to forget your card, invest in home exercise equipment. Who needs a gym card?

 # 34 I have trouble remembering if I've already added an ingredient to a recipe. How can I remember?

Your sponge cake didn't turn out the way it usually does. For some reason, it's a bit salty, and why do I still have all these eggs?

It's easy to get lost in the excitement of preparing a meal or dessert. Surrounding you is the bag of flour, brown sugar, salt, paprika, walnuts, eggs, baking soda, and everything else you need to make this concoction. You're doing everything correctly. The instructions include putting all the necessary ingredients on the counter. However, what's not included is how to remember if you've used them.

Be organized. After each item is added, transfer the container to the opposite side of the bowl. When you see the bag of sugar on your left, you'll know that ingredient has already been added. Hold off discarding eggshells. Instead, move them to the other side, as well. It's nice to maintain a clean work area, but once the eggshells are discarded, you're back to relying on your memory.

Say out loud what you're doing as if you are rehearsing for your own cooking show. Say, "I'm adding the flour. Look at it go into the bowl. Now, I'm adding the vanilla. The vanilla has been added."

As you begin, line up the ingredients against the back wall of the counter. Once they've been added, keep them off the wall. In doing so, you won't feel your back is up against there too, because you've remembered.

 # 35 **How can I remember the Books of the Bible?**

The minister is telling you to flip to *Philippians*, but you're still trying to find *Zephaniah*. Sometimes it's a job to find *Job*, numbing to find *Numbers*, and not so E Z to find *Ezra*.

While sitting in your pew waiting for the service to begin, take a look at the program and make note of the books of the Bible the preacher will cover. It's a time saver when you can follow along, instead of following behind.

Buy a Bible with tabs showing where each book begins. You won't have to fish for *Ephesians*, because you'll know where it is. Many Christian bookstores sell bookmarks with the books of the Bible listed. A quick glance will guide you where you need to turn.

Use the link system, and a little imagination, to remember the books.

Imagining a bottle of GIN EXITING the LAVATORY that's NUMB from the DEW, tells you the first five books are *Genesis, Exodus, Leviticus, Numbers,* and *Deuteronomy.*

If you think I'm JOSHING, then tell the JUDGE. He'll find the TRUTH under the laws of UNCLE SAM, yes UNCLE SAM and all the KINGS men. BOTH of them. It's been CHRONICLED on TWO occasions.

Remember that story and you'll know the next books are *Joshua, Judges, Ruth, 1 Samuel, 2 Samuel, 1 Kings, 2 Kings, 1 Chronicles,* and *2 Chronicles.*

The link pattern can take you all the way to *Revelation*, even if you start, "In the beginning..." Think you have a bad memory? Miracles do happen.

36   I often forget to add a fabric softener sheet. How can I remember?

After you remove the clothes from the dryer and clean the lint filter, (oh yeah, that too) put a fabric softener sheet into the dryer. It may feel lonely for a few days, but it will start mingling when the underwear and shirts come to town later in the week.

You could also put the whole box of sheets into the dryer. When you open the door to the dryer, that orange box cannot be missed. Take a sheet out and put the box on top of the machine. You'll never forget again.

Think of the sheet as a welcoming mat for the wet clothes. There's a mat by every door. Your dryer is no different. Spread the sheet on the bottom of the dryer, and then add clothes. Your clothes will love you for it.

#37 How can I remember the maze out of my friend's neighborhood?

You find your way back to Bob's house an hour after the party. "Sorry to bother you again Bob, but how do I get out of your neighborhood?"

How can you get lost? The house is only one hundred yards from the main road. Yet, like a football player scrambling up field, you keep searching for an opening; one that breaks free to get you home.

Look for landmarks each time you turn onto a street. Is it a right by the house with the flagpole in front? Are you turning by the house with the big elm tree? Are you making a left by the house with the pink flamingo in front? Pay close attention each time you're making turns, even though you're focused on arriving at the house on time.

Quickly turn your head over your shoulder to see streets you've passed. They'll be reminders when you leave later that night. Focus on landmarks if neighborhood street signs are hidden from view by weeping willows or broken street lights.

Make sure you know the exact address. Just knowing the house is *329 Bartlett* isn't enough. It just so happens Mr. Bartlett is the neighborhood developer and he has a big ego. So, is the address Lane, Avenue, Drive, Circle, Terrace, or Court? You'll need to know which.

Bring written directions and always ask the key question after you thank your host. "Bob, how do I get out of here?"

Psst. G ...P ... S.

38 How can I remember mathematical formulas?

When you put 2 and 2 together, it's easy to see why so many people have trouble with Math. Math is hard to figure. Sometimes it just doesn't add up and the confusion multiplies.

$$\text{QUADRATIC FORMULA}$$

$$f(x) = ax^2 + bx + c \qquad f(y) = ay^2 + by + c$$

$$x = \frac{-b \pm \sqrt{b^2 - 4ac}}{2a} \qquad y = \frac{-b \pm \sqrt{b^2 - 4ac}}{2a}$$

The Quadratic Formula becomes the Mnemonic Formula.

$f(x) = ax^2 + bx + c$, now becomes clearer with the story that a **fox** met up with **2** guys with an **ax** + a **box** by the **sea**.

Then, using their ax, the men drew a **long line** in the sand, and split them (2a). Suddenly, the men entered a **mine** (minus) where they came upon a swarm of **bees, plus** or **minus** a hundred (-b±). After falling, they climbed the mountain by walking along the top. Underneath, they heard **bees** walking **2**gether out of the **mine**. The leader said, "**4**ward march. Let's get the **air** **c**onditioner. It's hot in here." ($b^2 - 4ac$). A man turned to his friend and said, "**Y** don't we do this again?"

The techniques for memorizing formulas are the same for remembering any abstract piece. Finding familiar patterns and connections help make it memorable.

 # 39 Have you seen my glasses?

As we're putting our glasses down, we're already on our way doing something else. We might put them down as we walk into the kitchen, about to step outside, or settle back for a short nap. Our mind is seldom in focus when we lay our glasses down. And, without glasses it's difficult to stay in focus. Know what I mean?

Get into the habit of keeping your glasses in a permanent place when they're not across your nose. Sure, it's simpler to lay them down anywhere, but it's not that simple to remember where that place is 15 minutes later.

When you finish reading, put your glasses against the lamp. You can't read *The Gazette* without a glow and without glasses. You know where the lamp is, so put your glasses against it. Avoid putting your specs on objects that will be moved, such as papers. Family members may push them aside when searching for the comics or television section. Like a feather in the wind, your glasses will surely land somewhere else.

Follow the lead of your Kindergarten teacher or librarian and attach a chain to them. Even if you lose your head your glasses will be in good company.

Remove your glasses with both hands. This forces you to pay closer attention to what you're doing. If the right hand doesn't know what the left hand is doing, it only needs to ask.

Another effective hint: as you're putting your glasses down, imagine they're bursting into flames onto the object you put them on. Hours later, you'll recall where they are.

#40 How can I remember laps I've run around a track?"

If you lose count as to the number of laps you're doing, don't despair. One of your feet will let you know when you're on your last leg.

Your mind has to be alert when you run laps versus running from point A to point B. With track work you run from point A to point A, and continue doing so unless you remember where B is. The scenery all looks the same.

Pick up pebbles before beginning. Each pebble represents the number of laps you plan to run. Throw a pebble down after each lap. If you're in competition, replace the pebbles with tacks and throw them into your competitor's lane. This will increase your odds of winning.

If you'd rather your hands be free, then say out loud the lap you've just completed. Repeating "One, One, One," then, "Two, Two, Two," and so on, will help you remember.

The alphabet game will help you remember, as well. After each lap think of places that begin with A. As you're running say, "Asheville, Atlanta, Atlantic City, Athens." After your second lap think of places beginning with B. Say to yourself "Boston, Baton Rouge, Bakersfield, Bristol."

You'll be better in geography using this system, and once you get to Zanesville, you'll be a better runner, too.

41 Police need a description of the man who robbed the store. I'm having trouble remembering. How could I have paid more attention?

Go back to the spot you saw him. Were you seated behind the counter? Were you in front of the canned goods in the third aisle? Wherever it was, go there and put him into the picture. When he was standing close to you, was he taller than the top shelf? How much room was left from the top of his head to the doorway when he bolted?

Money and merchandise might have been stolen, but the fixtures remain fixed. If you remember he reached above the counter for the cigarettes, or only the top of his hat was visible when he walked by the *Mountain Dew* display, then you can determine his height.

Can't recall if he were right or left-handed? You do remember the weapon, don't you? Which side of his body did your eyes go to? When you recall that you solved another piece. What's the first thing you noticed about him? Dirty fingernails? The mole on his chin? The tattoo on his hand? The gold filling in his mouth? His high cheek bones? If you remember the long black hair, that may lead you to the dangling earring. That may remind you of something else. It's easier to recall in bits than trying to remember everything at once.

As soon as possible, write down as much as you can about the individual. As difficult as it may be, try to keep your emotions in check and start writing. Your act may prevent him from doing his next act.

42 I spend time looking up words that I should know how to spell. How can I become a better speller?

You can't tell the education level of a good speller, but you can get a hunch from a bad one. *Reatting a lettur ful uf mispeled wurds izn't verry becomeing.*

It's not uncommon to go to the dictionary looking up words we should know how to spell. Words, such as *necessary, maneuver,* and *efficiency* can be tricky.

Every word is made up of patterns that can help you remember. Be sure to look for them the next time you're stumped.

Here are 10 examples:

vacuum ...   U, U must vacUUm.

necessary ...   Is the CESSpool neCESSary?

kitchen ...   C a HEN in the kitCHEN?

martyr ...   Y be a martYr?

maneuver ...   The MANE U brush must be MANEUvered.

pavilion ...   There's a LION in the paviLION.

patient ...   PA, TIE the PATIEnt down.

bachelor ...   Do you ACHE to be a bACHElor?

manicure ... I C U R getting a manICURe.

efficiency ... I C I ENtered an effICIENcy.

There are hints to every word. The key is knowing where they are.

43 How can I remember to thaw the chicken?

You're sitting in front of the television when you start thinking about tomorrow's dinner. It's going to be chicken. Did the commercial about *chicken* remind you? Or, was it the wings of *Delta Airlines*, instead?

Either way, tomorrow the chicken needs to come out of the freezer.

If there's a sticker on the package, remove it and stick it onto your bathroom mirror. Hopefully, when you awake the next morning you'll still gargle, not cluck, and will remember to open the freezer.

As soon as you're reminded to take the chicken out, write *Chicken* on a piece of paper and put it in your cereal bowl or a place where you're bound to look tomorrow morning. Don't put the note on the freezer door, unless you eat frozen waffles each morning. The note must be in a place where your eyes are going to look before you leave for work.

Attach a string from the freezer door to the floor. You'll be reminded of it the next morning when you reach for your milk or eggs.

Wow, all this work just for chicken. Oh well, I didn't mean to ruffle your feathers.

44   My partner and I often lose count of the score when playing tennis. How can we remember?

Start playing with people who are less talented than you. Stronger players always know the score.

The rules of tennis say the server announces the score by saying his score, then the opponents. If you're holding the ball and say "Love serving 30," it means you're not winning. Be consistent, even if your backhand isn't, when keeping score.

If your opponent doesn't want the responsibility of scorekeeper, then it's your job to play the part. Give the score before each serve making sure your opponent can clearly hear you. After you hit your last ball over the fence and into the woods, repeat the score. "Okay, it's 30 all. Your serve when we continue," as both of you enter the poison ivy.

Sometimes your opponent will be adamant that he's leading by a point, not you. If so, let it go. Give him the benefit of the doubt and continue playing. It's not worth losing a friendship over and it will make you more determined to win the next point that you unjustly lost.

Recruit someone in the neighborhood to keep score. This way, all three of you have a job to do. If you still can't get the ball over the net, at least your memory will serve you right.

45 How can I remember what I just read?

You think you've subscribed to three newspapers. Instead, you're only reading the same story again and again in the same newspaper about Russian Potato farmers.

It's frustrating when we can't comprehend what we've just read. It's time consuming, too.

If possible, find a quiet place to read. Noise from the television, radio, and kids jumping onto you are mental blocks when you're trying to read and comprehend.

Read slowly. Imagine being there and try to feel the story.

Pick out key words and link one story to another and you'll remember much easier.

The CRUISE SHIP was on its way to HAWAII when a KANGAROO jumped onto the BUFFET TABLE. The animal, covered up to its neck with ROAST BEEF, shook the food off by swinging on a CHANDELIER. Suddenly, a FIRETRUCK entered the room and a PENGUIN got out and pulled the kangaroo off. Then, a MARCHING BAND began to play, until the DRUMMER walked into a LEMON PIE.

The 11 capitalized words piece the story together. Try it and see.

Cruise Ship ... Hawaii ... Kangaroo ... Buffet Table ... Roast Beef ... Chandelier ... Firetruck ... Penguin ... Marching Band ... Drummer ... Lemon Pie.

46 How can I remember where I parked my car after my plane trip?

I've seen it happen. July, 2001, five minutes after midnight at Baltimore/Washington Airport. I'm sitting on the shuttle bus as we enter the huge, full parking lot when a woman approaches the driver, saying "We can't remember where we parked." The look on her husband's face, sitting by the three children, wasn't good. Does the story have a happy ending? I don't know. I got off at the next stop.

The excitement of our trip, planned for months, is upon us. We jump out of our car and onto the shuttle looking forward to the flight. Five days later we wished we had looked backward to our car.

Count the number of car spaces to the shuttle stop and look up at the lot #. Can you remember it? Is it #5? Hey, that's the number of children I have. Is it #13? It's bad luck to lose my car. Is it #24? That's the first two numbers of my phone number. Is it T? If so, think *Tea*. Is it L? If so, think *L-ephant*. Try to find a memorable connection.

The people at *Walt Disney World* in Florida understand this. That's why parking lots are named *Sleepy*, *Happy*, and *Bashful*. They make them memorable so Dad doesn't feel Dopey for not finding the car.

On your parking ticket, write the location of where you parked. Days later when you grab your ticket, you're also grabbing your car.

#47 My daughter is in the school play. How can she remember her lines?

How do I get to Carnegie Hall? The same is true when it comes to school plays. You practice. However, if you learn a few memory tricks you can still plan to go out with your friends.

Bring the script wherever you go and read your lines when you have minutes to spare.

While at home go through your blocking, or movements, reading aloud a sentence at a time and overemphasizing each word. Continue when you have the sentence down cold. Link the last word to the first word of the next sentence. Find patterns that will aid your memory. As an example, look at the first two sentences of Lincoln's "Gettysburg Address."

Four score and seven years ago, our fathers brought forth on this continent a new nation, conceived in liberty and dedicated to the proposition that all men are created equal. Now, we are engaged in a great civil war ...

Note the pattern in the first sentence with the word *four*. There's 4 score and brought 4th. That's memorable. How can you remember *conceived* and *dedicate*? Conceive is a beginning, while DEAD-icate is an ending. That's a memorable pattern. How can you remember *created equal* to *Now, we are engaged..*? Think of equal rights. That's what NOW (National Organization for Women) stands for. *Equal rights* to *NOW* is a memorable connection, especially when you're married or *engaged*. Then, you hope you don't get into a *great civil war* with your partner.

You can find patterns throughout every speech or script. So look for them, practice, and ... break a leg.

#48 How can I remember directions of one-way streets?

It would be nice if we knew ahead of time which way traffic flows on Dearborn. If we knew, we'd take the next exit coming up onto Clairmont, instead. We are sure of one thing: The downtown one-way streets either go left or right. So, let's set ourselves straight. Hopefully, away from oncoming traffic.

Create a visual image for the four directions; *north, south, east,* and *west.* Create a visual image for the street name. Associate the two in a crazy fashion.

The word *north* is hard to picture, but the word *knot,* sounding similar to *north,* isn't. Visualize a huge rope tied in knots. *North* is now *knot. South* is similar to *Mouth. East* is similar to *Yeast.* Visualize *yeast,* or dough rising. *West* sounds like *vest,* and that can be visualized. The nouns *knot, mouth, yeast,* and *vest* are easier to picture than *north, south, east,* and *west.*

Canal Street runs South. Main Street runs West. Laurel Street runs East. Madison Street runs North. Unless you use your imagination, it will be difficult to remember.

Now, read and visualize. The *Canal* is flowing into your *Mouth.* In fact, hundreds of mouths are lapping up the canal. On the horse's *Mane* is a huge *Vest.* The *Laurel* wreath is covered with *Yeast.* See the dough hanging from the greenery. I'm *Mad* because I'm tied up in *knots.*

Without reviewing, which direction do Canal, Main, Laurel, and Madison go? Congratulations, you did it!

49 I'm receiving an award and want to thank people in my department. I'm afraid I may forget some names. How can I remember?

It's a memorable evening and you'll want to thank the folks who made it all happen, but be careful. Where do you draw the line?

If you thank the people in your department, shouldn't you thank Judy and Ted who came in from another department helping you those last two weeks? How about your husband and the moral support he gave you? Your parents coming in from Akron will be there. Don't they deserve to be thanked?

Avoid reading a laundry list of names. It's better to write them each "thank you" notes. In your acceptance speech, say what the award means to you and how you couldn't have done it without a strong support of team players, certainly too many to name here.

If you do want to thank a few people, create an acronym using their names. To remember to thank Gary, Tom, Cheryl, Hugh, and Sue, you can think of **GoaT CHeeSe**, or **SHaGgy CaT**. Be consistent with their names. If you're unsure of Hugh's last name don't mention the last names of the others.

Avoid using notes when offering thanks. You come across being more sincere when looking at them, instead of a paper, when saying their name. You've watched the *Academy Awards*, haven't you?

Before speaking find the key people in the audience. When acknowledging them you'll know where to look, instead of standing behind the lectern scanning the room like a bounty hunter.

50 I came home from work and realized I had left the stove on. How can I remember to turn it off?

As you know, turning the oven or stove off isn't your only task. You have to hurry to stir the beans, remember to take the bread out, and keep your eyes on your one-year-old making sure he doesn't fall over in his highchair. Turning off the stove? That's the least of your concern. Come back after dinner and we'll discuss it then.

Get into the habit of using both hands when you cook. One hand holds the pan, the other hand stirs the rice. One hand removes the pan, the other hand turns off the stove.

Incorporate the *DIAL* system when cooking. *D*elivering *I*ncredible *A*ppetizing *L*eftovers will remind you to check the dials. Or, *O*ffering *F*amily *F*ood, reminds you the oven needs to be turned *OFF*.

A pat on the back is always appreciated after a job well done. Do the same with your stove top. You couldn't have cooked the meal without them. So, give a quick pat on the four coils to say "thanks." Of course, it's best to wait after dessert is served to make this gesture.

51   How can I remember recipes?

While visiting your daughter up north you learn the recipe to her favorite cookies are at your home down south. If your memory can't dish up the recipe you won't be dishing out the dessert.

From *The Woman's Day Book of Baking*, here's a recipe for Maple Butter Thin Cookies:

1 cup all-purpose flour

½ cup cornstarch

½ cup confectioners' sugar

1 cup butter

¼ cup maple syrup

Mix flour, cornstarch, and confectioners' sugar. Add butter and syrup and mix with hands until smooth. Chill 1 hour. Shape into 1-inch balls and place at least 3 inches apart on an ungreased baking sheet. Bake in a preheated 300°F oven for 20 minutes. Now, let's make it memorable. Creating a story, with the lead actors being ingredients and measurements, helps us remember the recipe.

FLOWERS (flour), wearing a huge CAP (cup), attack an ear of CORN (cornstarch) HALF its size, when boxing great SUGAR Ray Robinson steps in ripping both of them in HALF. ADD to that, a BATTER (butter), wearing a CAP (cup), pays a QUARTER for SYRUP and MIXES it SMOOTHLY on an UNGREASED SHEET. A CHILL falls over the crowd for the next HOUR. Then, everyone INCHES up rolling into a BALL, 3 INCHES from each other, including the .300 hitter. 20 MINUTES later, the heat is off.

That's good brain food for remembering recipes.

#52 How can I remember to remove clothes from the dryer?

You've noticed you're running out of socks and underwear, yet the hamper is empty. Hmmm, perhaps they're in the dryer.

Your clothes have had quite a night. They've been soaked, spun, and hung out to dry, at least in the dryer. Isn't it about time you get them out of there?

If you're not within earshot of the loud buzzer signaling your clothes are done, good luck. You'll have to rely on your memory to get them out.

After you toss in a fabric softener sheet (see #36 if you forget), and clean the lint filter, bring the box into the family room or kitchen. It's out of its element. Seeing the box will remind you the clothes are in the dryer. Also, leaving a laundry basket within view will tell you something is up.

Leave the door open to the laundry room. The sight of the dryer, as well as the sound emitting from it, is a constant reminder your work is not done.

Also, leave a few coat hangers near the dryer, reminding you to hang some of those shirts that are not allowed in. Without the hangers you may think, *this time I'll let it go*. However, when your shrunken shirts come out, *letting it go* is what you'll do.

53 A family moved in across the street. How can I remember their names?

The moving van just pulled away leaving a new family behind. Of course, the family isn't new. They became new when they left their old neighborhood. Now, this new family is beginning a new life in a new town. They hope it's their last move. It's starting to get old. But then, what else is new?

Three weeks later (admit it) you introduce yourself. You meet husband Ken, wife Phyllis, daughters Courtney, Sheila, and son Matt. You figure, if the mother doesn't call all their names for dinner you'll never remember.

Write the names on a 3x5 card as soon as you have a chance, filing it in the kitchen drawer with the names of the other families on the block. Next time you see them playing in their yard, get the card and reacquaint yourself with the names.

Make an effort to call out their names when you see them. After a few weeks of "Hi Ken," you'll start to remember. Tweak the names to make it meaningful and create a story. For instance, FILL (Phyllis) the CAN (Ken) on the COURT (Courtney) with a MAT (Matt) and put a SHIELD (Sheila) on top, includes all their names.

Whether it's the family across the street or the nine members of the School Board, a story can be created.

 # 54   I got a great idea lying in bed, but had forgotten it in the morning. How could I have remembered?

Generally, when a "light goes on in our head," the lights are off in our room. Why is it our best ideas happen in the middle of the night?

You awake at 3:00 am with a brilliant idea that will help your company get off the ground. However, hours later when you get up your company stays down. Your idea never made it through the night.

Keep a large legal pad and an uncapped pen on your nightstand. When an idea hits you, write down key points. Speaking of ideas, it's not a bad one to make a practice run. While you're fully awake, close your eyes and write a sentence. If you're having trouble comprehending try writing again with your eyes closed. The rehearsal may come in handy when a moment of genius hits you in the middle of the night.

Also, to remember ideas, associate it to something in the room. For instance, throwing a crumpled piece of paper or a sock on the floor will mentally jolt your memory when you see it the next morning. If your bedroom is already messy adding a sock or crumpled paper won't help. Instead, straightening your room is the answer. You can also associate your idea to an open drawer or a lamp that you turn to the side. When you awake and notice these objects askew, you'll be reminded of your idea.

If your idea is so darn good, get up, turn the light on, and write it down. That will work.

55 I'd like to learn state and world capitals. Is there an easy way to do this?

By using your imagination, you can easily increase your learning in record time. Understanding a few memory tricks will have you standing at the head of the class.

The word *VIA*, meaning by way of, applies to memory, too.

V = Visualize. I = Imagination. A = Association.

How can we use *VIA* to remember Little Rock is the capital of Arkansas? Visualize, imagine, and associate *little rocks* (Little Rock) being filled into the *ark* (Arkansas). By breaking down the state and capital into a visual, and associating them in a bizarre way, it's hard to forget.

London is the capital of England. The words *London* and *England* need to be visualized and then linked. The word *Laundry* is similar to *London*. The word *Ink* is similar to *England*. Using your imagination, visualize dumping *Ink* into the *Laundry*. The ink is everywhere and it's ruining your clothes. *England* reminds us of *Ink*, and that reminds us the capital is *London*, similar to the word *laundry*.

If you can imagine a huge *Otter* in a *Can* you'll know *Ottawa* is the capital of *Canada*.

Imagine *Cauliflower* in a *Sack*, and you'll know the capital of *California* is *Sacramento*.

Visualize *Brussel Sprouts* in a giant *Bell* and you'll know *Brussels* is the capital of *Belgium*.

Once you put *VIA* to action, you can remember the capitals of every state and country.

56 I need to get a coupon in last Sunday's paper. How can I remember?

I remember seeing it, but how was I supposed to know I needed the coupon on ridding fleas? I didn't have a dog last Sunday. Now I do and I need to go into the garage to find that coupon. Could it have been in the Flea Market section?

Before you throw the scrambled newspaper into the recycling bin, spend a few moments to separate it. Take all that colored paper with coupons and put it aside. Do you see any coupons you need? If so, grab the scissors and go after it. Put the coupon in your "coupon file." What? You say you don't have one. Well, create one.

Coupons under the refrigerator magnet or left on counters are savings waiting to be lost. Let's face it. We do a good job of clipping the coupons, but what we do with them afterward is anyone's guess. It's not until we vacuum underneath the cushions when we find a jackpot, usually in expired coupons.

Invest in a coupon organizer and use it. Each time you go shopping, take it and you'll hold onto more money.

A bad memory not only can waste your time, but your money. Organizing everything in your life, even the Sunday newspaper, will save you time, save you money, and save you headaches. Everything has a place. Make sure you know where those places are.

#57 I can never remember how to pronounce Mr. Weinstein's name. How can I be sure?

Is it Wein*stein*, rhyming with *bean* or Wein*stein* rhyming with *sign*? Hmmm, maybe instead of calling, I'll send him a letter.

We know how to spell it, but aren't sure how to say it. Is it *Clough*, rhyming with *cow*, or *Clough* rhyming with *stuff*? Is it *Weiss* rhyming with *rice* or is *Weiss* rhyming with *peace*?

If it's a name that could go either way, quickly associate a word that rhymes with it, and create a little ditty. "Freddy Fertich has an itch, yes, Freddy Fertich is a witch."

Write the rhyming or recognizable word down when you hear it on the answering machine or when the secretary says, "Barbara Detrick is out." You'll know the correct pronunciation when you write (Debt-rick) the next time you call.

Remembering a name and calling it correctly is the first step in making a good first impression. Rewrite the name in a way you'll know how to pronounce it.

Names are important. Take the time to get them right.

 # 58 How can I keep my train of thought?

Losing our train of thought is not uncommon. For instance, just the other day .... I'm sorry, what was I talking about?

Our mind, without our permission, can jump from one thought to another at a fraction of a second. We have thoughts coming in, thoughts going out, and thoughts just not happening.

We may have important information to give, but struggle formulating our thoughts. How can we keep that train from derailing?

You can keep your thought on track by giving away the ending first. For example, "Brian and Wendy are getting married next Saturday. Last summer, while living in Winnipeg, Brian had met this wonderful girl ..."

Tell your listener, "Remind me to tell you about the circus incident." If your listener isn't bored after your boating incident, she'll remind you of the circus story.

Slow your rate of speech and look at your listener. You can't remember anything when you are looking at the waiter with the tray full of shrimp, or the ice sculpture of a horse.

When talking on the phone, jot down topics you want to discuss and points you want to make. Cross them off as you go into them.

#59 It's late at night and I can't remember where we pitched the tent. Help!

The campground is huge and you realize the folks from Michigan, Maryland, and Massachusetts bought the same tent you did at *Walmart*. You happily pitch the tent, not realizing you'll be doing it again Tuesday on trash day. Because the bugs are biting and the fish aren't, you take the family to the *Kountry Korral Kafe* down the road.

On your way back through the gates of *KOA*, you're not exactly sure which road to take. You don't remember it being this dark when you left for supper. You keep asking yourself, "Where did I go wrong?"

There's a reason why you were given a map of the campsite when you checked in. Become acquainted with it. Your site is #54, around the first curve and past the restrooms on the right. Study the map. This is your new neighborhood for the next 48 hours.

Set your odometer and measure the distance from your lot to the campground's entrance when you leave for the night. You'll be glad you did when you re-enter the grounds.

Make a mental note you're two sites past the family with the converted school bus and there's an open field across from yours.

Make certain where the road or trail is if you're camping in the woods. This way, you can easily find your way back after tomorrow's hike. Who knows? With proper planning, your wife and kids may want to stay another day.

60 I locked my keys in the car (again). How can I prevent this?

You own a car that gets 45 miles to the gallon. However, yesterday you lost a half of a tank of fuel while your car was idling in the driveway. You know you never should have gotten out to scrape your windshield.

There's something about closing doors with keys left behind. We know instantly what we've done. As soon as the door shuts we tell ourselves, "I don't think I should have done that." Yet, we do. In fact, before this day is out someone on your block will have locked themselves out of their house, or out of their car. Hopefully, it's not you. By following these key steps you'll always keep track of your keys.

Photographers know how to bring two subjects into focus. We need to do it, too. When closing doors, make certain you're looking at both the door and the key.

When leaving your home keep your keys in your hand. The times when you're sure they're in your pocket or purse may not turn out to be the case.

Please, trust me on this one. Never leave your vehicle with the engine running. I know, you're going to step out to only get the paper, or mail a letter, or drop off a video, but don't do it. You may be walking from here to eternity because your automatic lock automatically locked.

Go to the hardware store and spend $2 to have a spare key made. Keep it in your wallet or purse, and may you never have to use it.

61 I keep forgetting to mail those bills. How can I remember to go to the post office?

When your A/C won't run, your ice won't freeze, and your lights don't turn on anymore, you'll remember to head to the post office.

Keep a place on your desk or counter top specifically for mail. Buy a small container or box for your mail to sit. Remove the top. You'll want to make sure the envelopes are always visible. You know the old saying when it comes to forgetting to pay bills, "Out of sight, out of light."

Keep a roll of stamps in the container, too. If your mortgage lender provides you with envelopes, put stamps on them ahead of time. Hopefully, the stamps will be used before the post office raises the rate.

Before leaving the house, stick the mail in the doorjamb or put them on top of your purse. It will be impossible to forget the mail when it's right in front of your eyes.

Put a rubber band around the mail eliminating the chance a letter escapes. Your writing class may reward you for dropping a *y*, but when it comes to your mail you don't want any letters to fall.

Put the mail on your dashboard when you're driving away. It will be a constant reminder to go to the post office. Avoid putting the mail under the sun visor. It may be days before you remember, especially if you live in Seattle.

If it's in the budget, write bills as soon as they come in and get them out of the house. It's a nice feeling to know your cable is paid up for the next month and a half. Now, if I could only find a pen ...

62 I'd like to remember the floor to my doctor's office without checking the board in the lobby. How can I accomplish this?

You're already running late. The traffic was heavier than usual. The parking deck was full and now you're looking up at a menu board like you're ready to order a *Quarter Pounder*. But instead, you want to find the floor to get to Dr. Brunansky's office. Whatever happened to house calls?

Associate the floor to an action that makes it memorable. If it's the 2nd floor, think about your visit <u>2</u> see the doctor.

If it's the 3rd floor, associate the floor to the three very important people involved; you, the receptionist, and the Doctor.

If it's the 4th floor, remind yourself you're going <u>4</u> a checkup.

Is it the 5th floor? It's going to take your whole hand; four fingers and one thumb, to open the door to the office.

If it's the 11th floor, imagine your legs, shaped like the number 11, walking to the elevator.

Is it the 16th floor? Visualize driving up to it, like any 16-year-old would do on the first day of getting a driver's license.

Find a combination that links the floor to the purpose of your visit. The phonetic alphabet (pages 35-37) will help.

63 How can I remember keys points I want to make on a job interview?

The voice coming from behind the mahogany desk says, "Why should I hire you?" The voice on the other side says, "Well, if you give me a moment and allow me to make a phone call, I'll tell you." Better luck tomorrow.

Write down points you want to make, such as projects you carried through, awards you won, and experiences. Keep the points to a sentence. Then, reduce each sentence to a key word that will trigger your memory.

You want to mention your work on the Parks & Recreation project, your 4.0 grade average at Penn State and your volunteer work with *Habitat for Humanity*. In your "mind's eye" visualize a playground with a huge pencil coming down the slide falling into a house. The playground represents *Parks & Rec*, the pencil represents *Penn State*, and the house reminds you of your community service. Each topic is connected to another and even if the order is jumbled, you'll remember.

Make it memorable to the interviewer by saying upfront that your experience at the corporate, college, and community level qualifies you for the position. Then, go into each one.

Before the interview, do your homework on the company. Link the information the same way, and not only will you remember, but you'll be remembered, too.

You don't want to feel rushed on your big day, so decide early what you're going to wear. Get that decision out of your way soon. Take a practice run to the building you're going to so you won't get lost come Tuesday. Allow extra time for traffic. Now, you're free to organize your thoughts for the new position.

64 How can I remember to record my mileage each day?

The *Pasadena Tournament of Roses* has just finished and you're determined to begin the year keeping accurate records. All goes well until January 3rd when you forget to record your miles.

Drive to the office supply store and buy a booklet with entries to record mileage. While you're at it, buy two pens. When the ink runs out in June, the other will carry you the rest of the year. Make your first entry be the drive to the office supply store.

Keep the book in the glove compartment, but keep a sheet of paper marked *mileage*, in plain view. Fold the paper until you can slip it inside the handle of your door. You'll put your hand on it each time you exit your car. This will remind you to record your mileage. As you're stepping out of your car, leave the paper on your car seat. When you come back to your vehicle you'll automatically pick up the paper. What do you do with it? You slip it inside the door handle.

Keeping track of your business mileage can be a tough game to play. Some of your miles are business related, other miles aren't. In the car, out of the car, the pattern continues throughout the day. Forgetting to record the mileage is easy to do.

The act of slipping the paper inside the door handle cannot escape you. It's a constant reminder as you get out of the car to reach for the mileage book. The IRS will have to audit someone else.

65   How can I remember how Gladys likes her tea?

Demonstrating you know the likes and dislikes of your acquaintances' taste buds shows you care. It also shows you paid attention the last time the two of you met.

Listen when your friend places an order at the restaurant. She may be an invited guest at your home later in the year and you'll want to know her likes. For instance, if she prefers chicken only fried, visualize a huge chicken dancing in a frying pan on her head. Don't tell her what you're thinking, unless you don't want to see her again.

If your lunch partner likes tea, visualize a golf ball sitting atop a huge tee on her head. See yourself pouring sugar on the ball if she likes her tea sweetened. Hold the sugar if the preference is unsweetened.

If the drink of choice is *Mr. Pibb,* associate pebbles in the glass. Root Beer? Visualize a tree with roots in the glass. *Diet Pepsi?* Visualize popping (*Pepsi*) a balloon. The balloon dies (diet). Any dish or drink can be visualized in a funny and memorable way. Try it the next time you take a friend to lunch.

After meeting a client or prospect for lunch, record the date, restaurant, and your business associate's order on the back of their business card. The next time you meet for a bite, she'll be impressed when you slide the three packets of sweetener her way.

 # 66 How can I remember to stay awake in meetings?

This is for the thousands of people who just can't keep their eyes open in meetings. Who can blame them? Half the meetings we go to aren't worth remembering.

Some meetings last 20 minutes, others last a full day. It doesn't matter, we still fall asleep.

Before going to a meeting, grab change from your desk drawer and drop it into a vending machine. Press the drink you believe contains the most caffeine. Pour the contents into a plain mug. It looks more professional than drinking out of the can. Sip each time a yawn is coming on.

Choose a seat with a window view. You don't think it makes a difference? Who would you rather look at? That boring speaker you're instructed to look at each week, or the redwing blackbirds that frequent your office park?

Bring a pen and notepad with you. Even if you do nod off, your manager will assume you're taking notes.

From a nearby wall, remove the pushpin which holds the information on Amy's bridal shower. No one will miss it. There are 42 others around the 7th floor. Use the pin to gently poke yourself during times you think you're losing it. Be careful not to push too hard.

If you're only interested in getting an answer to one question, ask early. Then when you finally do fall asleep, at least you'll be informed.

67 I keep meaning to take my clothes to the dry-cleaners, but I forget. Any advice?

It's an awful feeling. The banquet is tomorrow night and the dress should have been at the cleaners. How did I forget? Maybe if I wear that huge scarf no one will notice the chocolate ice cream stain.

Get a separate laundry basket for dry-clean only. If you put your clothes meant for dry-cleaning into the usual basket, it gets lost. More importantly, it gets forgotten. If you throw your clothes in the corner of the room, that's not going to work, either. It's just like any other day around your house. You don't know if they're clean, dirty, or ready to be sent to the *Salvation Army*.

Plan on taking your clothes to the dry-cleaners on a specific day. Some businesses offer midweek savings if you bring laundry in on a Wednesday. If the store near you offers a deal, find out when that day is and stick with it.

Put your clothes into a bag or basket in the front seat of your car. If you lock them in the truck to be dropped off after work you may forget about them. You may not find them until the first nice Saturday in May when you grab your golf clubs.

Attach the copy of the dry-cleaning order to your laundry basket. This will remind you there are clothes to be picked up. It's a terrible feeling to see the old guy downtown wearing your blue blazer, because you failed to get your clothes after 30 days.

68 With my new job I have to know color patterns. How can I remember which color goes to which project?

Colors don't just add splash in our lives, they add meaning. White means "I surrender," black means "I made a profit," and yellow means "Hurry, drive faster." If your job depends on color-coding you need to be bright.

Let's say these five objects have to be color-coded: Picnic Table=Green; Telephone=Blue; Lamp=Violet; Bicycle=Red; Computer=Brown.

Since colors aren't tangibles, they're difficult to remember. Now, let's change them. Green becomes Green Beans, Blue becomes a Blue Diamond, Violet is a Velvet Robe, Red is Blood, and Brown means Brownie.

Colors transformed to objects make them memorable. Imagine a picnic table covered with a heaping pile of green beans. Visualize blue diamonds pouring out of the telephone receiver. Imagine your lamp is wrapped in a velvet robe, your bike is bleeding, and a brownie is wedged between computer keys. Test yourself. It works.

Color-coding works in every situation, such as remembering subway lines. In Boston, visualize blood spilling all over Mass General Hospital and you'll know it's the Red Line that takes you there.

In London, pretend the tennis racquet is strung with Green Beans, and you'll know the Green Line goes to Wimbledon.

In Chicago, visualize smuggling Blue Diamonds through O'Hare Airport, and you'll know the Blue Line gets you to the plane in time. That's providing you only visualize.

#69 I'm getting older and afraid of losing my memory. What can I do?

It's a question I hear often. Am I getting Alzheimer's disease? Losing your keys or forgetting someone's name is not a sign of the disease. It would be a concern having your keys, but not knowing what to do with them once you're in your car. Or, if you're unsure which goes on first; shoes or socks.

Alzheimer's is a serious disease and can only be diagnosed by a physician. It's important to have annual checkups, eat a well balanced diet, and to exercise regularly to help maintain good health.

The mind can be exercised, as well. Get into the habit of doing crossword puzzles or the *Jumble* word game found in most newspapers. Check out a book at the library and read. Reading helps keep our mind alert and our imagination on edge. Whether it's suspenseful novels or short stories, books are the calisthenics for our brain.

Practice remembering when the pressure is off. When you watch the evening news, ask yourself how you could remember the reporter's name and try to remember the last three commercials.

While waiting in line at the bank, read the names of the tellers and try to find hidden words. Seeing the name, *Barbara Rosewall*, you can find the words *bar*, *rose*, *sew*, and *wall*. If all the names are *Next Teller*, play the game at another bank.

Maintain a positive attitude. Stop telling yourself your memory is awful, and you can never remember anything. We become what we believe. Accentuate the positive, Say, "I'll remember," instead of, "I won't forget."

70   Is there a faster way to increase my vocabulary?

You storm out of your boss's office to clean out your desk, upset at the words Mr. Williams said, "You're a salient, perspicacious employee who I eminently regard." Don't quit yet. Brush up on your vocabulary. I think he likes you.

The best way to increase your vocabulary is to read. Get a library card, go to a bookstore, and fill your shelves. However, there's one book that doesn't belong on the shelf; the dictionary. Keep your dictionary on your desk and refer to it each time you meet a word you don't know. Like a smoke alarm, keep a dictionary on every floor of your home. You'll never know when you'll need it.

Use your imagination and associate the word to its meaning.

plenary ... complete, full. The PLANE was full.

baleful ... causing harm. Pitching a BALE FULL of hay is harmful.

campanile ... a bell tower. CAMPING by the bell tower is fun.

trumpery ... worthless, junk. Every TRUMPET is worthless.

torpid ... sluggish. The TORPEDO was very sluggish.

This system, like two graceful dancers, brings the two words together. They become inseparable. It's that connection that embeds the meaning into our mind.

The next time you meet a word you don't know, embrace it and welcome it to your increasing, magnifying, enhancing, ascending, and protracting vocabulary.

71 My 10-year-old keeps forgetting to zip his pants. What can I do to help him remember?

If you don't have a 10-year old, and the question is for you, that's okay. By the way, why did you sign this letter, "Name withheld by request?" Don't worry, my lips are sealed, which brings us to your question.

Zip before you button. If you button first, the zipper is hidden and you'll walk out of the convenience store thinking you're good to go. It won't be, until you have to go again when you realize your memory lapse. And, let's hope it's you who realizes it first.

Teach your son to say, "Zip to the bathroom," instead of, "Have to go to the bathroom." That will instill in his mind to "zip up" after he zips down.

Show your lad discretion on how to check his zipper. A hand on the belt, while the middle finger slips under, works in any public setting. So I've been told. Next question, please ...

72   How can I avoid the embarrassment of forgetting a name when I have to make introductions?

You see it coming and there's no escape. You're hoping for the floor to give way, a store alarm to go off, and for an opportunity to run. It's no use. It's not going to happen, because here she comes. It's the woman from work whose name you can't remember and she's coming your way. Good luck on this one buddy. I'm outta here.

This is the time when you need a friend. You're expected to make an introduction very soon and you have built up anxiety. You know this person, but can't think of her name. Quickly whisper to Sandy, "Help me please. Introduce yourself to this lady fast."

Your friend, we all need friends like this, will take the lead and say, "Hi, I'm Sandy and you are?" After you hear, "Madeline," say, "Madeline, how are you?" acting as if you knew her name all along.

You could always pretend you're about to sneeze giving your friend time to introduce herself. Pretending you have laryngitis works, too.

Hey, did someone mention honesty? Yes, there's nothing wrong with that. Simply say, "I'm sorry, your name is giving me a mental block."

So you forgot. Big deal. Get over it and continue shopping, but don't ever forget her name again. If you do, go with the laryngitis.

 # 73 **I have trouble concentrating on the telephone. How can I do a better job of this?**

The telephone is a wonderful tool. Where else can you present yourself in a professional manner without the listener knowing you're standing on your head smoking a pipe? The drawback is it takes you awhile to get to the call.

As convenient as the telephone is, it can be challenging when you can't see the person you're talking to. Instead, we're fumbling through papers, doodling on a scratch pad, or watching the fire on television.

Keep a pad and pen nearby so you can write down important information, such as times and dates you need to know. Get rid of clutter and distractions around you. Turn off the radio or TV. If you can't prevent the noisy environment, plug your exposed ear with a finger or fork, or tell the person you'll call back when you can think straight.

Ask questions and reiterate what you've heard avoiding misunderstandings. Use fewer contractions than you would in a face to face meeting. Saying, "I cannot go to the opera," is better understood than saying, "... can't ..." and eliminates the possibility of Richard honking his car horn in front of your condo Saturday night.

Close your eyes. This way, you're able to fully concentrate on the words traveling through the phone lines.

Pull off to the side of the road when you're on a cell phone. You can never give the listener your full attention when you're speeding down I-95 while the 18-wheeler carrying hogs is running you off the road.

74   On my way home from work I needed to get a few items at the store, but forgotten some things when I pulled into the lot. How could I have remembered?

You're speeding down the highway when you realize there are a few things you need at the store. *Bread, baking powder, eggs, laundry detergent,* and *toothpaste* are a must. Unfortunately, when you get to the store you only remember the baking powder. Well, at least you can brush your teeth.

Think of a story that strings the items together. Baking Bread in the Laundry room with an Egg stuck in my Tooth is a memorable scene.

You can also remember by linking the items together in a crazy way. Picture a loaf of bread stuffed with a huge egg. Then, imagine breaking an egg and toothpaste oozes out. Now, imagine brushing your teeth with laundry detergent and then, instead of using detergent, you're using baking powder to wash your clothes. It doesn't make sense, but it makes you get everything you need at the store.

Associate the items you need to parts of your car. Pick out five objects inside your car as you're driving. Associate an object to an item. Imagine the steering wheel is a huge loaf of bread. See yourself squeezing the bread as you're turning the wheel. Imagine the dashboard is covered in toothpaste. Visualize egg yolk dripping from the rearview mirror. Imagine the gear shift sprinkled with baking powder and visualize a full box of laundry detergent spilled onto the passenger seat.

When you get to the store a quick glance to the wheel, dashboard, mirror, gear shift, and seat will remind you what to buy.

#75   I forgot to send Aunt Mabel a postcard. How could I have remembered?

You could have taken her with you. She kept saying how much she wanted to see Niagara Falls. Now, your trip is over and you're feeling all wet, because the postcard your dear aunt patiently waited for never arrived. Of course, you could always mail one of your extra cards, hoping she doesn't notice the San Antonio postmark.

Buy postcards stamps before your trip. You don't want to cut short your visit to the California vineyards, because you need to go to the post office.

Write down names of the people you plan on sending postcards. Write clearly. You don't want your card to Uncle Luke going to 511 Maplewood Lane in Marietta, Georgia, when he lives on 511 Maplewood Lane in Marietta, Ohio.

Choose a time to write and send cards. Are mornings better for you? How about right before going to bed? Don't fret about not finding the post office. Leave the mail at the hotel desk or campground office. They'll be sure it's mailed.

Make a quick notation as to which card you sent to whom. If you sent Grampa a picture of a grizzly bear from Yellowstone, you'll know next time to send him another type of picture. A postcard of Denver's skyline would be better than the one of that city's zoo with a bear pictured.

On a personal note, never begin a postcard with, "How are you?" For once, it's not about them. This is all about you and the people you've met and the places you've seen. So, brag a little. Tell them what you've done. That's what postcards are for.

76 Why do they give me an appointment card six months before my next dental visit? Don't they know I'll forget?

They figure you will. That's why they'll call you a few days before. They don't want any cavities sitting in their appointment book.

Appointments are like mud thrown on a wall. Some will stick while others will be washed away.

Keep an appointment book by the telephone at work and at home. Refer to it before you say, "Yes." Use a pocket-sized calendar book when you're out or invest in a smartphone.

It's equally important to make sure the other party knows about the scheduled meeting. Always confirm appointments. Call a day or two ahead of time making sure the "green light" is still on. Also, sending a postcard or text is a great idea when you can add, "Looking forward to meeting you Monday at 9:00 to discuss your financial future."

77　How can I remember to take my medication?

Some prescriptions come with a handy memory aid; a dial or compartment labeled with dates. For medication without these devices, a sharp memory is needed.

Always leave the pill bottle in the same place in the cabinet or counter top. Having it in a familiar location will be one less thing you have to worry about. Leave the bathroom cabinet door open before going to bed. The next morning when you brush your teeth, the pills will be looking right back at you. You could also put your toothbrush on top of the pill bottle to help you remember.

With a pen nearby, tape a small calendar inside the bathroom cabinet or near the pills. Place a checkmark on the date each time you take a pill.

Get rid of old pill bottles. A quick phone call to the doctor's office will let you know which bottles to discard if you're unsure of their longevity. Clutter around the house transfers to clutter in the head.

78 The overdue library fee now exceeds the cost of the book. How can I remember to go to the library?

The librarian will give you a slip of paper with the date September 20th on it. That day means something. It's the day she wants her book back. Use the paper as a bookmark or clip it to the book's jacket.

On your calendar, make a notation when the book is due. The day before, put the book in front of your door so you will remember. Laying the book on the table near the door isn't enough for you to remember. The book must be in the direct path to the door. Do you think you'd forget if you stepped on Tom Clancy's name before leaving for work? You won't.

Lay the book on the dashboard when driving. I know. The reflection is awful. Well then, take it to the library and get rid of it.

79 How can I remember to turn off the coffee maker when I leave the office?

You've had a long day. You've made calls, been out on appointments, and filed reports. You're also the last person to leave the office. Tonight, it's your job to make sure computers are off, lights are out, and doors locked. And oh yes, the coffee maker, that needs to be off, too.

Put your coffee mug or *Styrofoam* cup on top of your computer while you're working. The coffee cup will remind you to turn off the machine before you leave.

Associate the C's before you leave. Computer off? Check! Calendar turned? Check! Counter cleaned? Check! Coffee maker off? Check! Now, time to go home. Coat? Check!

It will take only one week with a sign posted by the lights reading "*Coffee maker off?*" to remind you.

80   How can I remember what to pack?

A hockey player needs his skates, a track runner needs his shoes, and a moviegoer needs his ticket. There are some things we just can't do without and we must make sure they're packed.

Stand by your bags or luggage and visualize yourself naked after you've finished packing. Now, start getting dressed. Did you pack your underwear? Your socks? T-shirt? Shoes? Think about what you'll be wearing and needing on your excursion, making sure you have them packed.

The night before your trip, make a list of everything you'll need, including items you know you'll never forget. Check off items on the list as you're stuffing them into the suitcase.

Clear an area around your bags for what you need to pack. You may accidentally pack something you don't want, because it was near your socks when you threw them in. You don't want a can of dog food dropping from your blanket when you're on the Florida beach.

Always leave a plastic bag and clothes pins inside your luggage. The bag is for dirty laundry, and the pins are an excellent way to keep those hotel drapes closed.

Double-check essentials leaving nothing to chance, such as tickets, documents, and yes, skates.

81 I keep forgetting to remove my rings when I do dishes. How can I remember?

When a Las Vegas casino dealer comes to work, he/she will "High Ten" their replacement. It's standard practice so cameras can capture if dealers have money in their hands. A dishwasher needs to do the same.

"High Ten" the wall, above the sink, before turning on the faucet. Extended hands on the wall provide your eyes to check for rings. Why not just look down on your hands? You may forget to do that. It's not as memorable as a prewash slap to the wallpaper. If the day comes when you do lose your rings it will be a day when you didn't "High Ten" the wall.

Another idea is to run water over your hands before you fill the sink. As the water hits your fingers you can remove the rings.

The action of hitting the wall or running your hand underneath the faucet is a procedure giving you a final check to remove rings.

82 How can I remember to pick up my child at school?

Your child is a regular on school bus #324, however on this day, little Emma is working with a science tutor. She's depending on you to be there at 3 pm.

Set your watch alarm, or any other gadget you own that comes with a buzzing noise. When the alarm sounds, grab your car keys and go. Allow for extra time if you're at work, shopping, or a long way from the school.

Put a photo of your child near the front door, or by the stairs to remind you she needs to be driven home. If you're at work, tape the photo to your computer or phone.

Of course you love your daughter. Her picture is already in every room. However, moving the photo to a site that is out of the ordinary will trigger your memory. A picture of a bus will accomplish the same result, but who wants to explain that?

Do your best to arrive on time. She's ready to come home. You'll treasure those drive home moments long after she's grown up and moved away.

83   How can I remember to do the wash?

When your pants start walking down the stairs it's time to get the *Tide*. Let's hope no one needs to remind you on this one. But hey, sometimes we ... well ... forget to do the wash.

Soon after you come home from work, you'll be going out for the evening. It's important to do a load of laundry because tomorrow evening is the piano recital. Call your house while you're at work. Leave a message on the answering machine that the laundry needs to be done. What's the first thing we do when we come home from work? That's right. We look for the blinking light.

Visualize a huge washing machine blocking your front door. It's gigantic and suds are going everywhere. When you pull into your driveway and walk toward the door, you'll be reminded of the blockade. That image will remind you to do the laundry.

Keep a dirty sock by the door or wrap it around a table or chair. This simple procedure will remind you what to do when you come home from work. Come to think of it, a clean sock will have the same affect. Let's go with that.

#84 Twice last week I've forgotten to wear a belt. How can I prevent this from happening?

Leaning back in your chair, with arms at your hips, you've just concluded you have forgotten something. How did this happen?

In the closet, drape your belts over the hanger holding your pants. The belt will be in your hands before you know it. Somehow, get the belt touching your pants when they're in the closet. You needn't tell anyone.

Another reminder is to make sure your tie touches your belt buckle after you put it on.

When you first take hold of your belt, don't let go. Put your pants on with belt in hand. It's when you let go of it your mind does the same.

85 I can't remember the last time I changed the battery to the smoke alarm. How can I remember?

Grill those hamburgers in the den. Wait four seconds.

It has been well publicized Americans should change the smoke alarm battery on the days we observe daylight saving time. Why is that so? It's a simple memory aid reminding us to do it twice a year; the same number of times we change the clocks. One action reminds us of another.

The local news and daily newspaper suggest we change the battery when we *Spring Forward* and *Fall Back* the hour. Still, others forget. Usually, it's the people who are an hour late or early to church that day.

Because we get constant reminders of doing this, this question relates to more than changing the battery. It's about all those times we get reminded of doing things, but don't carry it through. We put it off.

Whenever possible, capture the moment now. When you think of something to do, to get, to send, do it now. When others remind you to "don't forget" or "you need to remember," do it then. Putting it off puts too much pressure on our mind to remember.

Procrastination is poison. Just ask the 45-year old man who never left home. His mother said, "Marvin, you'll never amount to anything because you procrastinate." Marvin looked at his mother and said, "I'll show you. You just wait."

When you're reminded to do something ... DO IT NOW.

86   How can I remember the order of downtown streets?

Okay, ready? Downtown San Diego; 1st, 2nd, 3rd, 4th, 5th, 6th, and 7th Street. Got that? Oh, you say you're visiting San Francisco. That's not so easy. When you know the series of streets in a city you're visiting, you'll never get lost. That's a feeling every traveler wants.

Let's go back to San Francisco and look at the order of 10 downtown streets; *Chestnut, Lombard, Greenwich, Filbert, Union, Green, Vallejo, Broadway, Pacific,* and *Jackson.*

See any patterns? Other than a Green Valle(y) it's going to take some work. The street names need to be nudged to make them memorable. The new word will remind us of the street.

Chestnut to Chest, Lombard to Lamb, Greenwich to Sandwich, Filbert to Film, Union to Onion, Green to Grin, Vallejo to Veil, Broadway to Board, Pacific to Pacifier, and Jackson to Jack-in-the-Box. Now, we can create a story.

A CHEST falls on a LAMB, which falls on a SANDWICH. Inside the Sandwich is a roll of FILM tied around an ONION. A man takes a bite and GRINS. Hiding his grin with a VEIL, he walks into a big BOARD. The board becomes a PACIFIER in his mouth. He begins to jump up and down like a JACK-IN-THE-BOX.

It takes only a minute to become familiar with the street names. The SANDWICH will remind you of GREENWICH and FILM reminds you of FILBERT. Use your imagination and you'll remember.

Visit a city soon. There's a story waiting for you.

87   How do I remember to flip the mattress prolonging its life?

It's always a good idea to turn your mattress over every few months to extend its durability. Families with teenagers always have the best mattress. Mothers have been known to flip mattresses quite frequently to get their child to school on time.

Here are six times during the year reminding you to flip the bed:

January 1. A new beginning. A time to TURN OVER a new leaf.

March 1. *MA*rch and *MA*ttress go together.

May 1. *MA*y and *MA*ttress go together.

July 4th. Did someone lay a firecracker underneath my bed?

Labor Day. The labor of turning the mattress over.

October 31. I know a good place to stash the candy.

You could also put a small dot on the calendar to remind you. Only you will know what it means. Therefore, when it comes to knowing when to turn the mattress, you'll always be on top of it.

88 My checkbook hasn't turned up in days. I can't remember where I put it. Any suggestions?

If you want to keep a check on your checkbook, leave it in one place. Each time you move it, the odds work against you. Keep it in the desk drawer where you write checks. Put it in the same spot after each use.

If the checkbook stays in your purse or wallet, then set aside a specific place for it and leave it there. Keep the checks and the register together by putting a rubber band around them. Toss the check covers out if you don't use them. Less is best; of course, not if you're referring to your balance.

Immediately record the amount in the register after you write the check. The wise guy behind you at the grocery store may grumble because you're taking too much time, but go ahead and do it now. It's a matter of checks and balances.

 # 89 How can I remember to water the lawn ?

If the grass is greener on the other side of the fence, your neighbor remembers to water the lawn.

Remember many years ago while pulling into the gas station the "ding, ding"'sound you heard while riding over the black tube? It signaled to the attendant for him to "fill 'er up." That "ding, ding" sound is seldom heard now, but the principle applies when needing to remember to water the lawn.

Stretch your hose over the driveway. When you come home from work, it's impossible for you to forget to turn the hose on. But, I know, you'll do it after dinner, or after the football game and before you go to bed. You won't forget, will you?

Reach down and pluck a couple of blades of grass on your way to the front door. Tape them to the remote control. After the game you'll be reminded to tend to your lawn.

Watch football games that are played only on natural grass. Any game played on artificial surface is not going to help you remember.

Suggest to your wife that she serve French style green beans. They look a lot like grass, and that will remind you to water the lawn.

Wives can play a major role, too. Pull the hose into the house and tie two loops around his neck. You might be headed for divorce court, but at least you'll have nice grass.

90 I often forget to turn off my car's turn signal. How can I remember?

At first, you think you're the most popular person in town. Everyone waves and makes interesting gestures to you. Of course, it only happens when you're behind the wheel of your car. Usually, it comes after you change lanes, turn corners, or go back the other way.

If you don't think this happens to you, would you know? Take this short quiz to see if you're one of those drivers who forget to turn off the turn signal.

Question #1. Do you keep hearing an irritating sound in your car that goes on for miles, thinking it's a truck backing up?

Question #2. Do you keep your eyes on the road, but never look at your control panel?

Question #3. Do you think you're sexy, because those two blondes in the red sports car keep honking the horn and mouthing words to you?

Keep your hand on the turn signal until you turn it off, especially on the Interstates when you're changing lanes.

Get into the habit of periodically checking the controls, making sure the turn signal is off.

Be gracious when your wife says, "You idiot, turn that thing off."

If the turn signal doesn't turn off after you make a turn, it's time to buy a new car. Yours is very outdated.

91   How do I remember to put the gas cap on?

Two days after leaving the *Shell* station you realize your gas cap is at *Exxon*, 423 miles back.

Some cars are equipped with gas caps that are connected by cord to the car. We hope our next car is like that. In the meantime, we have to rely on our memory. It's easy to place the cap on top of the pump while we're filling the tank. It's out of the way, but unfortunately, out of our mind.

Try keeping one hand on the door of the gas tank while you're filling up. This action is a constant reminder to get the cap.

Try wedging the cap in the empty slot where the pump is housed. It's impossible to forget because the pump is blocked from going back in. It's when you only remove the cap that you can return the pump to its original position. Now, the cap is in your hand.

As you're filling the tank, fill your free hand with the cap. If possible, slip on one of those flimsy plastic mitts to keep your hand clean. Later in the day, you don't want to be drinking unsweetened tea while smelling unleaded gas. There are some things you don't want to remember after you fill your tank.

Apply the verbal "IN/ON" method when refueling. When you return the hose back to the pump, say, "IN." This will prompt you to say, "ON" as you reach for the cap.

#92   How can I remember an author's book?

A friend asks if you've read any good books lately. You tell her the new one by Patricia Cornwell, but you can't remember the title.

You call the bookstore asking if they have the James Thurber book. When asked, "Which one?" You say, "The one with the blue cover."

Nine down in Sunday's crossword puzzle reads, *Author of Wuthering Heights*. All you know is that it has six letters.

Authors need for you to remember their work. That's why their name stands three inches high in bold letters on the front cover. Like the authors themselves, you need to write a story to remember. Here are five bestselling books for 2011.

Dreams of Joy, Lisa See. Can you *See Dreams of Joy*? Perhaps when you're at *Sea*.

Summer Secrets, Barbara Freethy. I have a *Secret*. I'm *Free* when *Summer* comes.

Buried Prey, John Sandford. I *Buried* the *Prey* in the *Sand*.

Just Like Heaven, Julia Quinn. *Queens* (Quinn) *Just Like Heaven*, nothing else.

A Game of Thrones, George Martin. *Martians* (Martin) are *playing Games* on *Thrones*.

Any book title can easily be associated with its author, including *ME*MORY! and *Mellor*.

93   How can I remember to wear a different dress the next time we get together with The Johnson's?

You recall the wonderful compliments you got, but you're uncertain as to which dress you were wearing. Now, the party is Saturday night and you want to make sure you're wearing a different outfit.

Does your husband remember? Oh well, it was worth asking. Is there anyone you can call who was at the party? Of course, it would be terribly embarrassing to find out she wasn't invited to this one. Maybe you can borrow her dress.

Save the literature from the functions you attend. Write on the back of the wedding program, ticket stub, or playbill what you were wearing. When you get the handout during your monthly club meeting, jot down on the back what you are wearing. This way, you won't wear the pink flowery dress with matching heels to next month's function.

Of course, you could always spill the contents of your glass on your lap. You might get a lot more stares, but at least you'll know not to wear the stained dress to next year's 3rd Annual Wine Festival.

 # 94 This morning I realized I was out of coffee filters. How could I have remembered to get some?

You can't go through the day without your coffee. How will you cope? How will you function? How will you survive? What do you have to say for yourself?

We need to get you some coffee.

When you're down to only a few filters, leave the box by the door so you'll remember to get more. Tearing off the box top may be the only reminder you'll need. Also, clean out the old filter after each use and replace it with a new one. You'll know immediately if you need to buy more later in the day.

If you've already discarded the box, bring another mug with you on your way to work. The empty coffee mug is a reminder to get filters.

95 How can I remember which way to turn the key when locking the door?

Okay, if you're wrong just turn it the other way. But wait, you've just wasted one second of your life. Multiply that by 5, then multiply it by 15. Add 3 and multiply it by 21. Wow! You've could have gone to Med School with all the time you squandered.

Do you turn the key to the *Left* to *Leave* or to the *Left* to *Lock*? Do you turn the key to the *Right* to *Return* or to the *Right* to *Ride away*?

Do you turn the key to the *Left* to *Let in* or to the *Right* to *Restrict* others from getting in? Or, do you press the button on that little device you have?

Which way does the key fit? Are the grooves up or down? If up, visualize raising the roof. If down, visualize my home is a foundation.

For safety purposes, grasp the key you're going to use before you walk outside or before you leave your vehicle. There are some seconds you don't want to waste.

96 By the time I walk upstairs I've forgotten what I was supposed to do. How can I remember?

Whether you live in a mansion in the mountains, or a boarding house in the burbs, walking from one room to another does something to our memory. There's something about that ninth step leading to the bedroom when we ask ourselves, "Why am I going upstairs?"

You may be on the phone, washing your hands, or putting the leftovers in the microwave when the thought occurs to you of retrieving the file from upstairs. Moments later you forget.

Once the idea hits you latch on to it. Are you on your way upstairs to fold clothes? Then, say it. "I'm on my way upstairs to fold the clothes." It's like snapping your fingers in front of your face forcing you to remember. Sing a song about what you're supposed to do. "Folding clothes, folding clothes, I'm on my way to folding clothes."

Use the Body Anchor method to remember. Visualize your *head* covered in towels, *elbowing* your computer, having your *waist* wrapped with plants and *kicking* toilet paper.

You may forget once you're upstairs, but you'll quickly remember when you think of those five body parts. Each one reminds you. Your head reminds you to fold towels, your elbow reminds you to turn off the computer, your waist reminds you to water the plants, and your foot reminds you to put a new roll in the bathroom.

Attaching new information (Computer) to what we already know (Elbow). That's how we remember.

97 The milk spoiled again. How do I train my kids to put the milk in the refrigerator?

Don't be too hard on your kids. They were only following directions. They simply misunderstood the date printed on the container. They thought they had 10 days left to put it away.

Telling them not to close the refrigerator door won't help either. Not only will your milk spoil, but your electric bill will go through the roof.

Associate the milk to their favorite sport. "Billy, taking the milk out is like playing catch. You have to return it quickly."

"Billy, the milk is like a big soccer ball (be careful with this one). The refrigerator is the goal."

"Billy, you get two points for pouring it into the glass, providing you return the milk in under 24 seconds."

"Billy, before you can play, put everything away."

If all else fails, "Billy, put the $%@*& milk away!"

98 How can I remember when the movie is playing?

It was sad to hear about the Minnesota couple who froze to death at the drive-in theatre. Too bad they misunderstood the sign by the entrance; "*Closed for the Season.*"

The movie you want to see is playing five times today. However, you remember only one of those times and that was 15 minutes ago; about the same time you tossed the movie section away. What time's the next showing?

Write down the time of the showings when you call the theatre. It will come in handy if you notice the waitress is going too slowly, or if the cops notice you going too quickly. Always have Plan B ready. Who knows? Your date may have trouble with the curling iron and the delay could cut into the movie.

Program your car radio dials to the times of the movie. If you ever forget, all you need to do is hit the buttons. Your date will be very impressed.

99 How can I remember to cover the plants on cold nights?

You spent an entire weekend last autumn designing the landscape around your home. The payoff has been worth it. You've also taught the neighborhood kids to kick the ball in someone else's yard. However, tonight another enemy is lurching; lower temperatures. It's time to cover the plants.

While you're in your stocking feet and about to sit for dinner, you hear Irv, channel 11's meteorologist, saying temperatures will drop overnight. Right now you'd rather tend to the greens on your plate than the ones outside in the cold. So, enjoy your meal.

Before you eat, pull the plant stand out from its present spot. Place the greenery in front of the television or slide it near the banister leading upstairs. This maneuver will remind you about the plants that need to be covered before you go to bed.

If the inside plants are too heavy to shift, leave them. Instead, find the empty plant holder in the back hall closet and put it in full view on the kitchen counter, on top of the TV, or on the stairs. Putting the object where you eventually have to move it reminds you to cover the plants.

Don't freeze when you hear about the frost warning. By taking some action now, you'll remember to take some action later.

If you do forget and your plants suffer, tell the neighborhood kids to return to your yard. Planting season will be back before you know it.

#100 On the few mornings I find a great parking space at work, I always walk to my usual spot in the back. How can I remember?

You've parked in this lot every morning for eight years. It's automatic the front rows are always taken. By habit you go to the back of the lot. This morning is different. There's an opening up front.

Stop and look back to your car before you enter your building. See it? It's over there, instead of way over there. That short pause will come in handy after you hear the 5:00 bell.

Don't fret if you forget and walk to your usual space. Remain calm and pretend you're taking a late afternoon walk. Or, walk to the red *Porsche* and fumble for your keys. Your co-workers will think you've gotten a raise. Hustle back to you car when you're sure no one is looking. Park in your usual space the next day. The walk will do you good.

#101 How can I remember the words inscribed at the base of the Statue of Liberty?

Imagine the excitement, as well as the uncertainty, of those who came before you on your visit to the Statue of Liberty, of immigrants wanting a better way of life. In Emma Lazarus' sonnet, "The New Colossus", she writes what the great statue represents, concluding with …

Give me your tired, your poor, your huddled masses yearning to breathe free. The wretched refuse of your teaming shore. Send these, the homeless, the tempest-tost to me, I lift my lamp beside the golden door!

To remember the first line, visualize Lady Liberty yelling for you to give her your *tie* (tired). She'll use that tie to *pour* (poor) water down to the *huddled masses*. Another example that *tired* comes before *poor*, is there are more letters in *tired* than *poor*. The longer word goes first.

Note the patterns of the letter *y*. There's *your, your, your,* and *yearn*. Imagine breathing free. Imagine *wrestlers* (wretched) *refusing* (refuse) to *team* up by the *shore*, and you'll remember the next line.

From *shore* it's *Send*. Both words begin with the letter *s*. Imagine the *homeless* have *tempers* (tempest-tost) as you lift *my lamp beside the golden door*! Note all those letter *t*'s, as in *the tempest-tost to…*

Make it a point to visit the Statue of Liberty. It's a destination every American should make.

Conclusion

Every March in New York City, a group of ordinary people, with extraordinary minds, compete in the *USA Memory Championship*.

A ticket to compete is less demanding than qualifying for the Boston Marathon. If you've celebrated your 12th birthday and have paid a modest fee, you're in.

Throughout the day, contestants memorize names and faces, long-digit numbers, over one hundred words, a long poem, and within five minutes attempt to memorize the order of a shuffled deck of playing cards.

Those in attendance, as well as the score of national media covering the event, are amazed at the incredible feats the human mind can produce. If they only knew. These contestants actually have less in their mind than those holding the program, because they never try to remember more than two things at the same time. They have trained their mind to associate new information to what they already know. They're skilled with strong anchors, strong imaginations, and strong links.

Learning the techniques in this book can put you in front of the cameras, too. More importantly, it will increase your productivity no matter your life's goals.

A trained memory increases the productivity of an attorney, waitress, bellhop, salesperson, student, clerk, physician, police officer, mechanic, librarian, engineer, and anyone else who gets out of bed to go to work.

These systems work and they'll work for you. Spend time learning each system. Realize that every example and every exercise in this book linked only two things at the same time.

Memory skills should be taught in grade school. It should be taught on college campuses, in large companies, small businesses, and retirement communities across the nation. *MEMORY!* is too big to ignore.

I've developed a passion for this subject because I know it has improved my life. It can improve yours, as well.

Number Directory

00 seesaw	41 rod	82 phone	023 use a name
01 seed	42 rain	83 foam	024 snare
02 sun	43 ram	84 fire	025 snail
03 sum	44 rear	85 file	026 snatch
04 soar	45 rail	86 fish	027 sink
05 soil	46 roach	87 fog	028 sniff
06 switch	47 rug	88 fife	029 snap
07 sick	48 roof	89 fob	030 swims
08 safe	49 rope	90 bus	031 summit
09 soup	50 lasso	91 bat	032 summon
10 toss	51 wallet	92 bone	033 swim home
11 Dad	52 lion	93 bomb	034 smear
12 tin	53 lamb	94 bear	035 smile
13 dime	54 lawyer	95 ball	036 smooch
14 door	55 lily	96 beach	037 smoke
15 tail	56 leash	97 bike	038 swim off
16 dish	57 leg	98 puff	039 swamp
17 dog	58 leaf	99 pipe	040 soars
18 TV	59 elbow	000 soy sauce	041 sword
19 tub	60 cheese	001 housesit	042 sworn
20 nose	61 shed	002 season	043 swarm
21 window	62 chain	003 says me	044 sore ear
22 onion	63 gym	004 Caesar	045 cereal
23 enemy	64 chair	005 sizzle	046 search
24 owner	65 jail	006 sees the show	047 icy - rocky
25 nail	66 judge	007 seasick	048 serve
26 notch	67 shake	008 seize half	049 syrup
27 neck	68 chef	009 icy soup	050 sails
28 knife	69 ship	010 seeds	051 sled
29 knob	70 keys	011 seated	052 saloon
30 mouse	71 cat	012 stone	053 slim
31 mat	72 gun	013 sodium	054 slower
32 money	73 gum	014 steer	055 slowly
33 mummy	74 car	015 steel	056 slash
34 hammer	75 eagle	016 stash	057 slug
35 mail	76 coach	017 stick	058 sleeve
36 match	77 cake	018 stove	059 slip
37 hammock	78 coffee	019 stop	060 switches
38 movie	79 cup	020 suns	061 switched
39 map	80 face	021 sand	062 switch on
40 rose	81 feet	022 use a noun	063 switch them

235

Numbers

064 switcher
065 satchel
066 switch shoe
067 switch week
068 switch off
069 switch pie
070 socks
071 socket
072 skin
073 skim
074 scar
075 scale
076 sickish
077 icy Coke
078 ice coffee
079 ice cap
080 saves
081 seafood
082 use phone
083 save me
084 safer
085 swivel
086 savage
087 so foggy
088 safe wave
089 safe hop
090 space
091 spit
092 spin
093 so balmy
094 spur
095 spill
096 speech
097 ice pack
098 so puffy
099 see the Pope
100 disease
101 test
102 tow away zone
103 days home
104 dizzier
105 tassel

106 dosage
107 desk
108 dizzy wife
109 day spa
110 toads
111 deadwood
112 hot town
113 daytime
114 detour
115 title
116 hot dish
117 hot dog
118 white dove
119 hot tip
120 tennis
121 tent
122 white onion
123 denim
124 toner
125 tunnel
126 teenage
127 tank
128 hide knife
129 tune-up
130 dimes
131 tomato
132 time in
133 time me
134 timer
135 oatmeal
136 dumb show
137 atomic
138 time off
139 tempo
140 tires
141 tired
142 train
143 drum
144 terrier
145 trail
146 trash
147 truck

148 driveway
149 trap
150 dolls
151 toilet
152 ate alone
153 tell me
154 taller
155 tell-all
156 wet leash
157 wet log
158 tea leaf
159 tulip
160 dishes
161 touched
162 wet chin
163 teach me
164 teacher
165 touch wall
166 touch shoe
167 touch wig
168 deja vu
169 touch up
170 dogs
171 ticket
172 token
173 Tacoma
174 taker
175 tackle
176 dog show
177 hot cocoa
178 hot coffee
179 teacup
180 TV's
181 tough hit
182 dive in
183 white foam
184 diver
185 hateful
186 TV show
187 tough guy
188 TV off
189 tough boy

190 tips
191 top hat
192 white pen
193 tip him
194 diaper
195 table
196 hot beach
197 tea bag
198 top off
199 wet baby
200 noses
201 nest
202 unseen
203 enzyme
204 answer
205 nozzle
206 wins show
207 nice guy
208 unsafe
209 nice boy
210 nets
211 knotted
212 Indian
213 anatomy
214 winter
215 needle
216 window wash
217 antique
218 handoff
219 no tip
220 onions
221 new window
222 an onion
223 no name
224 no winner
225 ninth hole
226 an inch
227 winning
228 new knife
229 onion pie
230 names
231 inmate

232 honeymoon	274 anchor	316 my dish	358 mail off
233 honey, I'm home	275 nickel	317 medic	359 my lip
234 no more	276 hang wash	318 motive	360 matches
235 animal	277 young guy	319 made-up	361 machete
236 no match	278 young wife	320 mayonnaise	362 machine
237 new hammock	279 hang up	321 mint	363 my shame
238 new movie	280 knives	322 ham, onion	364 major
239 new map	281 unfit	323 my name	365 match well
240 honors	282 no phone	324 minor	366 I'm the judge
241 honored	283 new fame	325 monthly	367 magic
242 no rain	284 unfair	326 munch	368 I'm the chef
243 no room	285 navel	327 monkey	369 matchup
244 in her hair	286 no fish	328 mean wife	370 mugs
245 unreal	287 no fog	329 mean boy	371 mugged
246 energy	288 Navy wife	330 Moms	372 mahogany
247 New York	289 new VP	331 homemade	373 home game
248 nerve	290 on the bus	332 my man	374 my car
249 unwrap	291 unpaid	333 my Mom	375 my gal
250 nails	292 now open	334 memory	376 make a wish
251 knelt	293 no bomb	335 home meal	377 my cookie
252 nylon	294 neighbor	336 my match	378 make off
253 only me	295 noble	337 mimic	379 make-up
254 only her	296 on the beach	338 home movie	380 movies
255 Honolulu	297 unpack	339 my map	381 moved
256 unleash	298 now behave	340 hammers	382 muffin
257 unlucky	299 new baby	341 mart	383 move him
258 only half	300 misses	342 homerun	384 mover
259 no help	301 mist	343 my room	385 muffle
260 nachos	302 Amazon	344 mirror	386 move the show
261 inched	303 museum	345 moral	387 I'm vague
262 nation	304 miser	346 march	388 move off
263 no shame	305 muzzle	347 mark	389 move up
264 injury	306 massage	348 I'm rough	390 mops
265 angel	307 music	349 more pie	391 mopped
266 enjoy the show	308 massive	350 malice	392 hambone
267 unshake	309 mess up	351 melt	393 my poem
268 inch off	310 mitts	352 melon	394 hamper
269 inch by	311 matted	353 I'm lame	395 maple
270 knocks	312 mitten	354 mailer	396 ambush
271 naked	313 medium	355 mail all	397 I'm back
272 noggin	314 motor	356 mulch	398 I'm above you
273 new game	315 motel	357 milk	399 my baby

400 roses	442 rerun	484 river	526 lunch
401 rest	443 war room	485 raffle	527 long
402 raisin	444 hear the roar	486 raw fish	528 yellow knife
403 resume	445 hear her yell	487 you're vague	529 lineup
404 razor	446 you're rich	488 rough wave	530 limes
405 wrestle	447 rework	489 rough up	531 helmet
406 horseshoe	448 rearview	490 ribs	532 lemon
407 rescue	449 rare buy	491 robot	533 hello Mom
408 receive	450 rolls	492 ribbon	534 yell more
409 recipe	451 world	493 hear poem	535 lame wheel
410 roads	452 hairline	494 rubber	536 I'll match you
411 rooted	453 realm	495 ripple	537 yellow mug
412 red wine	454 roller	496 rubbish	538 I'll move
413 redeem	455 really yell	497 air bag	539 lamp
414 radar	456 relish	498 rip off	540 walrus
415 rattle	457 relic	499 rip up	541 Lord
416 radish	458 relief	500 laces	542 learn
417 red wig	459 roll up	501 lost	543 yellow room
418 write-off	460 riches	502 loosen	544 layer hair
419 wiretap	461 reached	503 wholesome	545 laurel
420 rinse	462 Russian	504 loser	546 allergy
421 warrant	463 regime	505 loosely	547 yellow rug
422 reunion	464 richer	506 lose watch	548 lower half
423 uranium	465 hair gel	507 Alaska	549 yellow robe
424 runner	466 reach show	508 illusive	550 yellow wheels
425 renewal	467 a rush week	509 yells up	551 yellow wallet
426 ranch	468 rush off	510 lettuce	552 all alone
427 ring	469 worship	511 low tide	553 hollow limb
428 runoff	470 rocks	512 Aladdin	554 yell lawyer
429 rainbow	471 rocket	513 yell time	555 yell, yell, yell
430 rooms	472 raccoon	514 ladder	556 yellow leash
431 roomed	473 rock 'em	515 ladle	557 lilac
432 Roman	474 rocker	516 late show	558 lowlife
433 our Mom	475 regal	517 late walk	559 yell help
434 rumor	476 ricochet	518 loud wife	560 leashes
435 airmail	477 your kick	519 let up	561 lash out
436 rematch	478 rake off	520 lions	562 lotion
437 remake	479 your cup	521 walnut	563 I'll show him
438 war movie	480 reviews	522 linen	564 wheelchair
439 ramp	481 horrified	523 yell enemy	565 leash law
440 roars	482 raven	524 liner	566 yellow judge
441 reread	483 our fame	525 lonely	567 logic

568 he'll show off	610 jets	652 huge lion	694 chipper
569 hollow ship	611 cheated	653 huge lime	695 chapel
570 locks	612 showtune	654 jewelry	696 huge push
571 locket	613 showtime	655 huge lily	697 hatchback
572 log on	614 ashtray	656 geology	698 chip off
573 welcome	615 huge tail	657 chilly week	699 shape up
574 locker	616 huge dish	658 shelf	700 gases
575 legal	617 huge dog	659 huge lip	701 guest
576 luggage	618 showed off	660 judges	702 casino
577 yellow cake	619 showed up	661 judged	703 cosmo
578 lake view	620 Chinese	662 huge ocean	704 kisser
579 lockup	621 giant	663 judge him	705 castle
580 leaves	622 John Wayne	664 wash ashore	706 weak switch
581 loved	623 huge name	665 huge jail	707 weak, sick
582 leave on	624 January	666 show judge	708 ex-wife
583 leave home	625 channel	667 huge check	709 gazebo
584 lover	626 change	668 huge chef	710 cats
585 level	627 junk	669 huge ship	711 cadet
586 lavish	628 huge knife	670 Jacuzzi	712 kitten
587 yell fake	629 chin up	671 jacket	713 academy
588 leave off	630 jams	672 chicken	714 guitar
589 leave up	631 chimed	673 chew gum	715 cattle
590 lips	632 chimney	674 sugar	716 cottage
591 leaped	633 show Mom	675 juggle	717 catwalk
592 whale bone	634 wash my hair	676 huge catch	718 get off
593 album	635 huge mall	677 Chicago	719 get up
594 help her	636 huge match	678 shake off	720 wagons
595 lapel	637 jam key	679 checkup	721 Canada
596 I'll push	638 show movie	680 shaves	722 cannon
597 yellow bike	639 shampoo	681 shoved	723 economy
598 I'll pay half	640 chairs	682 huge van	724 canary
599 yellow pipe	641 shirt	683 shave him	725 canal
600 chases	642 journey	684 chauffeur	726 gun show
601 chest	643 germ	685 shovel	727 king
602 chosen	644 huge rear	686 huge fish	728 weak Navy
603 chase him	645 cheer - yell	687 JFK	729 canopy
604 chase her	646 church	688 shove off	730 combs
605 chisel	647 shark	689 show off pie	731 comet
606 Jazz show	648 sheriff	690 jobs	732 common
607 choose a week	649 cherry pie	691 chipped	733 come home
608 chase off	650 shoelace	692 wishbone	734 comb hair
609 choose up	651 child	693 huge bomb	735 camel

736 game show	778 kickoff	820 fence	862 fashion
737 comic	779 cake, pie	821 faint	863 fetch him
738 game off	780 caves	822 heavy onion	864 voyager
739 camp	781 coughed	823 venom	865 facial
740 cars	782 coffin	824 funny hair	866 a heavy judge
741 karate	783 give me	825 vinyl	867 heavy check
742 green	784 caviar	826 finish	868 heavy chef
743 cream	785 gavel	827 funky	869 heavy job
744 career	786 go fish	828 funny wife	870 fakes
745 grill	787 hockey fake	829 phone booth	871 faked
746 crash	788 give off	830 famous	872 heavy gun
747 crack	789 give up	831 foamed	873 vacuum
748 grave	790 cups	832 famine	874 faker
749 grape	791 Cupid	833 I have a Mommy	875 vehicle
750 calls	792 cabin	834 foamier	876 fake show
751 colt	793 keep them	835 family	877 heavy cake
752 clown	794 copper	836 heavy match	878 heavy cough
753 clam	795 cable	837 heavy mug	879 have a cup
754 clear	796 cabbage	838 have my half	880 heavy vase
755 ukulele	797 go back	839 have my pie	881 heavy food
756 clash	798 keep off	840 fires	882 have fun
757 clock	799 keep up	841 fried	883 half of me
758 glove	800 faces	842 frown	884 fever
759 clip	801 faucet	843 farm	885 heavy file
760 coaches	802 fasten	844 fire her	886 heavy fish
761 cashed	803 face me	845 farewell	887 heavy fog
762 cushion	804 VCR	846 fresh	888 off, off, off
763 catch me	805 vessel	847 frog	889 half off pie
764 catcher	806 heavy switch	848 very heavy	890 heavy bus
765 catch well	807 physique	849 frappe	891 heavy bat
766 catch show	808 face-off	850 falls	892 heavy piano
767 hockey check	809 faceup	851 flat	893 heavy bomb
768 catch a wave	810 fads	852 violin	894 halfway by her
769 ketchup	811 photo ID	853 flame	895 fable
770 cookies	812 half ton	854 flower	896 off the beach
771 kicked	813 feed me	855 follow all	897 halfback
772 cocoon	814 fatter	856 village	898 off by half
773 kick me	815 fiddle	857 flag	899 heavy baby
774 Quaker	816 fetish	858 fluff	900 passes
775 giggle	817 vodka	859 flip	901 pest
776 quick show	818 feet off	860 fishes	902 poison
777 cakewalk	819 fed up	861 fished	903 bus home

904 busier	946 brush	988 pay off half	0030 sees a mouse
905 puzzle	947 break	989 pay half up	0031 icy summit
906 passage	948 proof	990 babies	0032 seize money
907 bask	949 bathrobe	991 beeped	0033 says Mom
908 passive	950 pillows	992 baboon	0034 hazy summer
909 pea soup	951 plate	993 baby him	0035 he's smelly
910 boathouse	952 plane	994 paper	0036 sees my watch
911 potato	953 bloom	995 bubble	0037 hazy, smoky
912 button	954 player	996 baby shoe	0038 Swiss movie
913 bottom	955 pool hall	997 pay back	0039 Swiss map
914 butter	956 blush	998 pop off	0040 scissors
915 battle	957 black	999 pop up	0041 sees red
916 paid wage	958 bluff	0000 sees a seesaw	0042 see her now
917 paddock	959 apple pie	0001 he says stay	0043 Swiss army
918 paid off	960 bushes	0002 sassy son	0044 seas roar
919 bathtub	961 pushed	0003 house is the same	0045 seize roll
920 bones	962 passion	0004 seesaw soar	0046 so so rich
921 paint	963 push him	0005 icehouse sale	0047 Swiss rug
922 banana	964 pusher	0006 icehouse switch	0048 saucer heavy
923 Panama	965 bushel	0007 Swiss sock	0049 Swiss Air up
924 pioneer	966 pay the judge	0008 Swiss sofa	0050 icy scales
925 pinwheel	967 paycheck	0009 hisses - subway	0051 house salad
926 punch	968 push off	0010 suicides	0052 house salon
927 hopping	969 push up	0011 U.S. state	0053 see Salem
928 bowie knife	970 pucks	0012 sustain	0054 wise sailor
929 pinup	971 bucket	0013 system	0055 Swiss lily
930 poems	972 bacon	0014 sister	0056 weighs sludge
931 bombed	973 back home	0015 see Seattle	0057 wise slug
932 pay money	974 biker	0016 sauce dish	0058 house slave
933 pay Mom	975 buckle	0017 sassy dog	0059 wise slap
934 balmy weather	976 package	0018 Swiss TV	0060 sausages
935 pay me well	977 peacock	0019 sized up	0061 Swiss jet
936 pay my wage	978 back off	0020 seasons	0062 uses the john
937 pay my week	979 back up	0021 icy, sandy	0063 sees a chum
938 pay me half	980 beehives	0022 Swiss Nun	0064 icy, icy chair
939 pump	981 buffed	0023 season ham	0065 Swiss jail
940 press	982 buffoon	0024 see icy Norway	0066 sees the judge
941 port	983 above me	0025 seasonal	0067 house is shaky
942 brown	984 beaver	0026 sauce on watch	0068 Swiss chef
943 broom	985 buffalo	0027 his song	0069 sea was choppy
944 barrier	986 buff shoe	0028 Swiss knife	0070 Swiss kiss
945 barrel	987 pay off week	0029 he's snappy	0071 ice skate

Numbers

0072 seize the gun	0114 soda water	0156 stylish	0198 step off
0073 I say sick'em	0115 state law	0157 city look	0199 soda pop
0074 his cigar	0116 side dish	0158 stay alive	0200 sneezes
0075 his skull	0117 static	0159 saddle up	0201 snowsuit
0076 Swiss coach	0118 used TV	0160 stitches	0202 see Hawaiian sun
0077 Swiss cake	0119 stayed up	0161 stitched	0203 suns me
0078 Swiss coffee	0120 stones	0162 station	0204 sincere
0079 sauce cap	0121 stand	0163 city gym	0205 suns oil
0080 sassy face	0122 sweet onion	0164 wise teacher	0206 sneeze - achu
0081 sees food	0123 sit on him	0165 city jail	0207 sun soak
0082 sees phone	0124 stunner	0166 city judge	0208 snow is heavy
0083 sees fame	0125 stone wall	0167 sad joke	0209 sun's up
0084 cease fire	0126 stingy	0168 city chief	0210 sunny days
0085 sees fuel	0127 stung	0169 sweatshop	0211 sunny today
0086 sees fish	0128 used knife	0170 steakhouse	0212 suntan
0087 sees fog	0129 side knob	0171 stakeout	0213 house and home
0088 saws half off	0130 stems	0172 used wagon	0214 snow tire
0089 sees halfway up	0131 icy tomato	0173 used comb	0215 sundial
0090 icy subways	0132 stamina	0174 used car	0216 sandwich
0091 icy houseboat	0133 sweet Mom	0175 sad eagle	0217 San Diego
0092 saucepan	0134 steamer	0176 side coach	0218 Sony TV
0093 sees a bomb	0135 icy oatmeal	0177 sidekick	0219 sunny top
0094 icy supper	0136 sweat much	0178 yes, hot coffee	0220 use onions
0095 cesspool	0137 stomach	0179 stock up	0221 sign note
0096 he's so peachy	0138 sweet movie	0180 soda fizz	0222 CNN on
0097 use icepack	0139 stamp	0181 stay fit	0223 sign name
0098 sees above you	0140 stars	0182 stove on	0224 sign in here
0099 sues the Pope	0141 straw-hat	0183 sweet fame	0225 CNN will
0100 seduces	0142 acid rain	0184 city fire	0226 sunny, enjoy
0101 sawdust	0143 storm	0185 stifle	0227 sunning
0102 citizen	0144 his terrier	0186 see a TV show	0228 a sane Navy
0103 stays home	0145 stroll	0187 this TV week	0229 sun on the bay
0104 soda, sir	0146 starch	0188 has TV off	0230 wise names
0105 icy tassel	0147 strike	0189 has TV up	0231 sun made
0106 set switch	0148 strife	0190 steps	0232 snowman
0107 stays awake	0149 strap	0191 stopped	0233 zany Mom
0108 satisfy	0150 stalls	0192 step in	0234 sun more
0109 side swipe	0151 satellite	0193 sweaty palm	0235 sign my will
0110 statehouse	0152 stallion	0194 stopper	0236 sign my shoe
0111 statehood	0153 stall him	0195 staple	0237 ice on hammock
0112 sit down	0154 stole her away	0196 stopwatch	0238 seen a movie
0113 stadium	0155 sweet lily	0197 stay back	0239 sign me up

0240 snores	0282 sun fun	0324 seminar	0366 some judge
0241 snort	0283 sign of him	0325 seminole	0367 same joke
0242 sunny, rainy	0284 sign of her	0326 swim in a shoe	0368 same chef
0243 I see an Army	0285 sniffle	0327 swimming	0369 smash up
0244 sunnier here	0286 sunfish	0328 see men off	0370 smokehouse
0245 snarl	0287 sunny, foggy	0329 salmon up	0371 smoked
0246 synergy	0288 snow half off	0330 wise Moms	0372 smoke on
0247 see New York	0289 snow half up	0331 swim meet	0373 same game
0248 sunroof	0290 snow peas	0332 swim men	0374 smoker
0249 sun ripe	0291 snapped	0333 swim Mom	0375 smuggle
0250 snails	0292 snow bunny	0334 swim more	0376 swim coach
0251 sunlight	0293 sunbeam	0335 swim a mile	0377 swim - kick
0252 sign loan	0294 sniper	0336 swim much	0378 some cough
0253 ice on limb	0295 snowball	0337 use my mug	0379 some coffee
0254 ozone layer	0296 sunny beach	0338 his home movie	0380 see movies
0255 see Honolulu	0297 sign back	0339 use my map	0381 same food
0256 ice on eyelash	0298 snap off	0340 summers	0382 symphony
0257 swan lake	0299 snap up	0341 summer heat	0383 swim off me
0258 I was in love	0300 wise misses	0342 see a home run	0384 swim far
0259 snowy, help	0301 swim suit	0343 smear him	0385 some fail
0260 snowshoes	0302 wise mason	0344 hazy mirror	0386 swim fish
0261 snow shed	0303 see museum	0345 is moral	0387 some fog
0262 sunshine	0304 wise miser	0346 see the march	0388 swim half off
0263 sunny gym	0305 icy muzzle	0347 smirk	0389 some VP
0264 snow watcher	0306 same switch	0348 summer off	0390 same bus
0265 snow chilly	0307 hazy mask	0349 swimwear buy	0391 swamped
0266 snow the judge	0308 same sofa	0350 smells	0392 swim pony
0267 sign check	0309 his mishap	0351 he smiled	0393 swim by him
0268 snow chief	0310 housemates	0352 swim alone	0394 swim by her
0269 snow job	0311 swim to it	0353 smell them	0395 symbol
0270 snacks	0312 his hometown	0354 smaller	0396 some beach
0271 sneaked	0313 same time	0355 smelly hallway	0397 swim back
0272 sunken	0314 cemetery	0356 smallish	0398 swim above
0273 sink him	0315 icy metal	0357 ice milk	0399 some baby
0274 sneaker	0316 use my dish	0358 see him leave	0400 psoriasis
0275 snake oil	0317 use my deck	0359 small pie	0401 house arrest
0276 sink wash	0318 zoom TV	0360 smooches	0402 hazy Arizona
0277 synagogue	0319 Yes! a mudpie	0361 smudged	0403 his resume
0278 sneak off	0320 summons	0362 ice machine	0404 sorry sir
0279 sneak up	0321 cement	0363 smooch me	0405 yes, wrestle
0280 sunny face	0322 iceman won	0364 swim ashore	0406 see her switch
0281 snow fed	0323 same name	0365 see my shell	0407 his rescue

0408 see her sofa	0450 cereals	0492 icy ribbon	0534 silly hammer
0409 his hour is up	0451 his world	0493 is Aruba home	0535 seal mail
0410 house riots	0452 sirloin	0494 sour pear	0536 sell my shoe
0411 I swore today	0453 he's a real ham	0495 sewer bill	0537 slam week
0412 sardine	0454 sorry lawyer	0496 has rubbish	0538 silly movie
0413 his red home	0455 he's really well	0497 sore back	0539 slump
0414 icy radar	0456 use relish	0498 soar above	0540 sellers
0415 sore tail	0457 cereal, OK	0499 sorry, Papa	0541 sleigh ride
0416 sour dish	0458 see her leave	0500 slices	0542 silly run
0417 icy, red key	0459 see her lip	0501 he's lost	0543 sell rum
0418 see her TV	0460 has riches	0502 slow zone	0544 silly roar
0419 he's read up	0461 surge ahead	0503 slice ham	0545 slower whale
0420 sirens	0462 see Russia now	0504 slicer	0546 slow reach
0421 serenade	0463 is Russia home	0505 sells oil	0547 slower walk
0422 sour onion	0464 he's richer	0506 sells shoe	0548 slower half
0423 see her name	0465 a sorry jail	0507 see Alaska	0549 seal - wrap
0424 see runner	0466 a sorry judge	0508 sails off	0550 slow lasso
0425 ice, rain, hail	0467 see Russia, OK	0509 slows up	0551 sell wallet
0426 his ranch	0468 a sorry chef	0510 slides	0552 sell lion
0427 soaring	0469 serge by	0511 sold it	0553 slalom
0428 sour enough	0470 circus	0512 slow down	0554 cellular
0429 he's run by	0471 a sorry cat	0513 sold home	0555 silly lily
0430 icy rooms	0472 saw a raccoon	0514 salute her	0556 silly eyelash
0431 sorry mate	0473 sour gum	0515 salad oil	0557 silly league
0432 ceremony	0474 a sorry car	0516 slide show	0558 slow lava
0433 sorry Mom	0475 circle	0517 sell dog	0559 seal lip
0434 house warmer	0476 sorry, Coach	0518 sold off	0560 sell shoes
0435 sorry meal	0477 sour cake	0519 seal it up	0561 slashed
0436 sorry match	0478 a sorry cough	0520 saloons	0562 solution
0437 ceramic	0479 has a wreck up	0521 Iceland	0563 slash him
0438 sour movie	0480 sour face	0522 swollen knee	0564 slasher
0439 icy ramp	0481 sore feet	0523 slain him	0565 sell Jello
0440 a sorry rose	0482 icy ravine	0524 slain her	0566 slow choo-choo
0441 sore throat	0483 serve me	0525 salon oil	0567 slow check
0442 see a rerun	0484 icy river	0526 icy lunch	0568 silly chef
0443 sour aroma	0485 serve all	0527 sailing	0569 sail ship
0444 sore rear	0486 serve hash	0528 sell knife	0570 slugs
0445 has her role	0487 serve, OK	0529 has the line-up	0571 silk tie
0446 sorry Archie	0488 survive	0530 slams	0572 slogan
0447 sorry Iraq	0489 serve pie	0531 soulmate	0573 slug him
0448 sorry roof	0490 sour puss	0532 silly man	0574 sell car
0449 see through robe	0491 is Aruba hot	0533 sell my home	0575 he's legal

0576 sluggish	0618 switched off	0660 was she choosy	0702 his cousin
0577 eyes like a hawk	0619 switched pie	0661 was she shot	0703 ski some
0578 slack off	0620 icy chains	0662 association	0704 he's OK sir
0579 silly cowboy	0621 switch hand	0663 switch gym	0705 ski icy hill
0580 slaves	0622 see China now	0664 switch chair	0706 soaks wash
0581 slow feet	0623 switch name	0665 switch jail	0707 zig zag
0582 cell phone	0624 switch owner	0666 switch judge	0708 squeeze wife
0583 slave him	0625 switch nail	0667 switch joke	0709 sky is up
0584 silver	0626 see a change	0668 switch chef	0710 skits
0585 sea level	0627 switching	0669 switch job	0711 skated
0586 selfish	0628 switch knife	0670 switch keys	0712 ski down
0587 slave walk	0629 switch knob	0671 switch coat	0713 sick time
0588 sleeve off	0630 saw huge mouse	0672 switch gun	0714 skater
0589 sell off pie	0631 was she mad	0673 switch comb	0715 skate well
0590 silly boys	0632 switch money	0674 switch gear	0716 soak dish
0591 slipped	0633 switch mummy	0675 switch call	0717 sick dog
0592 sleep in	0634 switch hammer	0676 switch coach	0718 skate off
0593 sell poem	0635 switch mail	0677 see Chicago	0719 skate by
0594 slipper	0636 switch match	0678 switch coffee	0720 skins
0595 sleigh bell	0637 switch mug	0679 switch cap	0721 scant
0596 azalea bush	0638 switch movie	0680 switch office	0722 skin knee
0597 sleepwalk	0639 switch map	0681 switch food	0723 skinny Ma
0598 slip off	0640 his jersey	0682 switch phone	0724 scanner
0599 slip up	0641 his shirt	0683 switch fame	0725 signal
0600 switches house	0642 his journey	0684 switch over	0726 skinny shoe
0601 ice chest	0643 his germ	0685 such a fool	0727 skiing
0602 switch is on	0644 switch rower	0686 switch fish	0728 skinny half
0603 switches ham	0645 switch rail	0687 switch off, OK	0729 ski on by
0604 switches hour	0646 his church	0688 switch half off	0730 skims
0605 ice chisel	0647 see a shark	0689 switch VP	0731 soak meat
0606 switches shoe	0648 see the sheriff	0690 switch bus	0732 sick man
0607 switch sock	0649 his cherry pie	0691 switch bait	0733 sick Mom
0608 switch is off	0650 seashells	0692 switch pen	0734 use a camera
0609 switch soap	0651 switch wallet	0693 switch bomb	0735 see camel
0610 see jets	0652 switch line	0694 switch bar	0736 sick match
0611 switched tea	0653 switch lime	0695 switch ball	0737 soggy, muggy
0612 switched on	0654 switch lawyer	0696 was she pushy	0738 sick movie
0613 switch team	0655 was she loyal	0697 switchback	0739 skimpy
0614 ice shatter	0656 switch leash	0698 switch above	0740 cigars
0615 switch towel	0657 switch lock	0699 sewage pipe	0741 cigarette
0616 switch dish	0658 icy shelf	0700 squeezes	0742 screen
0617 switch dog	0659 switch help	0701 squeezed	0743 ice cream

0744 soak rear	0786 sick fish	0828 save the Navy	0870 save gas
0745 squirrel	0787 sick of the guy	0829 he's a funny boy	0871 save the cat
0746 scratch	0788 sick of ivy	0830 he's famous	0872 safe gun
0747 scary walk	0789 scuff up	0831 savvy maid	0873 save the gum
0748 scarf	0790 skips	0832 save money	0874 safe car
0749 scrub	0791 ice capped	0833 savvy Mom	0875 safe call
0750 sea gulls	0792 sick pony	0834 sophomore	0876 save cash
0751 skillet	0793 skip him	0835 save mail	0877 safe kick
0752 cyclone	0794 zookeeper	0836 safe match	0878 save coffee
0753 icy clam	0795 scapple	0837 safe hammock	0879 save the cub
0754 scholar	0796 skip wash	0838 safe move	0880 save face
0755 scale wall	0797 skip walk	0839 save the map	0881 safe food
0756 psychology	0798 the sky above	0840 sapphires	0882 safe haven
0757 sickly wig	0799 sick baby	0841 severed	0883 save the foam
0758 icy cliff	0800 see faces	0842 sovereign	0884 safe fire
0759 scallop	0801 save seat	0843 ice farm	0885 save fuel
0760 soggy shoes	0802 save the sun	0844 save your hair	0886 safe fish
0761 sketched	0803 saves a sum	0845 several	0887 save half, OK
0762 suction	0804 saves her	0846 he's fresh	0888 save, half off
0763 so catch me	0805 see fossil	0847 he's freaky	0889 save heavy boy
0764 he's a catcher	0806 saves wash	0848 safe roof	0890 safe bus
0765 sick jail	0807 saves the sick	0849 save our boy	0891 use heavy bat
0766 sick judge	0808 safe, safe	0850 save the whales	0892 use heavy baton
0767 sick joke	0809 saves up	0851 asphalt	0893 safe bomb
0768 sick chef	0810 see videos	0852 use a violin	0894 save par
0769 sick job	0811 soft head	0853 swivel him	0895 use heavy pail
0770 ice cakes	0812 save a ton	0854 Civil War	0896 safe beach
0771 sick cat	0813 save time	0855 swivel wheel	0897 save a buck
0772 soggy wagon	0814 software	0856 his flesh	0898 icy half above
0773 so kick him	0815 soft wheel	0857 U.S. Flag	0899 safe pipe
0774 he's the kicker	0816 soft shoe	0858 save a life	0900 use passes
0775 sick eagle	0817 Soviet guy	0859 has a flap	0901 he's a pest
0776 soggy cash	0818 save the TV	0860 ice fishes	0902 soup's on
0777 soggy cake	0819 he's fed up	0861 has fished	0903 sub swim
0778 see kickoff	0820 use fins	0862 save the ocean	0904 he's busier
0779 sick cub	0821 safe night	0863 save Jimmy	0905 subs awhile
0780 suck face	0822 save the union	0864 safe highchair	0906 see boys itch
0781 see hockey fight	0823 safe name	0865 safe jail	0907 see boys walk
0782 soggy van	0824 souvenir	0866 savvy judge	0908 see the boys off
0783 sick of him	0825 use vinyl	0867 safe joke	0909 soaps up
0784 sick of her	0826 see the finish	0868 safe shave	0910 spits
0785 scuffle	0827 saving	0869 safe ship	0911 spit out

0912 sew button	0954 spoiler	0996 use baby wash	1038 that's my wife
0913 sip it Ma	0955 spill oil	0997 swap back	1039 wet swamp
0914 spider	0956 splash	0998 see Pope wave	1040 tweezers
0915 hospital	0957 ice block	0999 see happy baby	1041 dessert
0916 soap dish	0958 spill half	1000 diseases	1042 it's rainy
0917 sip tea, OK	0959 he's a playboy	1001 deceased	1043 disarm
0918 was paid off	0960 speeches	1002 wet season	1044 it's a horror
0919 speed by	0961 soapy sheet	1003 it's so homey	1045 eat cereal
0920 spins	0962 has passion	1004 it was sorry	1046 it's rich
0921 spend	0963 so push him	1005 it's so oily	1047 it's rocky
0922 spin wine	0964 he's a pusher	1006 it's so chewy	1048 it's rough
0923 spy on him	0965 special	1007 it's sick	1049 disrobe
0924 spin hair	0966 a sub judge	1008 it's so heavy	1050 tassels
0925 spin wool	0967 sip, choke	1009 tosses up	1051 disallowed
0926 spinach	0968 so push off	1010 wet seeds	1052 twice alone
0927 sipping	0969 soapy ship	1011 tested	1053 hot salami
0928 spinoff	0970 swap keys	1012 Dizzy Dean	1054 eat celery
0929 spun by	0971 spaghetti	1013 toast him	1055 disloyal
0930 has bombs	0972 soup can	1014 hot cider	1056 hit, slash
0931 sip my tea	0973 soapy comb	1015 wet saddle	1057 dislike
0932 spy man	0974 subway car	1016 twice a day wash	1058 heats loaf
0933 spy Mom	0975 speckle	1017 wet sidewalk	1059 had a slip
0934 sip more	0976 icy backwash	1018 wood stove	1060 hot switches
0935 use up my oil	0977 sip cocoa	1019 heats it up	1061 it's shoddy
0936 use up my wash	0978 sip coffee	1020 it's noisy	1062 it's shiny
0937 use up my egg	0979 use a backup	1021 disowned	1063 it's a huge home
0938 sub movie	0980 swap vase	1022 it's neon	1064 it's cheery
0939 use a pump	0981 soapy feet	1023 it's on me	1065 it's jolly
0940 zippers	0982 soapy phone	1024 it's on her	1066 it's a choo-choo
0941 subway ride	0983 soapy, foamy	1025 it's on the wall	1067 it's shaky
0942 aspirin	0984 zap the fire	1026 it's in the wash	1068 eats huge half
0943 supreme	0985 swipe file	1027 tossing	1069 toss ship
0944 whisperer	0986 zap fish	1028 it's in the ivy	1070 disguise
0945 subway rail	0987 zap the fog	1029 it's in the pie	1071 wet socket
0946 use a brush	0988 sip half off	1030 dismiss	1072 it's gone
0947 iceberg	0989 zap the FBI	1031 eats meat	1073 it's a game
0948 has proof	0990 soapy bus	1032 that's a woman	1074 disagree
0949 use a prop	0991 swipe bat	1033 Idaho is my home	1075 it's ugly
0950 say please	0992 swipe pen	1034 eats more	1076 it's catchy
0951 split	0993 zap! bam!	1035 decimal	1077 eats cake
0952 spleen	0994 soap opera	1036 ate so much	1078 it's coffee
0953 spoil ham	0995 soapy pail	1037 that's my guy	1079 it's a wake-up

1080 it's fuzzy	1122 hid white onion	1164 heated chair	1206 twins age
1081 too soft	1123 titanium	1165 heated jail	1207 tiny sock
1082 it was fun	1124 eat dinner	1166 did huge wash	1208 what a nice wife
1083 it's foamy	1125 wet toenail	1167 do that joke	1209 tunes up
1084 hot sapphire	1126 tighten shoe	1168 had to shave	1210 doughnuts
1085 it's awful	1127 Titanic	1169 had a touch up	1211 dented
1086 it's fishy	1128 date on/off	1170 hot dogs	1212 downtown
1087 it's foggy	1129 had a tune-up	1171 dedicate	1213 Tiny Tim
1088 it's heavy, heavy	1130 dead mouse	1172 hit Tokyo now	1214 twin tower
1089 it's halfway up	1131 dead meat	1173 heated comb	1215 hot handle
1090 dispose	1132 dead man	1174 white tiger	1216 tiny dish
1091 dispute	1133 eat at my home	1175 hit the tackle	1217 tan dog
1092 teaspoon	1134 hit timer	1176 wet dog wash	1218 attentive
1093 it's a bomb	1135 eat oatmeal	1177 Diet Coke	1219 don't buy
1094 disappear	1136 too, too much	1178 eat at the cafe	1220 eat onions
1095 toss ball	1137 today muggy	1179 heated cup	1221 tenant
1096 hit icy patch	1138 do eat my half	1180 heed advice	1222 tiny nun
1097 toss back	1139 hot Tampa	1181 hot, hot, food	1223 tiny name
1098 it's up a half	1140 detours	1182 had TV on	1224 tiny honor
1099 it's a baby	1141 dehydrate	1183 wet, white foam	1225 down the Nile
1100 eat daises	1142 wide turn	1184 wet diver	1226 tiny notch
1101 dead city	1143 daydream	1185 hot devil	1227 tanning
1102 die too soon	1144 what a terror	1186 dead fish	1228 twin knife
1103 dates me	1145 hot trail	1187 today foggy	1229 tiny knob
1104 today's weather	1146 out with trash	1188 had TV off	1230 tan moose
1105 wet tassel	1147 tow truck	1189 hit TV up	1231 dynamite
1106 Dad's watch	1148 hot driveway	1190 hot tubs	1232 tinman
1107 today is OK	1149 tightrope	1191 deadbeat	1233 tiny Mummy
1108 date is off	1150 details	1192 dead pony	1234 eat no more
1109 heated soup	1151 detailed	1193 do tip him	1235 eat no meal
1110 eat toads	1152 dateline	1194 teddybear	1236 twin match
1111 outdated	1153 dead limb	1195 heated pool	1237 dynamic
1112 hit titan	1154 weed tiller	1196 eat at beach	1238 twin movie
1113 dead time	1155 dead lily	1197 tote bag	1239 tone me up
1114 dated her	1156 wet daily wash	1198 do the tipoff	1240 dinners
1115 do detail	1157 deadlock	1199 today be happy	1241 Tony Award
1116 hot, hot dish	1158 tidal wave	1200 downsize	1242 tune her in
1117 dead dog	1159 Dad, help	1201 twin city	1243 tiny room
1118 dead dove	1160 hot dishes	1202 tunes in	1244 dinnerware
1119 heat hot tub	1161 detached	1203 a tiny sum	1245 wooden rail
1120 titans	1162 dietician	1204 dinosaur	1246 tiny rash
1121 dead end	1163 head to gym	1205 tonsil	1247 tiny rug

1248 tin roof	1290 twin boys	1332 dumb man	1374 hate my car
1249 tiny rope	1291 wooden bat	1333 time my Mom	1375 he had me call
1250 tunnels	1292 tune piano	1334 tame my hair	1376 hide my cash
1251 tiny wallet	1293 tiny palm	1335 hid my mail	1377 demagogue
1252 tan line	1294 downpour	1336 time my wash	1378 heat my coffee
1253 tiny limb	1295 downplay	1337 time my walk	1379 do makeup
1254 tan lawyer	1296 tiny beach	1338 dumb movie	1380 at the movies
1255 tiny lily	1297 dune buggy	1339 dim my hope	1381 hide my fat
1256 tiny leash	1298 twin beehive	1340 timers	1382 hide my phone
1257 wooden leg	1299 tiny baby	1341 demerit	1383 hate my fame
1258 tiny leaf	1300 hi to the misses	1342 time the run	1384 time over
1259 tiny lip	1301 die, homicide	1343 heat my room	1385 hide my file
1260 wooden shoes	1302 time is now	1344 admirer	1386 eat my fish
1261 tiny shed	1303 hit the museum	1345 admiral	1387 dummy, fake
1262 tension	1304 do you miss her	1346 hot mirage	1388 eat my half off
1263 tiny gym	1305 hid the missile	1347 hit the mark	1389 eat my half up
1264 teenager	1306 time his wash	1348 dome roof	1390 dumps
1265 tiny jail	1307 tummy sick	1349 hid my ruby	1391 dump it
1266 tiny choo-choo	1308 hide my safe	1350 dumb laws	1392 hid my pony
1267 tiny check	1309 eat my soup	1351 dim light	1393 atom bomb
1268 tiny chef	1310 timeouts	1352 tame lion	1394 damper
1269 township	1311 demoted	1353 hot meal - ham	1395 temple
1270 tanks	1312 wet mitten	1354 hit molar	1396 dump wash
1271 hoodwinked	1313 dumb dumb	1355 dumb oil well	1397 dime back
1272 tin can	1314 diameter	1356 hid my eyelash	1398 tempo off
1273 tiny comb	1315 timidly	1357 time log	1399 Tampa Bay
1274 tanker	1316 heat my dish	1358 dumb love	1400 white roses
1275 heating oil	1317 automatic	1359 oatmeal pie	1401 trust
1276 do hang wash	1318 hit my TV	1360 wet matches	1402 treason
1277 tiny cake	1319 timid boy	1361 damaged	1403 dries him
1278 wedding vow	1320 demons	1362 admission	1404 dresser
1279 tin cup	1321 diamond	1363 dumb gym	1405 drizzle
1280 tiny office	1322 dominion	1364 dye my huge hair	1406 dressage
1281 tiny feet	1323 hate my name	1365 dumb jail	1407 to the rescue
1282 tiny phone	1324 demeanor	1366 dumb judge	1408 dries off
1283 tiny foam	1325 too menial	1367 dumb joke	1409 tree sap
1284 Denver	1326 hide my nacho	1368 dumb chef	1410 treats
1285 downfall	1327 timing	1369 dime shop	1411 traded
1286 tuna fish	1328 dummy knife	1370 tomahawks	1412 trade-in
1287 head in the fog	1329 do men obey	1371 tame cat	1413 Dartmouth
1288 tiny fife	1330 hide my mouse	1372 hide my gun	1414 trader
1289 tiny ivy hoop	1331 teammate	1373 dumb game	1415 turtle

1416 tradeshow	1458 true love	1500 white laces	1542 it will rain
1417 dry dock	1459 wet ear lobe	1501 deal set	1543 hotel room
1418 trade off	1460 trashes	1502 dials in	1544 taller oar
1419 dirty boy	1461 watershed	1503 tails him	1545 it will roll
1420 trains	1462 Trojan	1504 Dolly's here	1546 it will reach
1421 Toronto	1463 doorjamb	1505 till soil	1547 it will rock
1422 dry onion	1464 dry chair	1506 dials shoe	1548 tell her off
1423 train them	1465 dry jail	1507 white Alaska	1549 Delaware Bay
1424 trainer	1466 Dear Judge	1508 tells off	1550 it will lose
1425 drain well	1467 try a shake	1509 dials up	1551 tall load
1426 drench	1468 true chef	1510 toilets	1552 tall lion
1427 drink	1469 trash up	1511 diluted	1553 tall lamb
1428 attorney fee	1470 tear gas	1512 dial tone	1554 tell a lawyer
1429 doorknob	1471 target	1513 tell it, Ma	1555 tall oil well
1430 drums	1472 dragon	1514 tall door	1556 it will latch
1431 doormat	1473 drug him	1515 tall tale	1557 daily log
1432 doorman	1474 trucker	1516 tall dish	1558 tall leaf
1433 Dear Mom	1475 terry cloth	1517 tall dog	1559 hotel lobby
1434 drummer	1476 tire gauge	1518 tall TV	1560 delicious
1435 dry meal	1477 dry cake	1519 teletype	1561 tally sheet
1436 dry match	1478 drag off	1520 daily news	1562 hotel chain
1437 dream - awake	1479 trek by	1521 talent	1563 tall chum
1438 dream off	1480 drives	1522 wet linen	1564 daily chore
1439 tramp	1481 drift	1523 tell on him	1565 daily chili
1440 terrors	1482 drive in	1524 tell on her	1566 tell the judge
1441 try hard	1483 dry foam	1525 tall nail	1567 tell a joke
1442 dry run	1484 driver	1526 eat lunch	1568 tell the chef
1443 to your room	1485 travel	1527 dialing	1569 tall ship
1444 dry your hair	1486 try fudge	1528 hotel knife	1570 delicacy
1445 true, really	1487 terrific	1529 hot line up	1571 tailgate
1446 terror watch	1488 drive off	1530 tell him so	1572 tall can
1447 tire wreck	1489 drive up	1531 deli meat	1573 daily game
1448 dry her off	1490 troops	1532 tall man	1574 teal car
1449 tore, rip	1491 dropout	1533 tell Mom	1575 tall gal
1450 trials	1492 turban	1534 tall hammer	1576 tell the coach
1451 derailed	1493 drop me	1535 it will mellow	1577 tall cake
1452 water the lawn	1494 drapery	1536 it will match	1578 tall coffee
1453 tree limb	1495 doorbell	1537 tall mic	1579 tell a cop
1454 trailer	1496 out with rubbish	1538 tell him off	1580 hotel office
1455 heat really well	1497 drawback	1539 hot lamp	1581 hotel food
1456 door latch	1498 drop off	1540 tellers	1582 telephone
1457 hydraulic	1499 drop by	1541 tall award	1583 do you love me

1584 deliver	1626 white, shiny shoe	1668 teach the chef	1710 tickets
1585 tall fellow	1627 touching	1669 touch ship	1711 dictate
1586 tall fudge	1628 touch knife	1670 hot checks	1712 take down
1587 daily fog	1629 touch knob	1671 teach a kid	1713 dog team
1588 Tel Aviv	1630 touch a moose	1672 touch a gun	1714 doctor
1589 hotel phobia	1631 touch my head	1673 touch comb	1715 dog-tail
1590 tall boys	1632 teach me now	1674 touch car	1716 dog dish
1591 hotel patio	1633 teach Mom	1675 teach a gal	1717 ticktock
1592 tailbone	1634 touch my hair	1676 teach the coach	1718 talkative
1593 tell the poem	1635 touch the mail	1677 touch a cookie	1719 tack it up
1594 had a helper	1636 touch my shoe	1678 touch the cave	1720 Dickens
1595 white label	1637 teach my guy	1679 dish cup	1721 eat candy
1596 daily push	1638 touch him off	1680 touch face	1722 take onion
1597 tailback	1639 hide shampoo	1681 hot, itchy feet	1723 attack on home
1598 it will pay off	1640 teachers	1682 touch phone	1724 attack owner
1599 tell Papa	1641 T-shirt	1683 touch fame	1725 hot wagon wheel
1600 hot chases	1642 hot journey	1684 touch fire	1726 attack Nashua
1601 digest	1643 had a germ	1685 white shovel	1727 digging
1602 touch the sun	1644 touch rear	1686 touch a fish	1728 attack the Navy
1603 touches him	1645 teach her well	1687 touch fog	1729 take a nap
1604 touches her	1646 white church	1688 to shove off	1730 take my house
1605 teach us well	1647 dishrag	1689 dish a heavy pie	1731 take me out
1606 dishes wash	1648 hit sheriff	1690 odd jobs	1732 take me in
1607 teach us, OK	1649 hot, cherry pie	1691 touch bat	1733 take me home
1608 touch sofa	1650 wet shells	1692 touch pen	1734 tug my hair
1609 touches up	1651 touch wallet	1693 touch a bomb	1735 take the mail
1610 wet sheets	1652 eat chili now	1694 touch a bear	1736 take the match
1611 dish it out	1653 touch limb	1695 teachable	1737 take mug
1612 touchdown	1654 teach a lawyer	1696 touch up shoe	1738 take me off
1613 it shot him	1655 wet, shallow well	1697 touchback	1739 take me up
1614 white shutter	1656 touch eyelash	1698 touch above	1740 degrees
1615 dish towel	1657 touch leg	1699 teach baby	1741 ID card
1616 touch dish	1658 touch lava	1700 Texas	1742 take a run
1617 touch dog	1659 touch lip	1701 tuxedo	1743 diagram
1618 touch TV	1660 touch shoes	1702 hit casino	1744 tag rear
1619 touch it up	1661 touch a jet	1703 decks him	1745 heat grill
1620 touch nose	1662 had a shoe shine	1704 dogs her	1746 at the car show
1621 hid giant	1663 touch a chime	1705 white castle	1747 wet creek
1622 touch onion	1664 dishwasher	1706 dog switch	1748 autograph
1623 teach in Omaha	1665 touch a shell	1707 toxic	1749 take her up
1624 teach in Rio	1666 teach the judge	1708 takes off	1750 tackles
1625 teach in L.A.	1667 teach shag	1709 duck soup	1751 white cloud

251

1752 hide clown	1794 dog breath	1836 tough match	1878 day of coffee
1753 eat a clam	1795 duckbill	1837 tough hammock	1879 tough cabby
1754 tickler	1796 dog patch	1838 TV movie	1880 tough face
1755 tickle all	1797 take back	1839 tough map	1881 tough feet
1756 dog leash	1798 dig up ivy	1840 divorce	1882 day of fun
1757 white cloak	1799 dog puppy	1841 too afraid	1883 day of fame
1758 white glove	1800 wet faces	1842 tavern	1884 tough fire
1759 yacht club	1801 TV set	1843 deform	1885 dove flew
1760 dog chews	1802 TV is on	1844 tough roar	1886 tough fish
1761 tuck sheet	1803 TV zoom	1845 dive - roll	1887 tough fog
1762 education	1804 tough sir	1846 hot, fresh	1888 dove halfway off
1763 attack the jam	1805 hide fossil	1847 wet frog	1889 dive halfway up
1764 head cashier	1806 TV switch	1848 tougher half	1890 tough boss
1765 attack the jail	1807 TV is sick	1849 eat free pie	1891 dive boat
1766 attack judge	1808 TV is off	1850 devils	1892 day of pain
1767 a dog show, OK	1809 tough soap	1851 outfield	1893 dive bomb
1768 dog showoff	1810 divots	1852 Teflon	1894 tough bear
1769 dock ship	1811 divided	1853 hot flame	1895 tough pill
1770 dog wags	1812 out of town	1854 white flower	1896 tough beach
1771 take coat	1813 dive team	1855 tough yellow owl	1897 dive back
1772 attack wagon	1814 tough tire	1856 hot flash	1898 dive above
1773 dog comb	1815 daffodil	1857 out of luck	1899 tough baby
1774 take care	1816 divide wash	1858 tough love	1900 day passes
1775 attack! kill!	1817 Daffy Duck	1859 develop	1901 toothpaste
1776 take cash	1818 tough, tough	1860 TV shows	1902 eat poison
1777 duck - quack	1819 divide by	1861 TV watched	1903 tips him
1778 dog cough	1820 advance	1862 devotion	1904 tips her
1779 attack cop	1821 defined	1863 tough jam	1905 topsoil
1780 dog face	1822 tough nun	1864 TV chair	1906 tips a witch
1781 dog food	1823 dive on him	1865 tough jail	1907 toupee is a wig
1782 dog heaven	1824 divine hair	1866 tough judge	1908 tipsy wife
1783 dog fame	1825 tough nail	1867 ate a fish egg	1909 hit the busboy
1784 takeover	1826 divine witch	1868 tough shave	1910 diabetes
1785 dig - fill	1827 diving	1869 tough job	1911 hot potato
1786 take fudge	1828 TV on/off	1870 tough guys	1912 deep down
1787 attack fog	1829 divine hope	1871 TV Guide	1913 top team
1788 take halfway off	1830 white foams	1872 TV gone	1914 tap water
1789 attack halfway up	1831 tough meat	1873 tough game	1915 top hotel
1790 whitecaps	1832 tough man	1874 hot figure	1916 top dish
1791 tugboat	1833 tough Mom	1875 tough gal	1917 tape deck
1792 dog bone	1834 tough hammer	1876 tough cashew	1918 deep dive
1793 attack by him	1835 day of mail	1877 tough cookie	1919 tiptop

1920 head pains	1962 hot passion	2004 necessary	2046 nicer age
1921 wet paint	1963 tip jam	2005 nice sale	2047 Noah's ark
1922 eat banana	1964 tip chair	2006 nice switch	2048 nice roof
1923 top name	1965 eat a bushel	2007 niece is weak	2049 nice robe
1924 top owner	1966 top judge	2008 nice sofa	2050 noose loose
1925 wet pinwheel	1967 tip the shake	2009 noisy subway	2051 new sled
1926 hit - punch	1968 top chef	2010 nice days	2052 new salon
1927 tipping	1969 top shape	2011 nice Dad	2053 in slime
1928 tip knife	1970 tea bags	2012 nice tan	2054 wine cellar
1929 top knob	1971 topcoat	2013 nice time	2055 noisy oil well
1930 wet palms	1972 toboggan	2014 insider	2056 in sludge
1931 tie up meat	1973 top game	2015 nice deal	2057 knees - leg
1932 tie up man	1974 woodpecker	2016 nice touch	2058 no sleeve
1933 tie up Mom	1975 white buckle	2017 nest egg	2059 no sleep
1934 dip more	1976 top coach	2018 nose dive	2060 nice choice
1935 tie up mail	1977 dab cookie	2019 instep	2061 nice shot
1936 top match	1978 tip coffee	2020 nuisance	2062 nice shine
1937 tip mug	1979 tip cup	2021 nice window	2063 nice gym
1938 top movie	1980 dab face	2022 on CNN	2064 nice chair
1939 heat pump	1981 top video	2023 nice name	2065 nice jewel
1940 depress	1982 heat up oven	2024 nice honor	2066 nice judge
1941 tea party	1983 tape foam	2025 knees kneel	2067 no such guy
1942 white - brown	1984 tip over	2026 on his own show	2068 nice shave
1943 tapeworm	1985 top of hill	2027 unsung	2069 nice job
1944 hit barrier	1986 dopey fish	2028 niece / nephew	2070 nice guys
1945 top rail	1987 top half, OK	2029 nice nap	2071 nice kitty
1946 toothbrush	1988 hit above the ivy	2030 noisy mouse	2072 noisy gun
1947 wet park	1989 tip the FBI	2031 noisy maid	2073 NCAA game
1948 deprive	1990 tip bus	2032 insomnia	2074 nice car
1949 eat - burp	1991 tip boat	2033 nosy Mom	2075 unicycle
1950 tables	1992 tip piano	2034 owns more	2076 nice coach
1951 tablet	1993 dip palm	2035 nice meal	2077 nice kick
1952 Dublin	1994 white paper	2036 nice match	2078 nice cough
1953 diploma	1995 wet bubble	2037 no smog	2079 nice cop
1954 dip lower	1996 wet baby wash	2038 nice movie	2080 nice office
1955 hit blue whale	1997 tip bike	2039 in a swamp	2081 nice photo
1956 hot blush	1998 tip above	2040 nice raise	2082 nice van
1957 diabolic	1999 hit a pop-up	2041 nice hairdo	2083 wins fame
1958 double off	2000 nice oasis	2042 nice rain	2084 henhouse fire
1959 hot apple pie	2001 honey is sweet	2043 newsroom	2085 nice veil
1960 wet bushes	2002 nice son	2044 answer her	2086 wins a fish
1961 wet bushy head	2003 knows his math	2045 newsreel	2087 nice fog

2088 unsafe wife	2130 need my house	2172 nightgown	2214 non odor
2089 unsafe boy	2131 handmade	2173 night game	2215 no night owl
2090 no subs	2132 handyman	2174 need a car	2216 onion dish
2091 on Sabbath Day	2133 I need Mom	2175 nautical	2217 no, no doggy
2092 nice pen	2134 nightmare	2176 need cash	2218 on and off
2093 no soap, Ma	2135 windmill	2177 need a kick	2219 onion dip
2094 inspire	2136 need much	2178 handcuff	2220 no onions
2095 nice pal	2137 nutmeg	2179 handicap	2221 no one knew it
2096 nosy, pushy	2138 no time off	2180 window office	2222 no, no, no, no
2097 nice bag	2139 in Tampa	2181 need food	2223 no one knew him
2098 noisy beehive	2140 undress	2182 need a phone	2224 non owner
2099 nice baby	2141 nod your head	2183 want fame	2225 onion on the hill
2100 notices	2142 on a train	2184 need a fire	2226 a new neon show
2101 window seat	2143 new drum	2185 nightfall	2227 no yawning
2102 end zone	2144 underwear	2186 want fish	2228 own a new knife
2103 handsome	2145 new trial	2187 no TV week	2229 onion knob
2104 needs her	2146 no trash	2188 want half off	2230 no names
2105 window sill	2147 network	2189 hand off pie	2231 no one hummed
2106 window sash	2148 interview	2190 no tips	2232 union man
2107 new desk	2149 on a trip	2191 notepad	2233 I know now Mom
2108 need a sofa	2150 night owls	2192 window pane	2234 union hammer
2109 hand soap	2151 night light	2193 hunt bomb	2235 any new mail
2110 haunted house	2152 a night alone	2194 hunt berry	2236 onion match
2111 knitted hat	2153 needle him	2195 handball	2237 union mug
2112 hunt down	2154 antler	2196 need a push	2238 neon movie
2113 night time	2155 needle well	2197 notebook	2239 union map
2114 anteater	2156 indulge	2198 no tipoff	2240 win honors
2115 need a hotel	2157 night league	2199 naughty baby	2241 non road
2116 need a dish	2158 need love	2200 in a nice house	2242 the union ran
2117 hound dog	2159 antelope	2201 nuns eat	2243 Union Army
2118 nodded off	2160 need cheese	2202 no, no son	2244 neon rear
2119 knotted up	2161 window washed	2203 in a nice home	2245 union railway
2120 Indians	2162 window shine	2204 nuns hair	2246 in any rush
2121 night, night	2163 wind chime	2205 no nozzle	2247 in New York
2122 Indiana won	2164 window washer	2206 own a nice watch	2248 neon roof
2123 need a name	2165 wind chill	2207 nun is awake	2249 neon rope
2124 no dinner	2166 need a judge	2208 union is off	2250 no nails
2125 in denial	2167 not a joke	2209 onion soup	2251 neon light
2126 Indian shoe	2168 need a chef	2210 no windows	2252 new nylon
2127 knitting	2169 window shop	2211 in and out	2253 on any limb
2128 need a knife	2170 index	2212 no antenna	2254 onion layer
2129 antenna up	2171 no ticket	2213 on a new time	2255 own an oil well

2256 neon leash	2298 win one above	2340 no more ice	2382 on my phone
2257 neon leg	2299 own a new baby	2341 win my heart	2383 name of him
2258 neon leaf	2300 no misses	2342 no more honey	2384 enemy fire
2259 neon lip	2301 no mist	2343 in my room	2385 in my file
2260 no nachos	2302 no my son	2344 on my rear	2386 on my fudge
2261 on a new sheet	2303 new museum	2345 no moral	2387 name vague
2262 own a nation	2304 no miser	2346 in my reach	2388 now move off
2263 neon gym	2305 no missile	2347 in America	2389 win MVP
2264 knee injury	2306 name switch	2348 on my roof	2390 on my bus
2265 neon jail	2307 no mask	2349 on my robe	2391 on empty
2266 neon Judge	2308 in my safe	2350 animals	2392 on my piano
2267 Union Jack	2309 no mess up	2351 in my wallet	2393 enemy bomb
2268 non chef	2310 unmade house	2352 enemy line	2394 number
2269 union job	2311 animated	2353 unmail them	2395 honey maple
2270 winnings	2312 new mitten	2354 name a lawyer	2396 now I'm pushy
2271 union coat	2313 new medium	2355 animal hall	2397 on my back
2272 union gun	2314 new motor	2356 on my eyelash	2398 enemy above
2273 owning me	2315 win medal	2357 no milk	2399 name the baby
2274 neon car	2316 no muddy shoe	2358 in my loaf	2400 no roses
2275 a winning yell	2317 enemy attack	2359 on my lip	2401 unrest
2276 winning wage	2318 own my TV	2360 no matches	2402 in Arizona
2277 winning guy	2319 in my tub	2361 on my jet	2403 honors me
2278 non coffee	2320 no mayonnaise	2362 on a mission	2404 nursery
2279 owning up	2321 in my window	2363 in my gym	2405 no resale
2280 in a new office	2322 in my union	2364 in my chair	2406 owners wish
2281 own a new video	2323 in my name	2365 in my shell	2407 no rescue
2282 union phone	2324 in my honor	2366 numb judge	2408 New Years Eve
2283 non foamy	2325 name on wall	2367 no magic	2409 newer soap
2284 union free	2326 on my nacho	2368 win me a chef	2410 no radios
2285 union file	2327 numbing	2369 enemy ship	2411 honor the dead
2286 non fish	2328 on my knife	2370 in my gaze	2412 no radio on
2287 non foggy	2329 honeymoon pie	2371 in my coat	2413 on your dime
2288 onion half off	2330 in my maze	2372 own my gun	2414 no radar
2289 union VP	2331 now I'm mad	2373 on my comb	2415 on your dial
2290 on a new bus	2332 win my man	2374 in my car	2416 newer dish
2291 own a new boat	2333 I know my Mom	2375 on my call	2417 newer deck
2292 own a new piano	2334 no memory	2376 on my couch	2418 unheard of
2293 non bomb	2335 in my mail	2377 in my cocoa	2419 on your top
2294 new neighbor	2336 won my match	2378 in my coffee	2420 no runs
2295 in Nepal	2337 on my hammock	2379 in my cup	2421 no rent
2296 non bushy	2338 in my movie	2380 no movies	2422 no reunion
2297 non baggy	2339 union map	2381 on my feet	2423 own your name

2424 no rain here	2466 honor the Judge	2508 kneels off	2550 nail walls
2425 no rain, hail	2467 no rich guy	2509 nails up	2551 only a wallet
2426 on the range	2468 honor the chef	2510 annual dues	2552 only a loan
2427 honoring	2469 ownership	2511 annihilated	2553 only lamb
2428 no runoff	2470 new rugs	2512 nail down	2554 only a lawyer
2429 no run up	2471 new rocket	2513 annihilate them	2555 only a lily
2430 enormous	2472 in Oregon	2514 annihilator	2556 only a leash
2431 in warm heat	2473 narrow comb	2515 no ladle	2557 nail, lock
2432 win your man	2474 New Yorker	2516 nailed shoe	2558 only lava
2433 honor Mom	2475 on your call	2517 an old guy	2559 nail lip
2434 no rumor	2476 New York wish	2518 newlywed wife	2560 no eyelashes
2435 normal	2477 New York guy	2519 no let up	2561 unleashed
2436 win your match	2478 narrow cave	2520 nylon hose	2562 honey lotion
2437 in your hammock	2479 New York boy	2521 inland	2563 only jam
2438 honor the movie	2480 newer office	2522 new linen	2564 nail chair
2439 on ramp	2481 narrow foot	2523 only a name	2565 only jail
2440 no errors	2482 newer van	2524 nylon wire	2566 only a judge
2441 narrow road	2483 newer fame	2525 noel, noel	2567 only a shake
2442 Henry Aaron	2484 in the river	2526 no lunch	2568 only a shave
2443 honorarium	2485 won raffle	2527 nailing	2569 only a chip
2444 on your rear	2486 in her fudge	2528 nylon half	2570 no legs
2445 honor roll	2487 no rough guy	2529 no line-up	2571 unlocked
2446 honor the rich	2488 in rough ivy	2530 no limbs	2572 only a gun
2447 honor your guy	2489 honor the VP	2531 nail mat	2573 annual game
2448 on our roof	2490 newer bus	2532 only money	2574 onlooker
2449 honor the Rabbi	2491 unripped	2533 only Mom	2575 unlikely
2450 win or lose	2492 new hairpin	2534 nail hammer	2576 only cash
2451 new world	2493 near a bomb	2535 only a male	2577 only a cookie
2452 narrow lawn	2494 no riper	2536 only my wish	2578 only coffee
2453 no realm	2495 no ripple	2537 new yellow mug	2579 only a cup
2454 new ruler	2496 no rubbish	2538 only a movie	2580 no leaves
2455 near the oil well	2497 win her back	2539 in limbo	2581 unloved
2456 on your eyelash	2498 no rip-off	2540 no yellow rose	2582 only a phone
2457 on your leg	2499 honor the baby	2541 on alert	2583 only fame
2458 win her love	2500 new laces	2542 only rain	2584 unlover
2459 on your lip	2501 win lawsuit	2543 in a yellow room	2585 unlevel
2460 no riches	2502 kneel son	2544 kneel - roar	2586 unlavish
2461 unreached	2503 nails them	2545 kneel - roll	2587 only fog
2462 Norwegian	2504 new laser	2546 enlarge	2588 only half off
2463 newer gym	2505 nails wall	2547 nail rug	2589 only halfway up
2464 no richer	2506 nail switch	2548 nail roof	2590 no lips
2465 New Rochelle	2507 nails wig	2549 new yellow robe	2591 only a bat

2592 only a pen	2634 enjoy more	2676 enjoy the couch	2718 knock it off
2593 only a bomb	2635 enjoy the meal	2677 nacho - Coke	2719 hang it up
2594 only a bear	2636 enjoy the match	2678 no shakeoff	2720 nick nose
2595 no label	2637 enjoy my walk	2679 in a shake up	2721 knock on wood
2596 only a push	2638 enjoy the movie	2680 new chefs	2722 hang on now
2597 only a buck	2639 no shampoo	2681 enjoy food	2723 nickname
2598 only a beehive	2640 New Jersey	2682 unshaven	2724 weighing on her
2599 only a baby	2641 injured	2683 win huge fame	2725 in the canal
2600 no choices	2642 on a journey	2684 inch fire	2726 new gun show
2601 unjust	2643 inchworm	2685 Nashville	2727 honking
2602 unchosen	2644 no chair here	2686 one huge fish	2728 yank on/off
2603 nachos - yum!	2645 on a huge rail	2687 I knew JFK	2729 young'in boy
2604 when she's here	2646 in church	2688 inch halfway off	2730 win games
2605 new chisel	2647 knee jerk	2689 inch halfway up	2731 weighing meat
2606 enjoys the show	2648 no sheriff	2690 no chips	2732 young man
2607 nachos - OK	2649 no cherry pie	2691 on a huge boat	2733 weighing Mom
2608 enjoys the eve	2650 no jails	2692 in Japan	2734 weighing more
2609 inches up	2651 enchilada	2693 inch by him	2735 weighing mail
2610 no shots	2652 one huge loan	2694 inch by her	2736 weighing much
2611 when she died	2653 in a chilly home	2695 in a chapel	2737 yank hammock
2612 new showtune	2654 no chili here	2696 enjoy the beach	2738 knock him off
2613 new show time	2655 on a huge oil well	2697 inch back	2739 knock him up
2614 no chowder	2656 on a huge leash	2698 inch above	2740 new cars
2615 new huge toll	2657 no jelly, OK	2699 enjoy the baby	2741 new grad
2616 enjoyed show	2658 enjoy love	2700 no guesses	2742 unicorn
2617 new show dog	2659 no jelly pie	2701 no guest	2743 anagram
2618 no shut-off	2660 enjoy the shows	2702 Yankees win	2744 new career
2619 now shut up	2661 new huge jet	2703 wings me away	2745 uncurl
2620 nations	2662 no shoe shine	2704 Yankees hour	2746 Anchorage
2621 nationwide	2663 in a huge gym	2705 in a castle	2747 new crack
2622 now shine on	2664 in a huge shower	2706 new quiz show	2748 engrave
2623 now join me	2665 in a huge jail	2707 yanks wig	2749 neck rub
2624 engineer	2666 a hunch Judge	2708 knocks off	2750 wine glass
2625 national	2667 one huge shake	2709 wings up	2751 include
2626 no change	2668 on edge chef	2710 neckties	2752 unclean
2627 no junk	2669 one huge ship	2711 uncoated	2753 unclaim
2628 new huge knife	2670 when she goes	2712 knock down	2754 unclear
2629 enjoy a nap	2671 no jacket	2713 Yankee team	2755 an ugly whale
2630 new chums	2672 no shakin'	2714 knock door	2756 English
2631 unjammed	2673 enjoy the game	2715 in kettle	2757 an ugly guy
2632 enjoy money	2674 no joker	2716 Yankee Dutch	2758 no glove
2633 enjoy Miami	2675 unshackle	2717 naked guy	2759 unclip

2760 engages	2802 naive son	2844 no fire here	2886 knife a fish
2761 ink jet	2803 envies them	2845 unfurl	2887 in heavy fog
2762 win, coach, win	2804 no officer	2846 unfresh	2888 on/off, off, off
2763 young chum	2805 Navy Seal	2847 no frog	2889 Navy VP
2764 hung jury	2806 on/off switch	2848 on a heavy roof	2890 no fibs
2765 yank the shell	2807 envies the guy	2849 Navy rope	2891 Navy boat
2766 young judge	2808 new face-off	2850 no flies	2892 navy pen
2767 young jockey	2809 Navy soap	2851 inflate	2893 on a heavy bomb
2768 young chef	2810 new videos	2852 win a violin	2894 no vapor
2769 no ketchup	2811 invaded	2853 no volume	2895 navy blue
2770 no egg yokes	2812 invite in	2854 no valor	2896 an ivy patch
2771 now kick it	2813 invade them	2855 now flyaway all	2897 navy pack
2772 young again	2814 no food here	2856 no flesh	2898 on/off above
2773 no cake Ma	2815 knife dull	2857 no flack	2899 naive puppy
2774 new kicker	2816 new food show	2858 no fluff	2900 no passes
2775 young gal	2817 invade the guy	2859 envelope	2901 no pest
2776 young coach	2818 unfit wife	2860 no fishes	2902 no poison
2777 yank cookie	2819 navy top	2861 Navy jet	2903 no buys...hmmm
2778 no weak coffee	2820 no finesse	2862 no ovation	2904 honeybees here
2779 no cake, pie	2821 invent	2863 Navaho chum	2905 new puzzle
2780 young face	2822 unfunny hen	2864 in a heavy chair	2906 unhappy switch
2781 Yankee food	2823 uneven hem	2865 unofficial	2907 knapsack
2782 yank phone	2824 uneven hair	2866 naive judge	2908 now pass off
2783 Yankee fame	2825 no vinyl	2867 new fish egg	2909 no pass up
2784 no caviar	2826 unfinish	2868 Navaho Chief	2910 no pets
2785 no gavel	2827 knifing	2869 Navy ship	2911 unpadded
2786 young fish	2828 on/off, on/off	2870 no fakes	2912 unbutton
2787 yank fig	2829 now phone up	2871 navigate	2913 nap time
2788 yank off half	2830 infamous	2872 knife, gun	2914 no butter
2789 yank the VP	2831 knife the meat	2873 Navy game	2915 wine bottle
2790 young boys	2832 Navaho woman	2874 no figure	2916 unpaid wage
2791 now keep it	2833 a Navy Mom	2875 naïve gal	2917 nip/tuck
2792 new cabin	2834 no heavy hammer	2876 Navy coach	2918 now pay it off
2793 young bum	2835 no heavy mail	2877 knife - cake	2919 now pay it up
2794 wing by her	2836 Navaho match	2878 on/off coffee	2920 no pens
2795 no cable	2837 Navy mug	2879 Navaho cup	2921 one pint
2796 new cop show	2838 Navy movie	2880 Navaho face	2922 no opinion
2797 hang back	2839 Navy map	2881 Navy food	2923 unhappy gnome
2798 now keep off	2840 universe	2882 navy van	2924 wine opener
2799 young baby	2841 on Friday	2883 in heavy foam	2925 on a bony heel
2800 new faces	2842 no frown	2884 no fever	2926 Hawaiian Punch
2801 invest	2843 uniform	2885 in heavy foil	2927 new bank

2928 unhappy, naive	2970 unpacks	3012 messy den	3054 I'm slower
2929 nap, nap	2971 in a bucket	3013 I missed him	3055 muzzle well
2930 no bombs	2972 napkin	3014 hamster	3056 I'm a slouch
2931 unhappy maid	2973 NBA game	3015 messy doll	3057 I'm slack
2932 unhappy man	2974 no poker	3016 mustache	3058 myself
2933 unhappy Mom	2975 unbuckle	3017 mystic	3059 I'm a slob
2934 unhappy Mayor	2976 unhappy coach	3018 my staff	3060 massages
2935 unhappy male	2977 nab a cake	3019 messed up	3061 miss shot
2936 unhappy match	2978 win a bake-off	3020 messy nose	3062 homes join
2937 nap - hammock	2979 now bake a pie	3021 Amazon heat	3063 massage me
2938 unhappy movie	2980 unhappy face	3022 mess with no one	3064 massage her
2939 no bump	2981 honeybee food	3023 missin' him	3065 massage oil
2940 neighbors	2982 NBA fan	3024 missin' her	3066 massage show
2941 neighborhood	2983 honeybee off me	3025 I'm senile	3067 massage wig
2942 NBA arena	2984 a nap for you	3026 I'm a snitch	3068 mischief
2943 own a broom	2985 Napa Valley	3027 missing	3069 messy job
2944 no barrier	2986 unhappy fish	3028 messy knife	3070 miscues
2945 neighborly	2987 no beef, guy	3029 messin' up	3071 mosquito
2946 no brush	2988 nap halfway off	3030 museums	3072 miss again
2947 wine break	2989 unhappy FBI	3031 mass media	3073 miss game
2948 NBA ref	2990 no babies	3032 messy woman	3074 mascara
2949 no bribe	2991 unhappy body	3033 I miss Mom	3075 musically
2950 no apples	2992 unhappy pony	3034 messy Mayor	3076 music show
2951 an apple a day	2993 unhappy poem	3035 miss a meal	3077 messy cake
2952 no plane	2994 no paper	3036 mismatch	3078 mask off
2953 no blame	2995 new Bible	3037 may I smoke	3079 music boy
2954 unhappy lawyer	2996 new baby shoe	3038 museum fee	3080 messy face
2955 one blue whale	2997 unhappy book	3039 I'm so mopey	3081 messy feet
2956 no bleach	2998 honeybee above	3040 miseries	3082 messy van
2957 unplug	2999 nap baby	3041 misread	3083 I miss fame
2958 now I believe	3000 misses us	3042 miss the rain	3084 misfire
2959 an apple pie	3001 misused	3043 messy room	3085 misfile
2960 in the bushes	3002 Miss USA won	3044 mess her hair	3086 miss the voyage
2961 NBA shot	3003 misses him	3045 my cereal	3087 massive ache
2962 no passion	3004 I'm so sorry	3046 I'm so rich	3088 massive wave
2963 unhappy chum	3005 misses a wheel	3047 messy work	3089 massive boy
2964 unhappy jury	3006 misses a shoe	3048 messy roof	3090 mishaps
2965 one bushel	3007 I'm so sick	3049 my syrup	3091 mouse pad
2966 unhappy judge	3008 I'm so safe	3050 missiles	3092 messy pony
2967 knobby jug	3009 Mississippi	3051 mistletoe	3093 messy bum
2968 no push off	3010 moist eyes	3052 I'm so alone	3094 I'm super
2969 one push up	3011 misty-eyed	3053 mausoleum	3095 mass appeal

3096 messy beach	3138 meet my wife	3180 motives	3222 mean Nun
3097 messy book	3139 muddy map	3181 made a video	3223 mean name
3098 misbehave	3140 mattress	3182 muddy van	3224 mean owner
3099 messy baby	3141 maitre d'	3183 made fame	3225 women only
3100 my disease	3142 my train	3184 metaphor	3226 money in a shoe
3101 midwest	3143 humdrum	3185 medieval	3227 mining
3102 medicine	3144 motor here	3186 MTV show	3228 man 'n wife
3103 meets him	3145 motor oil	3187 I'm a tough guy	3229 men nap
3104 meets her	3146 mad rush	3188 meat, half off	3230 Minnie Mouse
3105 muddy soil	3147 Amtrak	3189 met halfway up	3231 a woman I met
3106 made a switch	3148 midriff	3190 mud pies	3232 man / woman
3107 I'm too sick	3149 home tribe	3191 made a bet	3233 mean Mom
3108 met his wife	3150 motels	3192 meaty - bony	3234 many more
3109 muddy soup	3151 meddled	3193 may I tip him	3235 main meal
3110 muddy toes	3152 medallion	3194 may I tip her	3236 mean match
3111 meditate	3153 Ma, tell me	3195 mud pile	3237 many may walk
3112 midtown	3154 I'm taller	3196 I'm at the beach	3238 mean move
3113 made it home	3155 metal wheel	3197 mudpack	3239 woman may buy
3114 matador	3156 metal watch	3198 met up with wife	3240 minors
3115 made it well	3157 motel key	3199 meet the baby	3241 human heart
3116 mad dash	3158 made you laugh	3200 a mean sis	3242 I'm in, you're in
3117 mad dog	3159 metal hip	3201 Minnesota	3243 main room
3118 mute TV	3160 muddy shoes	3202 monsoon	3244 I'm in error
3119 made it up	3161 he might shed	3203 mini swim	3245 monorail
3120 mittens	3162 I might join	3204 menswear	3246 money rich
3121 midnight	3163 Ma, teach me	3205 mean seal	3247 monarch
3122 mitten on	3164 I'm the teacher	3206 women's watch	3248 I'm on the roof
3123 made a name	3165 muddy jail	3207 women's wig	3249 minor boy
3124 hometown hero	3166 mad judge	3208 man's wife	3250 manuals
3125 my toenail	3167 muddy check	3209 mine sweep	3251 moon light
3126 I'm at a new age	3168 mad chef	3210 mints	3252 mean lion
3127 mating	3169 I might shop	3211 mandate	3253 I'm on a limb
3128 muddy knife	3170 medics	3212 mountain	3254 mean lawyer
3129 mitten boy	3171 my ticket	3213 menu item	3255 men will lie
3130 Mighty Mouse	3172 muddy gun	3214 monitor	3256 monthly wage
3131 medium height	3173 muddy game	3215 mantel	3257 monologue
3132 madman	3174 medicare	3216 main dish	3258 the woman I love
3133 meet Mom	3175 medical	3217 mean dog	3259 monthly pay
3134 medium hair	3176 meet the coach	3218 minute off	3260 munchies
3135 medium well	3177 made a cake	3219 Manitoba	3261 munch out
3136 medium age	3178 made coffee	3220 mean, nosy	3262 mansion
3137 muddy mug	3179 muddy cape	3221 manhunt	3263 manage him

3264 manager	3306 Moms age	3348 Miami rough	3390 Mom buys
3265 you manage well	3307 Mom's weak	3349 hem may rip	3391 memo pad
3266 mean judge	3308 Mom is a wife	3350 mammals	3392 my, my a pony
3267 money choke	3309 Mama's boy	3351 Mom will eat	3393 Miami bum
3268 mean shove	3310 my mates	3352 my melon	3394 member
3269 man the ship	3311 I'm mad at you	3353 Mom will hum	3395 mumble
3270 monkeys	3312 my hometown	3354 Miami lawyer	3396 Miami Beach
3271 mean cat	3313 Mom ate ham	3355 Mom will yell	3397 my hymn book
3272 my own gun	3314 Mommy dear	3356 Mom will age	3398 Mom, behave
3273 I'm in a coma	3315 my motel	3357 Yum! milk	3399 Miami baby
3274 manicure	3316 Mom hid wash	3358 Mom, I love you	3400 my roses
3275 mink oil	3317 Miami dog	3359 Mom, help	3401 Mayor's aide
3276 mean coach	3318 Mom ate half	3360 Miami chase	3402 I'm your son
3277 maniac guy	3319 homemade pie	3361 Mom should	3403 hammers me
3278 my young wife	3320 Mom knows	3362 my machine	3404 my rosy hair
3279 I'm a young boy	3321 Miami night	3363 Miami gym	3405 morsel
3280 mean face	3322 My man won	3364 Miami shore	3406 marry his wish
3281 many have wed	3323 Mom knew him	3365 Miami jail	3407 more sick
3282 minivan	3324 Miami owner	3366 Miami judge	3408 marry his wife
3283 money, fame	3325 Mom knew all	3367 a mummy shook	3409 more soap
3284 maneuver	3326 hey Mom, enjoy	3368 Miami chef	3410 merits
3285 many fail	3327 I'm my own guy	3369 Miami job	3411 marry today
3286 mean fish	3328 mummy in half	3370 a mime acts	3412 martini
3287 my Navy guy	3329 Mom, nap	3371 Miami cat	3413 maritime
3288 many have a wife	3330 Mom may see you	3372 Mom again	3414 murder
3289 man half boy	3331 Mom, may I eat	3373 Miami game	3415 marital
3290 Moon Pies	3332 Miami moon	3374 homemaker	3416 ham, radish
3291 money pit	3333 Mommy, Mommy	3375 Miami gal	3417 a married guy
3292 mean pony	3334 Mom may hear	3376 Miami coach	3418 mortify
3293 moonbeam	3335 my home meal	3377 Mom, the cook	3419 a married boy
3294 manpower	3336 my home match	3378 a mummy cave	3420 marathons
3295 monopoly	3337 Mom, may I go	3379 Miami cop	3421 marinate
3296 I'm on the beach	3338 Mom, move	3380 home movies	3422 my reunion
3297 money bag	3339 Miami map	3381 Miami food	3423 more numb
3298 men behave	3340 memories	3382 my I move in	3424 mariner
3299 my own baby	3341 Mom read	3383 Miami fame	3425 hammer nail
3300 I'm a misses	3342 my homerun	3384 Miami fire	3426 maroon shoe
3301 Miami's hot	3343 Miami room	3385 Mom flew away	3427 hammering
3302 Mom's a honey	3344 my mirror	3386 Miami fish	3428 I'm your new wife
3303 Mom's home	3345 memorial	3387 Miami fog	3429 may I run by
3304 Mom's here	3346 memory wish	3388 a mummy half off	3430 homerooms
3305 Mom's well	3347 memory weak	3389 a Miami VIP	3431 mermaid

3432 Mormon	3474 marker	3516 melt shoe	3558 my loyal wife
3433 me or Mom	3475 miracle	3517 mile to go	3559 a mile loop
3434 murmur	3476 mortgage	3518 mild wave	3560 mail cheese
3435 more mail	3477 more cake	3519 I'm laid up	3561 may I lash out
3436 I'm your match	3478 mark off	3520 melons	3562 Malaysian
3437 marry me, OK	3479 mark up	3521 melon head	3563 may I lash him
3438 humor my wife	3480 merry voice	3522 I'm alone now	3564 a mile shore
3439 humor me up	3481 more food	3523 millenium	3565 mail Jello
3440 more rosy	3482 morphine	3524 millionaire	3566 a male judge
3441 Mayor rode away	3483 more fame	3525 I'm lonely	3567 mail check
3442 more rain	3484 more fury	3526 melon wash	3568 a male chef
3443 more room	3485 marvel	3527 mailing	3569 a mail job
3444 hammer your hair	3486 more fudge	3528 melon half	3570 milks
3445 marry her wealth	3487 more fog	3529 melon pie	3571 milk it
3446 more rich	3488 hammer off half	3530 I'm all messy	3572 mulligan
3447 marry her, OK	3489 hammer half up	3531 malamute	3573 mail gum
3448 marry her off	3490 hem rips	3532 mailman	3574 mall walker
3449 hammer, rub	3491 I'm your buddy	3533 mail my ham	3575 mail call
3450 morals	3492 my ribbon	3534 a mile more	3576 mail cash
3451 my world	3493 hammer by him	3535 mail my will	3577 milk cow
3452 marlin	3494 home robber	3536 mail my shoe	3578 mail coffee
3453 more lamb	3495 marble	3537 mail my wig	3579 mail a cap
3454 hammer lower	3496 I'm rubbish	3538 home will move	3580 male voice
3455 moral law	3497 humor book	3539 home lamp	3581 mail food
3456 ham, relish	3498 more above	3540 molars	3582 I'm leavin'
3457 merrily you go	3499 I'm your baby	3541 mail route	3583 may I love him
3458 humor, laugh	3500 molasses	3542 mail run	3584 mull over
3459 Mayor will pay	3501 I'm lost	3543 mailroom	3585 I'm lovely
3460 marches	3502 I'm loose now	3544 mail her hair	3586 a male fish
3461 merged	3503 mauls him	3545 mail her heel	3587 mail fog
3462 martian	3504 mail is here	3546 mail her shoe	3588 mail off wife
3463 march him away	3505 meal is well	3547 mail her wig	3589 mail the VP
3464 merger	3506 meal is chewy	3548 mail her off	3590 mail bus
3465 marshall	3507 meal is OK	3549 mail robe	3591 mill about
3466 humor the judge	3508 mail is off	3550 a mile less	3592 mall open
3467 march, walk	3509 mail swap	3551 mail wallet	3593 mail bomb
3468 marriage off	3510 melodies	3552 mail a lion	3594 male bear
3469 march by	3511 melted	3553 meal, lamb	3595 mail bill
3470 marks	3512 mail it in	3554 a mile lower	3596 Malibu show
3471 market	3513 melt me	3555 homely lily	3597 mailbag
3472 American	3514 mild weather	3556 mail eyelash	3598 Malibu wave
3473 more gum	3515 melt hill	3557 homely look	3599 my yellow pipe

3600 my choices	3642 my journey	3684 much fury	3726 I'm gun-shy
3601 majesty	3643 mushroom	3685 my shovel	3727 mechanic
3602 match is on	3644 match your hair	3686 match fish	3728 magnify
3603 matches him	3645 mash her wheel	3687 much foggy	3729 my canopy
3604 matches her	3646 my church	3688 match off wife	3730 make a mess
3605 my chisel	3647 I'm a jerk	3689 match halfway up	3731 make my day
3606 matches shoe	3648 my sheriff	3690 my jobs	3732 make money
3607 match sock	3649 yum! cherry pie	3691 my huge boat	3733 mug Mom
3608 match is off	3650 much loss	3692 home Japan	3734 my camera
3609 match is up	3651 my child	3693 mash palm	3735 my camel
3610 matched his	3652 much alone	3694 mash the bear	3736 make me age
3611 I'm shut out	3653 much lamb	3695 match play	3737 make me go
3612 I'm shut in	3654 much lower	3696 mash peach	3738 make a move
3613 may I shoot him	3655 my shallow well	3697 match book	3739 home camp
3614 may I shoot her	3656 my jail wish	3698 mash beehive	3740 I'm crazy
3615 my huge deal	3657 my jail walk	3699 my huge baby	3741 migrate
3616 mash dish	3658 much love	3700 makes ice	3742 macaroni
3617 my huge deck	3659 much lip	3701 my guest	3743 macramé
3618 much TV	3660 much cheese	3702 magazine	3744 my career
3619 match it up	3661 I may judge it	3703 makes a home	3745 my girl
3620 machines	3662 magician	3704 makes war	3746 my garage
3621 my chant	3663 much shame	3705 my castle	3747 make her walk
3622 may I join in	3664 match the chair	3706 makes a show	3748 microwave
3623 match name	3665 much Jello	3707 Mexico	3749 I'm crabby
3624 machinery	3666 match the judge	3708 makes off	3750 my clothes
3625 emotional	3667 match the check	3709 makes up	3751 I'm cold
3626 my huge nacho	3668 match the chef	3710 maggots	3752 I'm clean
3627 matching	3669 my huge ship	3711 I'm a cadet	3753 my claim
3628 my huge knife	3670 much gas	3712 my kitten	3754 my glory
3629 machine boy	3671 my jacket	3713 make it home	3755 make a whale yell
3630 mash thumbs	3672 Michigan	3714 my guitar	3756 my cliche
3631 much meat	3673 match game	3715 make it well	3757 my clock
3632 much money	3674 I'm shakier	3716 make it chewy	3758 my glove
3633 mash my thumb	3675 me juggle	3717 make it walk	3759 home club
3634 match my hair	3676 magic show	3718 make it wave	3760 make a choice
3635 much mail	3677 much cocoa	3719 make it up	3761 mug shot
3636 match my shoe	3678 much coffee	3720 my guns	3762 make a shine
3637 match my wig	3679 I'm shook up	3721 magnet	3763 make shame
3638 match my half	3680 match office	3722 mug a Nun	3764 make a chair
3639 my shampoo	3681 much food	3723 magnum	3765 make Jello
3640 measures	3682 much fun	3724 mug the owner	3766 mug a judge
3641 measured	3683 much fame	3725 magnolia	3767 make a check

Numbers

3768 mug a chef	3810 my videos	3852 my violin	3894 move by her
3769 make cheap	3811 I'm faded	3853 my flame	3895 move ball
3770 make the case	3812 move it now	3854 Mayflower	3896 move bush
3771 make a kite	3813 move it home	3855 move the lily	3897 move back
3772 make again	3814 move the door	3856 my flesh	3898 move above
3773 make a comb	3815 movie deal	3857 my flag	3899 move baby
3774 make cry	3816 move dish	3858 I'm fluffy	3900 home bases
3775 make a call	3817 move dog	3859 muffle boy	3901 I'm a pest
3776 make a catch	3818 move the TV	3860 move shoes	3902 I'm busy now
3777 make cocoa	3819 I'm fed up	3861 my wife should	3903 mops the home
3778 make coffee	3820 muffins	3862 my ovation	3904 I'm busier
3779 make a cup	3821 move on it	3863 move huge ham	3905 maybe a sale
3780 make a face	3822 move onion	3864 move chair	3906 maybe a switch
3781 make a video	3823 move on home	3865 move jail	3907 I'm a busy guy
3782 megaphone	3824 move in here	3866 move judge	3908 I'm a busy wife
3783 make fame	3825 my final	3867 muff joke	3909 maybe soup
3784 makeover	3826 my funny shoe	3868 move - shove	3910 empty house
3785 my gavel	3827 moving	3869 move ship	3911 emptied
3786 make fudge	3828 muffin half	3870 move keys	3912 empty wine
3787 muggy, foggy	3829 move on up	3871 move coat	3913 empty home
3788 make wife wave	3830 move my house	3872 move gun	3914 I'm better
3789 make wife happy	3831 move my head	3873 move comb	3915 embattle
3790 make a pass	3832 move my wine	3874 move car	3916 empty shoe
3791 may I keep it	3833 move Mom	3875 I'm fickle	3917 mop deck
3792 my cabin	3834 move my hair	3876 move the couch	3918 I'm paid off
3793 may I keep him	3835 move the mail	3877 movie kick	3919 I'm paid up
3794 I'm a keeper	3836 move the match	3878 my wife gave	3920 my bonus
3795 make a pile	3837 move my wig	3879 move cup	3921 homebound
3796 make a patch	3838 move him off	3880 move vase	3922 Yum! banana
3797 make a buck	3839 move me up	3881 move foot	3923 mop in home
3798 Ma, keep off	3840 home fries	3882 move van	3924 I'm a pioneer
3799 I'm OK, baby	3841 I'm fired	3883 move off me	3925 map on wall
3800 my voices	3842 my frown	3884 move over	3926 homey bunch
3801 I'm fast	3843 my farm	3885 move file	3927 mopping
3802 move son	3844 move your hair	3886 move the fish	3928 maybe the Navy
3803 moves home	3845 I'm frail	3887 move fig	3929 my pin up
3804 move sir	3846 I'm fresh	3888 move halfway off	3930 my poems
3805 moves wall	3847 maverick	3889 move halfway up	3931 I'm bombed
3806 moves watch	3848 move her off	3890 move bus	3932 map man
3807 movie is OK	3849 move her up	3891 move bat	3933 maybe Mom
3808 move is off	3850 muffles	3892 amphibian	3934 I'm happy, merry
3809 moves up	3851 home field	3893 move by him	3935 I'm a happy male

3936 maybe I'm wishy	3978 maybe coffee	4020 raisins	4062 rise / shine
3937 maybe I'm awake	3979 may I pack up	4021 Arizona heat	4063 rosy, chummy
3938 maybe a movie	3980 mopey face	4022 resign now	4064 raise chair
3939 maybe, maybe	3981 map of Idaho	4023 reassign me	4065 wears shawl
3940 umpires	3982 maybe Vienna	4024 Arizona air	4066 hires a judge
3941 import	3983 maybe fame	4025 raisin hill	4067 rosy cheek
3942 I'm a Brownie	3984 map fire	4026 you're a snitch	4068 where's the chef
3943 my broom	3985 map file	4027 rising	4069 raise ship
3944 emperior	3986 maybe fish	4028 raise a knife	4070 rescues
3945 umbrella	3987 maybe foggy	4029 raisin pie	4071 risk it
3946 my brush	3988 maybe half off	4030 resumes	4072 raise cane
3947 hamburg	3989 maybe the VP	4031 raise my head	4073 rescue me
3948 improve	3990 mop the bus	4032 raise money	4074 race car
3949 I'm preppy	3991 my baby wed	4033 rosy Mom	4075 recycle
3950 my pals	3992 my baby won	4034 raise a hammer	4076 raise cash
3951 home plate	3993 may I pop him	4035 you're smelly	4077 rescue cow
3952 my plane	3994 my paper	4036 raise my shoe	4078 risky wife
3953 emblem	3995 my Bible	4037 you're smoky	4079 horoscope
3954 mop lower	3996 mop the beach	4038 where's my wife	4080 raise voice
3955 maybe I'll lie	3997 humpback	4039 raise me up	4081 raise feet
3956 maybe I'll show	3998 mop above	4040 razors	4082 you're so funny
3957 maybe I'll go	3999 maybe baby	4041 resort	4083 receive a ham
3958 maybe I'll wave	4000 raises his eye	4042 Rice-A-Roni	4084 rosy fire
3959 maybe I'll buy	4001 resist	4043 rosy room	4085 raise veil
3960 my beach house	4002 raise a son	4044 raise her hair	4086 raise fish
3961 mop the shed	4003 racism	4045 ears hear well	4087 you're so vague
3962 my passion	4004 rice, sir	4046 research	4088 receive half
3963 me push him	4005 hears so well	4047 rosy rug	4089 raise the VP
3964 me push her	4006 raise switch	4048 raise the roof	4090 recipes
3965 maybe she will	4007 you're so sick	4049 our syrup	4091 rosebud
3966 maybe a judge	4008 race is off	4050 wrestles	4092 horse pen
3967 mop, shave	4009 raises up	4051 result	4093 air is balmy
3968 mop the ship	4010 rest easy	4052 hair salon	4094 hair spray
3969 mop the ship	4011 rusted	4053 wrestle him	4095 Rose Bowl
3970 my bucks	4012 rest in	4054 wrestler	4096 rosebush
3971 my bucket	4013 rest home	4055 wrestle well	4097 hurry's back
3972 ham bacon	4014 rooster	4056 you're a slouch	4098 rise above
3973 maybe a comb	4015 hairstyle	4057 you're slack	4099 hears baby
3974 my big hair	4016 wristwatch	4058 yourself	4100 red houses
3975 my buckle	4017 we're stuck	4059 you're asleep	4101 artist
3976 maybe coach	4018 raise the TV	4060 horseshoes	4102 redesign
3977 maybe a cake	4019 rest up	4061 year is shot	4103 writes home

4104 rotisserie	4146 road rage	4188 write half off	4230 ruin my house
4105 yard sale	4147 yard work	4189 rose halfway up	4231 run him out
4106 yard is huge	4148 rude, rough	4190 rodeo pass	4232 Rain Man
4107 red sock	4149 ear drop	4191 red bat	4233 run Mom
4108 radio is off	4150 rattles	4192 red pen	4234 rain more
4109 ride the subway	4151 retaliate	4193 write poem	4235 run mail
4110 rodeo days	4152 ride alone	4194 root beer	4236 run the match
4111 red toad	4153 redial him	4195 red apple	4237 ruin my walk
4112 red town	4154 retailer	4196 red patch	4238 run him off
4113 right time	4155 red lily	4197 read book	4239 rain maybe
4114 red door	4156 red leash	4198 ride above	4240 runners
4115 radio dial	4157 right leg	4199 rude baby	4241 run right
4116 red dish	4158 hearty laugh	4200 runs house	4242 run run
4117 heart attack	4159 red lip	4201 runs out	4243 our new room
4118 radio / TV	4160 radio shows	4202 runs in	4244 you're in the rear
4119 road top	4161 radish weed	4203 ransom	4245 you're unreal
4120 red nose	4162 radiation	4204 rinse hair	4246 you're in reach
4121 right-hand	4163 radish, ham	4205 rinse well	4247 ruin rug
4122 red onion	4164 red cherry	4206 runs wash	4248 year in review
4123 write name	4165 red Jello	4207 ransack	4249 runner-up
4124 award winner	4166 rude judge	4208 rinse off	4250 run loose
4125 through tunnel	4167 Radio Shack	4209 runs by	4251 run wild
4126 rotten shoe	4168 rude chef	4210 warrants	4252 run alone
4127 writing	4169 red chip	4211 rented	4253 hire a new limo
4128 written off	4170 retakes	4212 run-down	4254 run lower
4129 radio knob	4171 red kite	4213 random	4255 where? Honolulu
4130 your dimes	4172 red wagon	4214 reindeer	4256 ruin whole wash
4131 red meat	4173 red comb	4215 rental	4257 run the league
4132 rude men	4174 red car	4216 round shoe	4258 ruin love
4133 write Mom	4175 radical	4217 run, eat, walk	4259 run, leap
4134 here tomorrow	4176 rude coach	4218 rendezvous	4260 oranges
4135 read mail	4177 red cookie	4219 roundup	4261 orange tea
4136 right match	4178 throat, cough	4220 runny nose	4262 rain / shine
4137 radio mic	4179 rodeo cowboy	4221 rainy night	4263 run the gym
4138 write him off	4180 red face	4222 reunion on	4264 rain shower
4139 road map	4181 red feet	4223 rain on me	4265 run the jail
4140 writers	4182 red phone	4224 rain on her	4266 orange shoe
4141 red heart	4183 award fame	4225 rain on all	4267 rain check
4142 return	4184 red fire	4226 rain on shoe	4268 ranch wife
4143 redo room	4185 rightful	4227 running	4269 we're on a ship
4144 road warrior	4186 red fish	4228 reunion off	4270 rings
4145 rod / reel	4187 rude, havoc	4229 run - nap	4271 raincoat

4272 rain again	4314 warm water	4356 warm leash	4398 room above
4273 ring him	4315 armadillo	4357 arm, leg	4399 warm baby
4274 rain gear	4316 armed with shoe	4358 you're my love	4400 her roses
4275 wrinkle	4317 arithmetic	4359 warm lip	4401 rear seat
4276 ring wash	4318 hear my TV	4360 our matches	4402 her reason
4277 ruin cake	4319 you're my type	4361 room aged	4403 roars home
4278 ruin coffee	4320 romance	4362 row machine	4404 her razor
4279 run cowboy	4321 remount	4363 warm gym	4405 rehearsal
4280 run the office	4322 hear my union	4364 armchair	4406 rewire switch
4281 ruin food	4323 hear my name	4365 warm chili	4407 air rescue
4282 we're in heaven	4324 Roman war	4366 warm judge	4408 rear is off
4283 runny, foamy	4325 Roman wall	4367 Army shack	4409 rears up
4284 run far away	4326 warm nacho	4368 Army chef	4410 your rights
4285 rainfall	4327 harmonica	4369 Army job	4411 rewrite it
4286 run, fetch	4328 Army - Navy	4370 room keys	4412 your radio on
4287 rainy, foggy	4329 roman pie	4371 Army cot	4413 you're right Ma
4288 run off wife	4330 room messy	4372 Army gun	4414 rear door
4289 run the FBI	4331 roommate	4373 warm gum	4415 your rattle
4290 rainbows	4332 Army man	4374 Army car	4416 our radish
4291 run by it	4333 hear my Mom	4375 you're my gal	4417 rear deck
4292 rain upon	4334 weary memory	4376 Army coach	4418 hear your TV
4293 run by me	4335 Army mail	4377 rum cake	4419 your radio up
4294 runaway bear	4336 Army match	4378 warm coffee	4420 reruns
4295 rain pail	4337 roomy hammock	4379 rummy cube	4421 rear end
4296 run the beach	4338 warm movie	4380 warm face	4422 a rerun on
4297 run back	4339 Army map	4381 removed	4423 hear your name
4298 rain above	4340 rumors	4382 remove wine	4424 you're a runner
4299 run puppy	4341 remarried	4383 remove him	4425 here or in hell
4300 weary misses	4342 ram ran	4384 warm over	4426 their ranch
4301 you're misty	4343 Army room	4385 removal	4427 roaring
4302 hire me soon	4344 hear me roar	4386 remove shoe	4428 hear the runoff
4303 hair museum	4345 room with a rail	4387 remove wig	4429 rear knob
4304 room is airy	4346 arm reach	4388 remove ivy	4430 war rooms
4305 arm is well	4347 room with a rug	4389 remove hip	4431 rare meat
4306 hour massage	4348 room with a roof	4390 ramps	4432 rare money
4307 hear the music	4349 hear me rip	4391 armpit	4433 our hero Mom
4308 room safe	4350 arm loose	4392 warm pen	4434 our rumor
4309 arms up	4351 Army lad	4393 room by him	4435 rare meal
4310 remedies	4352 room alone	4394 warm beer	4436 rare match
4311 hear my Dad	4353 warm lime	4395 rumble	4437 rare make
4312 hear me out now	4354 you're my lawyer	4396 rampage	4438 rare move
4313 you're a medium	4355 warm lily	4397 roam back	4439 rare map

4440 rewire ours
4441 rare art
4442 roar rain
4443 our war room
4444 roar! roar!
4445 hear her rule
4446 roar, reach
4447 rare rug
4448 hear our review
4449 wear your robe
4450 rare loss
4451 roar lady
4452 roar lion
4453 our real home
4454 hair roller
4455 rare lily
4456 our relish
4457 our relic
4458 our relief
4459 we're your help
4460 our riches
4461 roar jet
4462 our ration
4463 you're our chum
4464 you're richer
4465 rare shell
4466 roar choo choo
4467 roar - shake
4468 hire our chef
4469 rare ship
4470 hairy rugs
4471 wore her coat
4472 hairy raccoon
4473 rework him
4474 hear our choir
4475 hear your call
4476 hear the ricochet
4477 her Oreo cookie
4478 hear your cough
4479 wore her cape
4480 hear the reviews
4481 hear her feet

4482 hear the raven
4483 hear her fume
4484 wore her fur
4485 our raffle
4486 her raw fish
4487 our review week
4488 her ear half off
4489 rewire FBI
4490 her ribs
4491 row your boat
4492 your ribbon
4493 rewire bomb
4494 here hour by hour
4495 hear her bell
4496 our rubbish
4497 rare book
4498 rare beehive
4499 rare pipe
4500 releases
4501 really sweet
4502 real sunny
4503 roll, swim
4504 real sore
4505 really silly
4506 rail switch
4507 really sick
4508 real safe
4509 rolls up
4510 relates
4511 related
4512 roll down
4513 real dumb
4514 realtor
4515 worldly
4516 real touchy
4517 real dog
4518 worldview
4519 roll the tape
4520 hairlines
4521 real neat
4522 a real nun
4523 real name

4524 row the liner
4525 you're lonely
4526 our lunch
4527 reeling
4528 real naive
4529 early nap
4530 real messy
4531 real mad
4532 real man
4533 really Mom
4534 a reel mower
4535 early meal
4536 hourly match
4537 real muggy
4538 roll movie
4539 real mopey
4540 rollers
4541 railroad
4542 relearn
4543 real roomy
4544 real roar
4545 hourly, yearly
4546 real rush
4547 real rocky
4548 real rough
4549 roll hair up
4550 real loose
4551 real loud
4552 real lion
4553 roll lime
4554 real lawyer
4555 roll yellow wheel
4556 real eyelash
4557 roll log
4558 real love
4559 roll lip
4560 relishes
4561 aerial shot
4562 relation
4563 real chum
4564 roll the chair
4565 real jail

4566 real judge
4567 real check
4568 real chef
4569 real cheap
4570 hairy legs
4571 roll a cat
4572 real gun
4573 you're welcome
4574 roll the car
4575 roll call
4576 real cash
4577 roll cookie
4578 real coffee
4579 roll cup
4580 relieves
4581 relieved
4582 real funny
4583 real foamy
4584 reliever
4585 you're lovely
4586 roll fudge
4587 roll fog
4588 roll wife off
4589 roll halfway up
4590 ear lobes
4591 rollaway bed
4592 roll pen
4593 real bomb
4594 real bear
4595 whirlpool
4596 real peachy
4597 rollback
4598 real beef
4599 real baby
4600 reach his house
4601 hairy chest
4602 reach the sun
4603 reaches me
4604 reaches her
4605 reaches all
4606 reach the switch
4607 reaches egg

4608 your age is off	4650 roachless	4692 war with Japan	4734 wreck my hair
4609 reaches up	4651 our child	4693 rush by him	4735 hairy camel
4610 reach toes	4652 rush alone	4694 Hershey bar	4736 rocky match
4611 rich Dad	4653 reach limb	4695 reachable	4737 rock hammock
4612 reached in	4654 rich lawyer	4696 reach beach	4738 Rocky movie
4613 reached him	4655 our shallow well	4697 reach back	4739 our camp
4614 reach door	4656 reach leash	4698 reach above	4740 riggers
4615 roach hotel	4657 rich league	4699 reach baby	4741 required
4616 arched shoe	4658 rush love	4700 your guesses	4742 rocky run
4617 rich Doc	4659 reach lip	4701 request	4743 rec room
4618 reach the TV	4660 hire judges	4702 rakes in	4744 your career
4619 reached up	4661 rush the shot	4703 wrecks home	4745 hairy gorilla
4620 Russians	4662 your huge chin	4704 wrecks hair	4746 our garage
4621 rich aunt	4663 rich chum	4705 rakes well	4747 rock her wig
4622 rich nun	4664 reach the jury	4706 rugs wash	4748 rocky roof
4623 arch enemy	4665 rechew chili	4707 rookies walk	4749 regroup
4624 rich owner	4666 rich judge	4708 rocks heavy	4750 hourglass
4625 rational	4667 rich shake	4709 racks up	4751 air quality
4626 your chance	4668 rich chef	4710 rockets	4752 recline
4627 reaching	4669 rich chap	4711 wear coat / tie	4753 reclaim
4628 arch knife	4670 Hershey Kiss	4712 rag town	4754 regular
4629 rush on up	4671 wear jacket	4713 rag time	4755 wreck the lily
4630 reach my house	4672 reach gun	4714 rocketeer	4756 archeology
4631 rich maid	4673 recheck him	4715 rocket oil	4757 rookie league
4632 rich man	4674 you're a joker	4716 rocket watch	4758 rake leaf
4633 rich Mom	4675 rich gal	4717 raggy dog	4759 our club
4634 Rushmore	4676 rich coach	4718 rock TV	4760 ricochets
4635 rush meal	4677 rich cookie	4719 rocket up	4761 ricocheted
4636 rush the match	4678 Irish coffee	4720 raccoons	4762 hear the action
4637 reach mug	4679 wear huge cap	4721 recount	4763 rock gem
4638 rush move	4680 rich voice	4722 Reagan won	4764 rocky shore
4639 you're jumpy	4681 rich food	4723 wreck new home	4765 hear coach yell
4640 rich horse	4682 reach phone	4724 rookie owner	4766 rookie judge
4641 orchard	4683 reach fame	4725 Erie Canal	4767 our cash cow
4642 our journey	4684 hair shaver	4726 hurricane watch	4768 rookie chef
4643 your germ	4685 our shovel	4727 rocking	4769 workshop
4644 richer war	4686 reach fish	4728 rock the Navy	4770 earthquakes
4645 richer oil	4687 reach fog	4729 year gone by	4771 earthquake hit
4646 our church	4688 reach heavy wave	4730 a year comes	4772 rock wagon
4647 you're jerky	4689 reach halfway up	4731 hair - comb it	4773 war - kick him
4648 richer wife	4690 rich boys	4732 rake money	4774 wreck car
4649 our cherry pie	4691 reach boat	4733 wreck my home	4775 hear the gaggle

4776 rookie coach	4818 rough TV	4860 refugees	4902 rubs in
4777 wreck cake	4819 rooftop	4861 throw fish out	4903 rips me
4778 rocky cove	4820 ravens	4862 hear ovation	4904 rubs her
4779 rookie cop	4821 refund	4863 rough gym	4905 wraps well
4780 eerie caves	4822 rough Nun	4864 rough chair	4906 rubs watch
4781 wreck food	4823 rough name	4865 we're official	4907 rubs wig
4782 rock van	4824 refinery	4866 rough judge	4908 rubs off
4783 rock fame	4825 roof nail	4867 roof check	4909 rips up
4784 recover	4826 orphanage	4868 rough chef	4910 rabbits
4785 rock fell	4827 roofing	4869 rough shape	4911 riptide
4786 rockfish	4828 rough knife	4870 rough guys	4912 rebutton
4787 rocky, foggy	4829 rough nap	4871 rough cat	4913 rubbed him
4788 throw calf off	4830 we're famous	4872 review again	4914 rubbed her
4789 here, I give up	4831 rough meat	4873 our vacuum	4915 reptile
4790 rock bus	4832 rough woman	4874 refigure	4916 robbed watch
4791 rock boat	4833 rough Mom	4875 you're fickle	4917 robotic
4792 our cabin	4834 rough hammer	4876 rough coach	4918 rubbed off
4793 Iraqi bomb	4835 rough meal	4877 rough cookie	4919 wrapped up
4794 you're a keeper	4836 rough match	4878 rough cave	4920 ribbons
4795 rock pile	4837 arrive home OK	4879 rough gap	4921 Robin Hood
4796 rocky beach	4838 review movie	4880 revives	4922 wrap onion
4797 rock back	4839 revamp	4881 revived	4923 rob enemy
4798 rake above	4840 rivers	4882 review oven	4924 hire a pioneer
4799 rock baby	4841 Harvard	4883 revive him	4925 harpoon whale
4800 rough seas	4842 refrain	4884 revive her	4926 our bunch
4801 revisit	4843 reform	4885 revival	4927 wrapping
4802 refasten	4844 rough roar	4886 revive show	4928 wrap knife
4803 rough sum	4845 you're frail	4887 rough fog	4929 ribbon boy
4804 hear the officer	4846 you're fresh	4888 revive wife	4930 wire bombs
4805 refusal	4847 riverwalk	4889 revive boy	4931 wrap meat
4806 rough switch	4848 rave review	4890 review boys	4932 wrap money
4807 roof is OK	4849 rough rope	4891 rough bite	4933 rob Mom
4808 reviews wave	4850 raffles	4892 review pony	4934 rob hammer
4809 revs up	4851 raffled	4893 review poem	4935 wrap meal
4810 rivets	4852 our violin	4894 rough bear	4936 ruin my shoe
4811 riveted	4853 rough limb	4895 review play	4937 rip hammock
4812 rough town	4854 rough lawyer	4896 rough peach	4938 rip movie
4813 rough time	4855 refill oil	4897 review book	4939 air pump
4814 rough water	4856 rough leash	4898 roof above	4940 wrappers
4815 rough hotel	4857 our flag	4899 rough puppy	4941 airport
4816 refit shoe	4858 you're fluffy	4900 rubs eyes	4942 airborne
4817 rough dog	4859 rough lip	4901 rhapsody	4943 wire broom

4944 wire barrier	4986 rub fish	5028 loose Navy	5070 lose keys
4945 rubber wheel	4987 repave walkway	5029 loosen up	5071 lose cat
4946 hairbrush	4988 rip off half	5030 loose moose	5072 loose gun
4947 air brake	4989 rip off hobo	5031 less meat	5073 lose game
4948 reprove	4990 our babies	5032 lose money	5074 lose car
4949 rhubarb	4991 rub bat	5033 lazy mummy	5075 Law School
4950 rubbles	4992 rip open	5034 less / more	5076 yellow squash
4951 ear bled	4993 rob bomb	5035 lose mail	5077 lose cookie
4952 airplane	4994 our paper	5036 lose match	5078 less coffee
4953 rebloom	4995 our Bible	5037 L.A. smog	5079 lazy cowboy
4954 repay lawyer	4996 ripe peach	5038 lays him off	5080 lose face
4955 rebel yell	4997 rub back	5039 lose map	5081 lose food
4956 repolish	4998 rip above	5040 lasers	5082 lose phone
4957 wrap leg	4999 wrap baby	5041 lacerate	5083 lose fame
4958 our belief	5000 loses us	5042 less rain	5084 less fur
4959 rub lip	5001 loses head	5043 less room	5085 lose file
4960 wrap cheese	5002 lose sun	5044 lose rear	5086 lose fish
4961 rubbish out	5003 lose sum	5045 lose her will	5087 less fog
4962 rub chin	5004 loses hair	5046 laser show	5088 lose half off
4963 rob huge home	5005 loose soil	5047 wheels rock	5089 wills of hope
4964 rapture	5006 loses shoe	5048 lose roof	5090 loose pass
4965 wrap Jello	5007 loses wig	5049 lose rope	5091 low speed
4966 robe / judge	5008 yells safe	5050 yellow sails	5092 lose pen
4967 rob shack	5009 looses hope	5051 lose wallet	5093 loose bomb
4968 rip the chef	5010 lazy days	5052 lose alone	5094 loose bear
4969 weary pushup	5011 lazy Dad	5053 lose limb	5095 oil spill
4970 repacks	5012 Yellowstone	5054 lazy lawyer	5096 lazy beach
4971 rebuked	5013 low sodium	5055 wheel slowly	5097 lays back
4972 rob gun	5014 wool sweater	5056 lose eyelash	5098 less above
4973 rub comb	5015 last will	5057 lose leg	5099 lose puppy
4974 rob car	5016 lost shoe	5058 yellow sleeve	5100 lighthouses
4975 rebuckle	5017 elastic	5059 loose lip	5101 lights out
4976 rub cash	5018 lost wife	5060 less cheese	5102 yield sign
4977 wrap cake	5019 lost hope	5061 lose, cheat	5103 leads him
4978 ruby cave	5020 loosens	5062 lose shine	5104 leads her
4979 wrap cowboy	5021 loosen tie	5063 less shame	5105 holiday hassle
4980 rub face	5022 listen in	5064 lazy jury	5106 light switch
4981 rub feet	5023 loosen me	5065 lose shell	5107 yellow desk
4982 ripe vine	5024 lazy owner	5066 lazy judge	5108 leads off
4983 rope off home	5025 loose nail	5067 lose check	5109 lights up
4984 rub off hair	5026 loosen shoe	5068 lazy chef	5110 lightweights
4985 we're hopeful	5027 leasing	5069 lose job	5111 latitude

5112 lot to win	5154 little hair	5196 old peach	5238 lion movie
5113 lead it home	5155 little hill	5197 ladybug	5239 line me up
5114 light tower	5156 little shoe	5198 loud above	5240 liners
5115 loud hotel	5157 lady luck	5199 loud baby	5241 lion heart
5116 loaded wash	5158 wildlife	5200 low noises	5242 lion ran
5117 old dog	5159 little boy	5201 lines out	5243 align room
5118 loud TV	5160 yellow dishes	5202 leans in	5244 lion roar
5119 loaded up	5161 loud jet	5203 lonesome	5245 lean, roll
5120 loud noise	5162 Yale tuition	5204 lancer	5246 low energy
5121 late night	5163 old gym	5205 hollow nozzle	5247 loan rug
5122 loud nun	5164 loud cheer	5206 lane switch	5248 line roof
5123 old name	5165 old jail	5207 lion is weak	5249 line her up
5124 loud owner	5166 loud judge	5208 leans off	5250 lonely house
5125 hollow tunnel	5167 late check	5209 lines up	5251 lonely day
5126 old niche	5168 hail to the chief	5210 walnuts	5252 lonely one
5127 oil tank	5169 old job	5211 landed	5253 linoleum
5128 light knife	5170 hail taxi	5212 London	5254 lonelier
5129 light nap	5171 loud cat	5213 alone at home	5255 lonely eel
5130 loud mouse	5172 load gun	5214 laundry	5256 lonely shoe
5131 ultimate	5173 late game	5215 lion tail	5257 lonely guy
5132 old man	5174 Law degree	5216 lion dish	5258 lonely wife
5133 loud Mom	5175 late call	5217 lion attack	5259 lonely boy
5134 loud hammer	5176 loud coach	5218 alone with TV	5260 lunches
5135 light meal	5177 loud quake	5219 line it up	5261 lunch out
5136 light match	5178 light coffee	5220 linens	5262 luncheon
5137 old mug	5179 yellow tea cup	5221 Halloween night	5263 launch him
5138 Hollywood movie	5180 loud wives	5222 the lone nun	5264 lunch hour
5139 old map	5181 lead foot	5223 the lone enemy	5265 launch whale
5140 willow trees	5182 lot of honey	5224 a lone owner	5266 launch a shoe
5141 loud radio	5183 Hollywood fame	5225 well-known wall	5267 loan a check
5142 loud rain	5184 wildfire	5226 linen wash	5268 lunch off
5143 lit room	5185 lot of yellow	5227 leaning	5269 lone ship
5144 yellow terrier	5186 light fudge	5228 well-known wife	5270 links
5145 elderly	5187 light fog	5229 lion nap	5271 linked
5146 holiday rush	5188 light fife	5230 lion / mouse	5272 Lincoln
5147 yellow truck	5189 lot of hope	5231 lean meat	5273 lone game
5148 low driveway	5190 loud bus	5232 loan money	5274 lawn care
5149 ladder up	5191 light bat	5233 alone with Mom	5275 yell uncle
5150 ladles	5192 loud piano	5234 lawn mower	5276 language
5151 yell outloud	5193 loud bomb	5235 a lone mile	5277 long ago
5152 loud lion	5194 wild boar	5236 lone match	5278 lion cave
5153 little home	5195 yellow table	5237 lion may go	5279 link-up

5280 yellow knives	5322 lemon honey	5364 lame jury	5406 lowers age
5281 lion food	5323 aluminum	5365 lime shell	5407 yell rescue
5282 loan phone	5324 lemon war	5366 lame judge	5408 lowers ivy
5283 alone with fame	5325 lemon oil	5367 lime shake	5409 lower subway
5284 lion fur	5326 lemon wash	5368 lame chef	5410 lords
5285 low on fuel	5327 oily mink	5369 lamb chop	5411 alerted
5286 alone with fudge	5328 lime knife	5370 yellow mugs	5412 lower down
5287 line off walkway	5329 lemon pie	5371 we'll make out	5413 alert him
5288 line halfway off	5330 hail Moms	5372 lame gun	5414 oily radar
5289 line halfway up	5331 lamb meat	5373 lime gum	5415 yellow rattle
5290 lineups	5332 lame man	5374 lime car	5416 lower dish
5291 lean body	5333 helium mummy	5375 lame call	5417 lower deck
5292 loan pen	5334 hollow memory	5376 lame coach	5418 lower the TV
5293 alone with a bum	5335 lame male	5377 lime cake	5419 lower top
5294 hello neighbor	5336 lame match	5378 lime coffee	5420 learns
5295 line pool	5337 lime mug	5379 lime cup	5421 learned
5296 oil on beach	5338 lame movie	5380 lime office	5422 Law reunion
5297 lineback	5339 lame map	5381 lame feet	5423 learn math
5298 line above	5340 all Mothers	5382 lime phone	5424 learner
5299 alone with baby	5341 lame heart	5383 lame fame	5425 learn well
5300 hello misses	5342 lime horn	5384 lime fur	5426 holy ranch
5301 lime soda	5343 will you marry me	5385 limb fell	5427 layering
5302 limousine	5344 lame roar	5386 lime fudge	5428 lower knife
5303 Law museum	5345 low morale	5387 lime fog	5429 lower knob
5304 lime sour	5346 all march	5388 I'll move off	5430 yellow rooms
5305 lambs wool	5347 limerick	5389 I'll move up	5431 layer meat
5306 oily massage	5348 lime roof	5390 lamps	5432 Holy Roman
5307 lime is OK	5349 lame rope	5391 limped	5433 lower mummy
5308 limb is off	5350 hilly malls	5392 lima bean	5434 lower hammer
5309 limb is up	5351 limelight	5393 helium bomb	5435 lower my wall
5310 limits	5352 yellow melon	5394 lumber	5436 lower match
5311 limited	5353 lime, lime	5395 lamp oil	5437 lower hammock
5312 yellow mitten	5354 lame lawyer	5396 yellow rubbish	5438 lower my half
5313 lime dime	5355 lime lily	5397 Olympic	5439 oily ramp
5314 lime door	5356 lime leash	5398 limp off	5440 lower / raise
5315 William Tell	5357 whole milk	5399 lame puppy	5441 lower road
5316 lime dish	5358 lime leaf	5400 yellow roses	5442 lawyer ran
5317 lame duck	5359 lime lip	5401 leather seat	5443 lower arm
5318 lame TV	5360 yellow matches	5402 lawyers win	5444 lower rear
5319 all made up	5361 lame shot	5403 lures me	5445 lower rail
5320 lemons	5362 oily machine	5404 lowers hair	5446 lower her age
5321 lemonade	5363 lime chime	5405 lower sail	5447 layer rock

5448 lower roof	5490 yellow robes	5532 yellow lemon	5574 ale, liquor
5449 lower rope	5491 yellow rabbit	5533 lay low Mom	5575 Yale likely
5450 yellow rails	5492 yellow ribbon	5534 lay low Mayor	5576 lowly coach
5451 whole world	5493 lower the boom	5535 hail, hail mail	5577 lolly gag
5452 we'll roll in	5494 all rubber	5536 we'll all match	5578 lowly cave
5453 lower limb	5495 lower pail	5537 oil well may go	5579 I'll lock up
5454 liar, liar	5496 lower bush	5538 we'll all move	5580 yellow leaves
5455 lower lily	5497 lower back	5539 oil lamps	5581 we all love it
5456 lower leash	5498 holier above	5540 all lawyers	5582 loyal fan
5457 lower league	5499 lower baby	5541 lay low right away	5583 I'll love him
5458 yell relief	5500 all losses	5542 you'll learn	5584 I'll love her
5459 lower lip	5501 all lost	5543 holy, holy rum	5585 yellow level
5460 leather shoes	5502 law lesson	5544 hello, hello roar	5586 lowly fish
5461 Lear jet	5503 we'll lose him	5545 low wheel, really	5587 lowly fog
5462 low region	5504 all lose hair	5546 we'll all reach	5588 I'll leave half
5463 large home	5505 hole, lose wheel	5547 oily, yellow rug	5589 I'll leave pie
5464 leather chair	5506 you'll lose a shoe	5548 oily, yellow roof	5590 oily lips
5465 largely	5507 lily is weak	5549 oily, yellow rope	5591 lily pad
5466 large shoe	5508 oil well is heavy	5550 oily, yellow lace	5592 lethal weapon
5467 allergic	5509 oil well is up	5551 holy, holy lady	5593 I'll lap him
5468 large wave	5510 yellow wallets	5552 yell, yell lion	5594 yell, yell bear
5469 large hippo	5511 lay low today	5553 oily, oily, lamb	5595 yellow label
5470 lower case	5512 oil Aladdin	5554 lowly lawyer	5596 we'll all push
5471 hollow rocket	5513 oily, oily dime	5555 yell, yell, yell hello	5597 I'll lay back
5472 lower gun	5514 yellow ladder	5556 oily, yellow leash	5598 I'll lie above
5473 I'll work home	5515 well hello Dolly	5557 oily, yellow log	5599 lollypop
5474 lower car	5516 hello, hello teach	5558 lowly love	5600 lashes us
5475 we'll work well	5517 loyal dog	5559 holy, holy leap	5601 lashes out
5476 lower couch	5518 all let off	5560 lowly choice	5602 latches on
5477 layer cake	5519 we'll let up	5561 lay low jet	5603 lashes him
5478 lower cave	5520 yellow lines	5562 oil lotion	5604 leashes her
5479 I'll work up	5521 holy land	5563 lowly gym	5605 I'll chisel
5480 lower voice	5522 yellow linen	5564 lowly jury	5606 lashes wash
5481 lower foot	5523 yell, yell name	5565 lowly jail	5607 lashes wig
5482 lower van	5524 lowly owner	5566 lowly judge	5608 whale shows off
5483 lower the FM	5525 all lonely	5567 low, low check	5609 whale shows up
5484 lower fire	5526 oily lunch	5568 lowly chef	5610 yellow jets
5485 lower file	5527 all yelling	5569 oily, yellow chip	5611 lashed out
5486 lower fudge	5528 hello, hello Navy	5570 lowly case	5612 latched on
5487 lower fog	5529 all line up	5571 well liked	5613 latch the dome
5488 I'll revive you	5530 hollow limbs	5572 I'll log on	5614 latch door
5489 lower the FBI	5531 we'll all meet	5573 lowly game	5615 lash tail

5616 lash, touch	5658 latch love	5700 Law cases	5742 Lake Huron
5617 leash dog	5659 latch lip	5701 he likes it	5743 luke warm
5618 I'll show it off	5660 latch cheese	5702 logs on	5744 Law career
5619 all showed up	5661 latch jet	5703 locksmith	5745 all girl
5620 lotions	5662 latch chain	5704 I like his hair	5746 licorice
5621 legend	5663 latch chime	5705 look silly	5747 legwork
5622 leash a Nun	5664 latch chair	5706 likes the watch	5748 leaky roof
5623 lotion me	5665 latch shell	5707 look sick	5749 oily crab
5624 lash owner	5666 lash judge	5708 lock safe	5750 legalize
5625 lotion oil	5667 latch check	5709 looks up	5751 legal aid
5626 oil change	5668 lash chef	5710 yellow cats	5752 all clean
5627 whale watching	5669 latch job	5711 leg it out	5753 lay claim
5628 I'll show a knife	5670 latch keys	5712 look down	5754 like a lawyer
5629 latch knob	5671 yellow jacket	5713 I liked him	5755 legal will
5630 leash a moose	5672 I'll show a gun	5714 alligator	5756 legal age
5631 lash him out	5673 I'll check him	5715 I liked L.A.	5757 wall clock
5632 lash men	5674 yellow shaker	5716 lick dish	5758 look alive
5633 leash a mummy	5675 I'll juggle	5717 locked key	5759 lock lip
5634 leash my hair	5676 I'll show cash	5718 all get off	5760 look cheesy
5635 leash mail	5677 yell Chicago!	5719 hello / goodbye	5761 leaky shed
5636 lash mash	5678 latch coffee	5720 look nice	5762 election
5637 latch mug	5679 we'll check by	5721 leaky window	5763 logjam
5638 I'll show a movie	5680 latch office	5722 low cannon	5764 lecture
5639 yellow shampoo	5681 latch food	5723 leak name	5765 lock jail
5640 yellow jersey	5682 latch van	5724 I like the owner	5766 look, Judge
5641 yellow shirt	5683 we'll shave him	5725 look in hallway	5767 look shaky
5642 L.A. journey	5684 hail a chauffeur	5726 look in wash	5768 I like the chef
5643 yellow germ	5685 yellow shovel	5727 logging	5769 like a chip
5644 I'll shower her	5686 latch fish	5728 look naive	5770 lock keys
5645 leash rail	5687 latch the fog	5729 yellow canopy	5771 lock gate
5646 Holy Church	5688 we'll shove off	5730 yellow combs	5772 look again
5647 latch rug	5689 lash the FBI	5731 look mad	5773 I'll kick him
5648 latch roof	5690 low jobs	5732 look mean	5774 lock car
5649 latch rope	5691 we'll ship it	5733 look Mom	5775 lucky gal
5650 yellow shells	5692 yell Japan!	5734 look merry	5776 I like the coach
5651 oily child	5693 I'll show a bomb	5735 hail a camel	5777 lick cake
5652 latch line	5694 ill shopper	5736 I like my age	5778 I like coffee
5653 latch limb	5695 Holy chapel	5737 leaky mug	5779 like a cup
5654 latch layer	5696 I'll chew a peach	5738 like movie	5780 lock office
5655 latch lily	5697 lash back	5739 lock him up	5781 like food
5656 leash, leash	5698 latch above	5740 lacrosse	5782 lock van
5657 latch leg	5699 leash puppy	5741 low grade	5783 like fame

5784 like fur	5826 all finish	5868 love the chef	5910 yellow beads
5785 yellow gavel	5827 loving	5869 leave a chip	5911 oily potato
5786 lake fish	5828 leave Navy	5870 leave keys	5912 yellow button
5787 look foggy	5829 I'll have you nap	5871 love the kitty	5913 well bottom
5788 we'll give half	5830 leave my house	5872 love again	5914 yellow butter
5789 I'll give up	5831 love me, too	5873 leave game	5915 we'll battle
5790 look busy	5832 love a woman	5874 love the car	5916 I'll buy dish
5791 look bad	5833 love Mom	5875 live gala	5917 lap to go
5792 yellow cabin	5834 leave more	5876 leave cash	5918 leaped off
5793 like a bum	5835 leave mail	5877 love cake	5919 laptop
5794 look happier	5836 love match	5878 love coffee	5920 whale bones
5795 likeable	5837 love my wig	5879 leave cab	5921 yellow paint
5796 look boyish	5838 love the movie	5880 leave office	5922 yellow banana
5797 lock bike	5839 leave map	5881 love food	5923 I'll buy new home
5798 leak above	5840 lovers	5882 leave phone	5924 the ole pioneer
5799 like a baby	5841 oily, fried	5883 hall of fame	5925 I'll buy a nail
5800 ill faces	5842 love the rain	5884 love affair	5926 I'll punish you
5801 love seat	5843 law firm	5885 lava flow	5927 leaping
5802 loves on	5844 love her hair	5886 live fish	5928 I'll buy a knife
5803 loves me	5845 ill, frail	5887 love fog	5929 wall pin-up
5804 loves her	5846 all fresh	5888 leave off half	5930 all poems
5805 loves all	5847 yell Africa	5889 life of hope	5931 help me out
5806 leaves a shoe	5848 leave her off	5890 leave bus	5932 help me win
5807 lovesick	5849 love her up	5891 alphabet	5933 help Mom
5808 loves wife	5850 levels	5892 love piano	5934 I'll pay more
5809 loves up	5851 leaflet	5893 live bomb	5935 help me all
5810 loved the house	5852 lifeline	5894 love a bear	5936 help my show
5811 loved it	5853 lovely home	5895 loveable	5937 help me walk
5812 leave town	5854 lovely hair	5896 love the beach	5938 help my wife
5813 we'll feed him	5855 lovely whale	5897 love back	5939 help my boy
5814 elevator	5856 lovely age	5898 leave above	5940 oil price
5815 leave it all	5857 yellow flag	5899 love baby	5941 leopard
5816 loved the show	5858 love life	5900 hall passes	5942 yellow, brown
5817 love the dog	5859 lovely pie	5901 leaps ahead	5943 yellow broom
5818 liftoff	5860 live shows	5902 I'll buy soon	5944 library
5819 leave it be	5861 live shot	5903 I'll buy some	5945 liberal
5820 love the noise	5862 wall of China	5904 I'll pass her	5946 yellow brush
5821 elephant	5863 love the gym	5905 whole puzzle	5947 yellow brick
5822 love no one	5864 leave the jury	5906 lips age	5948 I'll prove you
5823 love the name	5865 love Jello	5907 we'll bask	5949 loop rope
5824 Leavenworth	5866 love the judge	5908 I'll pass off	5950 labels
5825 all vinyl	5867 leave a check	5909 hail busboy	5951 I'll be late

276

5952 help line	5994 wallpaper	6036 watches match	6078 juice, coffee
5953 the whole plum	5995 Holy Bible	6037 show smog	6079 juice cup
5954 labeler	5996 he'll be pushy	6038 chose movie	6080 washes face
5955 label wall	5997 I'll be back	6039 huge swamp	6081 washes food
5956 I'll blush	5998 loop above	6040 huge sores	6082 chase van
5957 yellow black	5999 help baby	6041 chose a route	6083 chase fame away
5958 label off	6000 chooses a house	6042 chase rain away	6084 chose fur
5959 label up	6001 chooses it	6043 washes arm	6085 she's full
5960 yellow pages	6002 chase scene	6044 washes her hair	6086 she's fishy
5961 we all pushed	6003 chooses me	6045 she's real	6087 she's foggy
5962 I'll buy China	6004 chooses her	6046 she's rich	6088 she's half off
5963 help the gym	6005 chooses well	6047 she's a wreck	6089 she's halfway up
5964 help the jury	6006 shows his watch	6048 shows her off	6090 chess piece
5965 whole bushel	6007 watches us go	6049 shows her up	6091 she's beat
5966 help the judge	6008 chases off	6050 chisels	6092 chews bone
5967 I'll buy a shake	6009 chooses up	6051 chiseled	6093 chose a poem
5968 we'll push off	6010 justice	6052 chose a loan	6094 she's poor
5969 we'll push up	6011 watch us Dad	6053 chisel ham	6095 chase ball
5970 law books	6012 chase down	6054 she's slower	6096 she's pushy
5971 lab coat	6013 just me	6055 chew slowly	6097 she's back
5972 help - a gun	6014 jester	6056 she's all wishy	6098 she's above you
5973 I'll back him	6015 chase tail	6057 huge slug	6099 chase puppy
5974 help / care	6016 washes dish	6058 choose life	6100 shoots us
5975 yellow buckle	6017 chase dog	6059 huge slip	6101 huge test
5976 loop cash	6018 watches TV	6060 chews cheese	6102 jets in
5977 I'll be quick	6019 juice it up	6061 she's shot	6103 jets home
5978 I'll back off	6020 show signs	6062 Jay's chin	6104 shoots her
5979 we'll back up	6021 washes window	6063 choose a gym	6105 shot a seal
5980 lip / voice	6022 chosen one	6064 she's cheery	6106 shoot, swish
5981 well behaved	6023 a chosen hymn	6065 she's jolly	6107 jet ski
5982 yellow pay phone	6024 huge snare	6066 shows judge	6108 jets off
5983 I'll buy fame	6025 huge snail	6067 shows check	6109 shoots up
5984 I'll be fair	6026 choose a niche	6068 she's a chef	6110 she dates
5985 helpful	6027 chasing	6069 she's chubby	6111 she dieted
5986 I'll buy fudge	6028 washes knife	6070 wash socks	6112 shot down
5987 help the fog	6029 huge snap	6071 chase cat	6113 cheated me
5988 leap of faith	6030 she swims	6072 chose again	6114 shut door
5989 help the VP	6031 chase him out	6073 chews gum	6115 shoddy hotel
5990 hello Pops	6032 choose a man	6074 chase car	6116 chewed dish
5991 help beat	6033 choosy Mom	6075 show a skill	6117 shot dog
5992 I'll buy a pony	6034 huge summer	6076 huge squash	6118 watched TV
5993 help pay him	6035 chews meal	6077 cheese cake	6119 shot it up

6120 show tunes	6162 huge tuition	6204 Chinese year	6246 join her show
6121 shut window	6163 she ate jam	6205 Chinese wall	6247 generic
6122 chewed onion	6164 huge teacher	6206 Chinese shoe	6248 shiny roof
6123 shout name	6165 judicial	6207 Chinese guy	6249 shiny robe
6124 chewed on hair	6166 shot judge	6208 Chinese wife	6250 channels
6125 huge tunnel	6167 should I jog	6209 shines up	6251 shine light
6126 chewed on shoe	6168 shot chef	6210 wash hands	6252 huge nylon
6127 shouting	6169 huge touch up	6211 chanted	6253 chain limb
6128 showed a knife	6170 washed dog	6212 Chinatown	6254 Asian lawyer
6129 chewed knob	6171 shot a goat	6213 shiny dime	6255 wish - Honolulu
6130 showed my house	6172 shotgun	6214 ocean water	6256 shiny leash
6131 chewed meat	6173 chewed gum	6215 China doll	6257 join league
6132 shot a man	6174 washed car	6216 shiny dish	6258 shiny leaf
6133 showed Mom	6175 huge tackle	6217 chain dog	6259 shiny lip
6134 huge timer	6176 shot coach	6218 shine TV	6260 changes
6135 chewed meal	6177 chewed cookie	6219 shiny tub	6261 changed
6136 showed match	6178 should I cough	6220 shiny nose	6262 change wine
6137 shot my hog	6179 chewed cup	6221 shiny window	6263 change him
6138 showed movie	6180 sheet of ice	6222 shine onion	6264 ginger
6139 huge dump	6181 chewed food	6223 shine name	6265 June - July
6140 shutters	6182 shoddy oven	6224 Asian owner	6266 change shoe
6141 shattered	6183 showed fame	6225 genuinely	6267 change wig
6142 shut her in	6184 I should fire you	6226 show an inch	6268 change off
6143 showed room	6185 jet fuel	6227 joining	6269 change up
6144 showed rear	6186 chewed fish	6228 join Navy	6270 chunks
6145 huge trial	6187 showed fog	6229 shiny knob	6271 junket
6146 showed her age	6188 showed off wife	6230 Asian mouse	6272 shine gun
6147 sheet rock	6189 chewed off pie	6231 wage unmade	6273 join game
6148 huge driveway	6190 huge tips	6232 Asian woman	6274 shiny car
6149 huge trap	6191 shot put	6233 Asian mummy	6275 wishing well
6150 shuttles	6192 shut / open	6234 shine my hair	6276 junky show
6151 she told you	6193 shut up mouth	6235 chain mail	6277 shiny cake
6152 shot lion	6194 chewed berry	6236 join the match	6278 showing off
6153 shuttle me	6195 huge table	6237 shiny mug	6279 showing up
6154 shuttle her	6196 chewed up shoe	6238 shown movie	6280 shiny face
6155 shot the oil well	6197 shot back	6239 Asian map	6281 Asian food
6156 chewed leash	6198 shout above	6240 shiners	6282 shiny van
6157 jet lag	6199 shout baby	6241 generate	6283 join the fame
6158 chewed leaf	6200 Chinese house	6242 ocean rain	6284 Asian fur
6159 chewed lip	6201 Ash Wednesday	6243 Gin Rummy	6285 watch the NFL
6160 wash dishes	6202 shines on	6244 shinier hair	6286 Asian fish
6161 chit chat	6203 chains him	6245 General	6287 Asian fog

6288 shy Navy wife	6330 show my mouse	6372 jam gun	6414 short hair
6289 she knew a fib	6331 show my maid	6373 jam gum	6415 short wall
6290 chin-ups	6332 show me money	6374 show me my car	6416 shortage
6291 Asian beauty	6333 show my Mom	6375 age my gal	6417 shower dog
6292 shiny penny	6334 show me more	6376 jam couch	6418 shirt off
6293 Asian poem	6335 jam mail	6377 jam cake	6419 cherry top
6294 chain bear	6336 jam my shoe	6378 jam coffee	6420 journeys
6295 shiny ball	6337 show Mom, OK	6379 huge make-up	6421 journey ahead
6296 China beach	6338 show my movie	6380 show my face	6422 journey on
6297 June bug	6339 show Mom up	6381 show me food	6423 geranium
6298 shine above	6340 watch Mars	6382 jam phone	6424 wage earner
6299 shiny baby	6341 huge mart	6383 show me fame	6425 journal
6300 huge messes	6342 show me rain	6384 show me the fire	6426 huge orange
6301 jams it	6343 chew my arm	6385 shameful	6427 cheering
6302 jams, honey	6344 huge mirror	6386 show me the fish	6428 watch her wave
6303 shames me	6345 huge mural	6387 show me fog	6429 watch her nap
6304 she may swear	6346 huge march	6388 show my wife off	6430 germs
6305 huge muzzle	6347 shamrock	6389 show him the VP	6431 shower mate
6306 watch massage	6348 jam roof	6390 champs	6432 Germany
6307 huge mask	6349 jam rope	6391 jumped	6433 sure Mom
6308 shame is off	6350 shameless	6392 champion	6434 charmer
6309 jams up	6351 show me a lady	6393 jump him	6435 huge airmail
6310 shammed us	6352 huge melon	6394 chamber	6436 jury may age
6311 jammed toe	6353 jam lamb	6395 jumble	6437 share hammock
6312 huge mitten	6354 huge mailer	6396 jumbo wash	6438 share movie
6313 jammed thumb	6355 jam oil well	6397 gym bag	6439 cheer me up
6314 geometry	6356 jam leash	6398 jump off	6440 huge roars
6315 she may tell	6357 jam leg	6399 jumbo pie	6441 share the road
6316 she may teach	6358 show me love	6400 huge raises	6442 show a rerun
6317 jammed key	6359 jam lip	6401 shower is hot	6443 share a room
6318 show me a TV	6360 huge matches	6402 shower is on	6444 shower her hair
6319 jammed up	6361 she may cheat	6403 showers home	6445 chair rail
6320 jam nose	6362 age machine	6404 shower is here	6446 share her wash
6321 chewy mint	6363 shame, shame	6405 juries lie	6447 chair, rug
6322 show me a nun	6364 show my jury	6406 cherries age	6448 share her age
6323 shame on me	6365 jam shell	6407 huge rescue	6449 cheer her up
6324 shame on her	6366 jam choo-choo	6408 shower is off	6450 Jerry Lewis
6325 jam nail	6367 show magic	6409 shores up	6451 Charlotte
6326 huge munchy	6368 show me a chef	6410 shirts	6452 share a line
6327 jamming	6369 show me a job	6411 shirt / tie	6453 share a limb
6328 jam knife	6370 jam keys	6412 shorten	6454 share a lawyer
6329 show man up	6371 jam coat	6413 short hem	6455 jury will yell

6456 huge relish	6498 sharp wife	6540 jailers	6582 shallow oven
6457 chair leg	6499 chirp up	6541 huge alert	6583 shallow fame
6458 huge relief	6500 shoelaces	6542 chilly rain	6584 huge liver
6459 cherry lip	6501 wish list	6543 chilly room	6585 shy, lovely
6460 churches	6502 chill is on	6544 chilly rear	6586 jellyfish
6461 charged	6503 jails him	6545 chilly rail	6587 chilly, foggy
6462 huge ration	6504 chills her	6546 she'll reach	6588 she'll have half
6463 charge him	6505 chilly seal	6547 shell, rock	6589 jolly VP
6464 charger	6506 chili is chewy	6548 chilly roof	6590 jail pass
6465 church wall	6507 huge - Alaska	6549 cello, harp	6591 she'll bite
6466 church show	6508 chill is off	6550 shallow wells	6592 chili bean
6467 church week	6509 chili soup	6551 shallow wallet	6593 she'll bomb
6468 charge fee	6510 shields	6552 shallow lawn	6594 chilly bear
6469 charge up	6511 childhood	6553 chilly lamb	6595 huge lapel
6470 jerks	6512 a child won	6554 jolly lawyer	6596 shallow beach
6471 shark tooth	6513 jail time	6555 shallow oil well	6597 she'll bug you
6472 sure I can	6514 shoulder	6556 chilly leash	6598 she'll be off
6473 chew her gum	6515 a child will	6557 chilly leg	6599 chilly puppy
6474 sure I care	6516 childish	6558 shallow love	6600 judges house
6475 cherry cola	6517 chili dog	6559 chilly lip	6601 judges it
6476 share couch	6518 shield off	6560 chili cheese	6602 judge is in
6477 Cherry Coke	6519 shield up	6561 she'll shoot	6603 judges me
6478 share coffee	6520 show lines	6562 shallow ocean	6604 judges her
6479 shower cap	6521 chilly night	6563 she'll show him	6605 judges well
6480 share office	6522 huge linen	6564 chilly shower	6606 judges show
6481 sheriff wed	6523 chill on him	6565 jolly, jolly	6607 judge is weak
6482 share fun	6524 huge liner	6566 jolly judge	6608 judge is heavy
6483 sure fame	6525 shy, lonely	6567 shell shock	6609 judges boy
6484 surefire	6526 challenge	6568 jolly chef	6610 wash sheets
6485 cheerful	6527 shelling	6569 jolly chap	6611 judged it
6486 share fudge	6528 jelly knife	6570 Shell gas	6612 huge show tune
6487 sheriff awoke	6529 huge line-up	6571 huge locket	6613 judged him
6488 shower of faith	6530 chilly moose	6572 shall we go now	6614 judged her
6489 shower off boy	6531 chili meat	6573 shell game	6615 judged well
6490 cherry pies	6532 shallow man	6574 age the liquor	6616 judged show
6491 chirped	6533 shallow mummy	6575 she'll kill you	6617 judge a dog
6492 huge ribbon	6534 chilly mare	6576 chilly couch	6618 judged wife
6493 cherry bomb	6535 chilly mall	6577 chilly cocoa	6619 she chewed pie
6494 sharper	6536 chilly match	6578 chilly cave	6620 huge chains
6495 share a ball	6537 shallow mug	6579 shallow cup	6621 she joined
6496 share beach	6538 shallow movie	6580 shelves	6622 Jewish nun
6497 sharp wig	6539 huge lamp	6581 jail food	6623 Jewish name

6624 judge winner	6666 Jewish judge	6708 checks off	6750 wash clothes
6625 huge, shiny wall	6667 judge joke	6709 checks up	6751 chocolate
6626 huge change	6668 Jewish chef	6710 checked house	6752 huge clown
6627 judging	6669 judgeship	6711 checked out	6753 huge clam
6628 judge Navy	6670 judge case	6712 checked in	6754 huge gallery
6629 huge shiny ape	6671 judge a cat	6713 checked me	6755 juggle wheel
6630 huge chimes	6672 show huge gun	6714 shocked her	6756 huge clash
6631 judge my hat	6673 judge game	6715 shake it well	6757 shake a leg
6632 Jewish man	6674 judge car	6716 checked watch	6758 huge glove
6633 Jewish Mom	6675 judge call	6717 shaggy dog	6759 huge club
6634 judge more	6676 judge the coach	6718 shake it off	6760 chew cashews
6635 judge mail	6677 judge cake	6719 shake it up	6761 she coached
6636 judge match	6678 huge shock wave	6720 chickens	6762 ejection
6637 judge him, OK	6679 huge checkup	6721 chew candy	6763 gee, cash them
6638 judge movie	6680 judge office	6722 huge cannon	6764 huge catcher
6639 judge my pie	6681 judge food	6723 check name	6765 check jail
6640 huge chairs	6682 judge van	6724 shock the winner	6766 check with judge
6641 wash shirt	6683 judge fame	6725 huge canal	6767 shaky check
6642 huge journey	6684 huge, huge fire	6726 huge gun show	6768 shaky chef
6643 huge germ	6685 huge shovel	6727 shaking	6769 shaky job
6644 judge her hair	6686 judge fish	6728 jackknife	6770 huge cookies
6645 judge her well	6687 huge chef awoke	6729 jog on by	6771 Chicago day
6646 huge church	6688 show chef off	6730 shake mouse	6772 chuck wagon
6647 huge shark	6689 judge the FBI	6731 checkmate	6773 Chicago home
6648 huge sheriff	6690 huge chaps	6732 check menu	6774 Chicago weather
6649 gee, shower up	6691 she shopped	6733 shook Mom	6775 shake eagle
6650 huge shells	6692 show Japan	6734 jackhammer	6776 shake coach
6651 Jewish lady	6693 huge, huge bomb	6735 check mail	6777 shake, kick
6652 huge, huge lion	6694 huge, huge bear	6736 shake my shoe	6778 check coffee
6653 judge a lamb	6695 huge chapel	6737 shake mug	6779 Chicago boy
6654 judge, lawyer	6696 huge, huge beach	6738 check movie	6780 shock waves
6655 judge a lily	6697 huge, huge bug	6739 shook him up	6781 shake feet
6656 show huge leash	6698 judge above you	6740 checkers	6782 check phone
6657 huge, huge log	6699 Jewish Pope	6741 checkered	6783 shake fame
6658 huge shelf	6700 shakes us	6742 huge grin	6784 check fire
6659 huge, huge lip	6701 checks out	6743 chew crumb	6785 huge gavel
6660 show judges	6702 wage - casino	6744 huge career	6786 shake fish
6661 shy judge hid	6703 checks him	6745 showgirl	6787 check fog
6662 huge, huge shine	6704 checks hair	6746 huge crash	6788 shake off half
6663 huge, huge gym	6705 shakes well	6747 shag rug	6789 check halfway up
6664 judge, jury	6706 checks wash	6748 geography	6790 chickpeas
6665 huge, huge shell	6707 jogs OK	6749 sugar pie	6791 shake butt

6792 shake pen	6834 shave my hair	6876 show off cash	6918 chipped off
6793 check palm	6835 shove mail	6877 shove cake	6919 chip tub
6794 show keeper	6836 shave much	6878 show off cave	6920 Japanese
6795 chew cable	6837 shove my key	6879 show off cape	6921 job hunt
6796 huge cabbage	6838 shave my half	6880 shave face	6922 chop onion
6797 check back	6839 shove my pie	6881 shove food	6923 jab enemy
6798 check above	6840 shavers	6882 shove off now	6924 show up owner
6799 check baby	6841 shave her head	6883 show off fame	6925 chop only
6800 shaves us	6842 chevron	6884 show off fur	6926 huge punch
6801 chef's hat	6843 huge farm	6885 shove off whale	6927 shopping
6802 chef is in	6844 shave her hair	6886 show off fish	6928 chip knife
6803 chef is home	6845 shave her well	6887 shove the fog	6929 choppy nap
6804 shaves hair	6846 shy, fresh	6888 shave off half	6930 huge bombs
6805 huge fossil	6847 huge frog	6889 shave half up	6931 chop meat
6806 chef's wage	6848 shove her off	6890 chief pays	6932 cheap man
6807 chef's wig	6849 shove her up	6891 shave body	6933 shop Mom
6808 shaves off	6850 shovels	6892 shove piano	6934 shop more
6809 shoves by	6851 shovel out	6893 show off bomb	6935 shop - mall
6810 show videos	6852 huge violin	6894 shove bear	6936 job match
6811 shifted	6853 huge flame	6895 shove ball	6937 cheap mug
6812 chieftain	6854 huge failure	6896 show off beach	6938 cheap movie
6813 shaved him	6855 shovel well	6897 shove back	6939 cheap map
6814 shaved hair	6856 huge village	6898 shave above	6940 shoppers
6815 chew off tail	6857 shovel walk	6899 shave the Pope	6941 shepherd
6816 shove dish	6858 shovel off	6900 choppy seas	6942 chaperone
6817 shave dog	6859 huge flop	6901 cheap seat	6943 cheap room
6818 shaved off	6860 shave cheese	6902 chip in	6944 huge barrier
6819 shave top	6861 she fished	6903 chops ham	6945 cheap reel
6820 huge phones	6862 huge ovation	6904 chops hair	6946 gibberish
6821 edge of night	6863 show off gym	6905 chips wall	6947 shipwreck
6822 shave onion	6864 shove jury	6906 job switch	6948 chop hair off
6823 shove enemy	6865 show off jail	6907 chops egg	6949 ship her up
6824 shove owner	6866 show off judge	6908 chops off	6950 chapels
6825 watch the final	6867 show off check	6909 chops up	6951 show blood
6826 show finish	6868 chief, chief	6910 chop toes	6952 chaplain
6827 shaving	6869 show off ship	6911 chipped tooth	6953 huge bloom
6828 shove knife	6870 shove keys	6912 chipped in	6954 shapely hair
6829 chew off knob	6871 show off cat	6913 chopped ham	6955 cheap, lowly
6830 she fumes	6872 shove gun	6914 chapter	6956 shoe polish
6831 shave my head	6873 chew off game	6915 huge battle	6957 shopoholic
6832 shave a man	6874 Chevy car	6916 chip dish	6958 shapely wife
6833 shave mummy	6875 huge vehicle	6917 shop talk	6959 chap lip

6960 huge beaches	7002 cases won	7044 kiss her hair	7086 kiss fish
6961 she pushed	7003 kisses him	7045 casserole	7087 walks foggy
6962 show passion	7004 kisses her	7046 kiss her shoe	7088 goes half off
6963 cheap gym	7005 excel	7047 kiss her OK	7089 goes half up
6964 chubby jury	7006 kisses shoe	7048 hockey's rough	7090 gossips
6965 huge bushel	7007 kisses egg	7049 egg, syrup	7091 goes batty
6966 chubby judge	7008 kisses wife	7050 castles	7092 go spin
6967 cheap joke	7009 kisses up	7051 go slide	7093 goes by me
6968 chubby chef	7010 guests	7052 gasoline	7094 Casper
6969 shipshape	7011 custody	7053 whack, slam	7095 gospel
6970 shoe box	7012 keystone	7054 go slower	7096 Cosby Show
6971 huge pocket	7013 custom	7055 go slowly	7097 goes back
6972 shop again	7014 kissed her	7056 castle show	7098 goes above
6973 cheap game	7015 coastal	7057 gas log	7099 goes bye bye
6974 cheap car	7016 go stash	7058 goes all off	7100 cats house
6975 huge buckle	7017 hockey stick	7059 go asleep	7101 good city
6976 cheap couch	7018 hockey stuff	7060 key switches	7102 good son
6977 chop cookie	7019 coast by	7061 a guy is shot	7103 cats meow
6978 cheap coffee	7020 casinos	7062 oxygen	7104 gets her
6979 cheap cab	7021 accent	7063 whacks a chum	7105 waggy tassel
6980 ship vase	7022 kiss no one	7064 hugs jury	7106 gets wish
6981 cheap food	7023 kiss enemy	7065 hugs jelly	7107 get sick
6982 cheap fun	7024 eggs on hair	7066 hugs the judge	7108 go to sofa
6983 cheap fame	7025 go snail	7067 walks shaky	7109 gets up
6984 job fair	7026 go snitch	7068 kiss the chef	7110 got dizzy
6985 chop, fall	7027 kissing	7069 goes choppy	7111 cut it out
6986 chop fish	7028 Casanova	7070 kiss, kiss	7112 good town
6987 chop off wig	7029 weak snap	7071 cascade	7113 good time
6988 chop off half	7030 eggs messy	7072 ex-con	7114 good tire
6989 chop off pie	7031 eggs made	7073 go sock him	7115 coattail
6990 chop peas	7032 kiss a woman	7074 hockey score	7116 get a dish
6991 cheap bat	7033 kiss Mom	7075 thick skull	7117 guide dog
6992 cheap piano	7034 kiss more	7076 egg squash	7118 good TV
6993 cheap bomb	7035 weak smile	7077 goes coo coo	7119 good tip
6994 chew paper	7036 kiss my shoe	7078 hacks cough	7120 kittens
6995 huge bubble	7037 go smoke	7079 gas cap	7121 goodnight
6996 chop up shoe	7038 kiss my wife	7080 kiss face	7122 good onion
6997 cheap bike	7039 kiss me bye	7081 kiss feet	7123 good name
6998 shop above	7040 kissers	7082 hockey is fun	7124 good wiener
6999 cheap pipe	7041 kiss the road	7083 hockey's fame	7125 cotton, wool
7000 excess	7042 kiss her now	7084 eggs over	7126 good inch
7001 exhaust	7043 case room	7085 week is full	7127 kidding

7128 cotton weave	7170 walk dogs	7212 canteen	7254 a con, liar
7129 kidnap	7171 kitty cat	7213 canned ham	7255 OK, Honolulu
7130 cat meows	7172 octagon	7214 country	7256 acknowledge
7131 get mad	7173 good game	7215 candle	7257 canal walk
7132 cat woman	7174 good car	7216 can't she	7258 gain love
7133 a good Mom	7175 cat call	7217 Kentucky	7259 can I help
7134 egg timer	7176 good coach	7218 hug new TV	7260 quenches
7135 weak oatmeal	7177 good cake	7219 wagon top	7261 quenched
7136 got a match	7178 good coffee	7220 cannons	7262 ignition
7137 academic	7179 good cup	7221 walk on net	7263 go in gym
7138 get me half	7180 cute face	7222 walk on onion	7264 walk on chair
7139 get a map	7181 cat fight	7223 walk on enemy	7265 walk on shell
7140 actress	7182 get the phone	7224 gain honor	7266 con a judge
7141 catered	7183 get off me	7225 walk on nail	7267 gun check
7142 coat worn	7184 cat fur	7226 cannon show	7268 gain a chef
7143 get a room	7185 good / evil	7227 gaining	7269 gun shop
7144 caterer	7186 got a fish	7228 awake on knife	7270 kings
7145 go trolley	7187 get off walk	7229 wake no one up	7271 conked
7146 get rich	7188 go dive off	7230 weak enemies	7272 going on
7147 coat rack	7189 get off hoop	7231 gain a maid	7273 king me
7148 go drive	7190 octopus	7232 con man	7274 kangaroo
7149 ego trip	7191 go to bat	7233 again Mom	7275 going well
7150 kettles	7192 good pen	7234 gain more	7276 wagon coach
7151 go tell it	7193 get by him	7235 walk in mall	7277 going OK
7152 guideline	7194 go tip her	7236 walk in my shoe	7278 going off
7153 walk to Lima	7195 code blue	7237 can / mug	7279 going up
7154 get a lawyer	7196 go to beach	7238 walk-in movie	7280 canvass
7155 walk to lily	7197 cut back	7239 cane my boy	7281 confetti
7156 good leash	7198 get above	7240 co-winners	7282 confine
7157 catalog	7199 get a puppy	7241 I can read	7283 walk on foam
7158 get a life	7200 Kansas	7242 I can run	7284 gunfire
7159 godly boy	7201 conceit	7243 gun room	7285 gainful
7160 goat cheese	7202 gain a son	7244 Cannery Row	7286 awaken fish
7161 good shot	7203 consume	7245 walk on rail	7287 walk in fog
7162 quotation	7204 cancer	7246 awake in rush	7288 again half off
7163 good chum	7205 counsel	7247 go New York	7289 connive boy
7164 good chair	7206 walks in shoe	7248 walk on roof	7290 walk on bus
7165 good Jello	7207 cans egg	7249 walk on rope	7291 walk in boot
7166 good Judge	7208 conceive	7250 canals	7292 walk on piano
7167 good check	7209 walk on subway	7251 kenneled	7293 awaken by him
7168 good chef	7210 weekends	7252 go online	7294 awaken bear
7169 good job	7211 ignited	7253 kennel him	7295 cannibal

7296 walk on beach	7338 calm movie	7380 game face	7422 corn on the ...
7297 gain back	7339 come home boy	7381 OK, move it	7423 acronym
7298 awaken by wife	7340 cameras	7382 OK muffin	7424 corner
7299 awaken baby	7341 comrade	7383 go move him	7425 green wall
7300 calm seas	7342 camera on	7384 game for you	7426 greenish
7301 chemist	7343 calm room	7385 OK, I'm full	7427 crying
7302 hug my son	7344 calmer weather	7386 calm fish	7428 green ivy
7303 comes home	7345 calmer whale	7387 calm, foggy	7429 grown up
7304 combs hair	7346 calmer show	7388 OK, move off	7430 crumbs
7305 camisole	7347 camera week	7389 OK, move up	7431 crammed
7306 OK message	7348 camera off	7390 camps	7432 crewman
7307 combs wig	7349 hog my robe	7391 camp out	7433 carry me home
7308 comes off	7350 camels	7392 company	7434 creamer
7309 comes up	7351 calm lady	7393 camp home	7435 crummy law
7310 comedies	7352 hog my line	7394 camper	7436 carry my shoe
7311 committed	7353 camel home	7395 gumball	7437 cram week
7312 comedian	7354 camel hair	7396 comb the beach	7438 carry my half
7313 game time	7355 calm lily	7397 come back	7439 Grampa
7314 combed hair	7356 comb eyelash	7398 calm above	7440 careers
7315 comb tail	7357 whack my leg	7399 calm baby	7441 car radio
7316 comedy show	7358 the game I love	7400 caresses	7442 carry her now
7317 walk my dog	7359 calm lip	7401 crest	7443 carry the Army
7318 whack my TV	7360 game shows	7402 greasy hen	7444 carry her here
7319 combed up	7361 wig matched	7403 greasy ham	7445 carry the rail
7320 commons	7362 commotion	7404 grocery	7446 carry her shoe
7321 community	7363 calm gym	7405 carousel	7447 car wreck
7322 communion	7364 calm jury	7406 greasy shoe	7448 car roof
7323 hack my name	7365 game show law	7407 crazy week	7449 carry her up
7324 cow manure	7366 calm judge	7408 caress wife	7450 girls
7325 common law	7367 OK magic	7409 grows up	7451 grilled
7326 common show	7368 calm chef	7410 crates	7452 Carolina
7327 combing	7369 go match up	7411 greeted	7453 cruel home
7328 common wife	7370 comics	7412 accordion	7454 curly hair
7329 common boy	7371 comb cat	7413 greet him	7455 curly wall
7330 hug the Moms	7372 come again	7414 quarter	7456 girly show
7330 hug my mouse	7373 calm, calm	7415 Great Wall	7457 garlic
7332 come home now	7374 comic hour	7416 great age	7458 cry wolf
7333 hug my Mom	7375 comical	7417 critic	7459 curl up
7334 comb my hair	7376 comic show	7418 gratify	7460 gorgeous
7335 come home all	7377 gamecock	7419 great boy	7461 crashed
7336 game, match	7378 comic wife	7420 cranes	7462 creation
7337 a weak mimic	7379 comic boy	7421 crowned	7463 carry shame

Numbers

7464 creature	7506 glass shoe	7548 clear off	7590 claps
7465 crucial	7507 classic	7549 call her up	7591 galloped
7466 crash the show	7508 closed off	7550 kill lice	7592 clip on
7467 car check	7509 close by	7551 cool lady	7593 kill bomb
7468 carry chef	7510 cleats	7552 goal line	7594 clipper
7469 crash up	7511 clotted	7553 kill lamb	7595 global
7470 crooks	7512 guillotine	7554 call lawyer	7596 calabash
7471 cracked	7513 equal time	7555 kill a lily	7597 call back
7472 carry gun	7514 cold weather	7556 cool leash	7598 clip off
7473 crack him	7515 cold ale	7557 cool leg	7599 clay pipe
7474 cracker	7516 gold watch	7558 kill / alive	7600 catch z's
7475 crackle	7517 cold week	7559 coil lip	7601 weak chest
7476 Greek show	7518 clay dove	7560 colleges	7602 cashes in
7477 crack egg	7519 called up	7561 clashed	7603 catches him
7478 crack wave	7520 clowns	7562 coalition	7604 catchers her
7479 crack up	7521 clarinet	7563 clash with me	7605 catch seal
7480 graves	7522 clean hen	7564 glacier	7606 catch show
7481 gravity	7523 clean him	7565 call jail	7607 catches egg
7482 car phone	7524 cleaner	7566 call judge	7608 catches wave
7483 carve ham	7525 colonial	7567 kill the joke	7609 catches up
7484 carver	7526 clench	7568 call the chef	7610 coached us
7485 careful	7527 clinic	7569 call - show up	7611 coached at Iowa
7486 carry fish	7528 clean off	7570 clocks	7612 cash it in
7487 graphic	7529 cleanup	7571 Calcutta	7613 coach team
7488 carry wife off	7530 clams	7572 clock in	7614 coached her
7489 acrophobia	7531 climate	7573 call game	7615 catch a tail
7490 grapes	7532 coal mine	7574 clicker	7616 catch dish
7491 carpet	7533 claim him	7575 go local	7617 catch dog
7492 Caribbean	7534 gloomy weather	7576 clock show	7618 catch TV
7493 car bomb	7535 claim all	7577 goal kick	7619 go shut up
7494 grabber	7536 call match	7578 click off	7620 kitchens
7495 grapple	7537 claim key	7579 call a cab	7621 hockey joint
7496 garbage	7538 claim half	7580 gloves	7622 lower nun
7497 carry bike	7539 clump	7581 golf tee	7623 catchy name
7498 crabby wife	7540 colors	7582 kill phone	7624 action hero
7499 cry baby	7541 Colorado	7583 kill fame	7625 hockey channel
7500 glasses	7542 chlorine	7584 clover	7626 wig change
7501 closet	7543 wiggle room	7585 kill file	7627 catching
7502 calls in	7544 cooler weather	7586 kill fish	7628 catch knife
7503 coliseum	7545 killer whale	7587 kill fog	7629 weak chin up
7504 calls her	7546 cooler wash	7588 glove off	7630 catch mouse
7505 colossal	7547 cooler week	7589 call the VP	7631 gosh, me too

7632 coachman	7674 catch car	7716 cake dish	7758 quickly wave
7633 catch Mom	7675 catch eagle	7717 kick dog	7759 quickly up
7634 catch more	7676 go check wash	7718 kicked off	7760 kick shoes
7635 catch mail	7677 catch a cookie	7719 kick it up	7761 cookie sheet
7636 catch match	7678 catch a cough	7720 cocoons	7762 go / action
7637 gosh, I'm weak	7679 catch a cab	7721 coconut	7763 go catch him
7638 catch movie	7680 catch vase	7722 kick no one	7764 cookie jar
7639 go jump	7681 catch food	7723 kooky name	7765 kick shell
7640 cashiers	7682 catch phone	7724 kick owner	7766 quick judge
7641 catch ride	7683 catch fame	7725 kick in wheel	7767 quick Joke
7642 week journey	7684 catch fire	7726 Coke on shoe	7768 kick, shove
7643 catch her home	7685 catch flu	7727 cooking	7769 go catch up
7644 catch her here	7686 catch fish	7728 cake knife	7770 cakewalks
7645 catch, roll	7687 catch a thief, OK	7729 quick nap	7771 kick cat
7646 ok church	7688 go shove off	7730 quick mouse	7772 quick gun
7647 go Jerico	7689 coach the VP	7731 kick him, too	7773 quick game
7648 weak sheriff	7690 catch bus	7732 quick money	7774 quacky car
7649 weak chirp	7691 catch a boat	7733 quick Mom	7775 Coca-Cola
7650 eggshells	7692 OK Japan	7734 cook more	7776 quick cash
7651 weak child	7693 catch a bomb	7735 guacamole	7777 quick kick
7652 catch a lion	7694 cash bar	7736 quick match	7778 quacky cough
7653 catch a lamb	7695 catchable	7737 kick him, OK	7779 kick cab
7654 catch lower	7696 catch the beach	7738 quick movie	7780 cookie face
7655 catch lily	7697 cash back	7739 hockey camp	7781 quick feet
7656 catch a leash	7698 whack, chop off	7740 Quakers	7782 cook, oven
7657 catch log	7699 catch baby	7741 go-cart	7783 quick fame
7658 catch a leaf	7700 kicks us	7742 quick run	7784 quick fire
7659 coach help	7701 cookie is hot	7743 quick Army	7785 cake file
7660 catch shows	7702 hog casino	7744 OK career	7786 quick fish
7661 catch jet	7703 cooks ham	7745 cog railway	7787 kick off week
7662 OK shoe shine	7704 kicks her	7746 quicker show	7788 kick wife off
7663 catch shame	7705 cake sale	7747 weak crack	7789 kick the VP
7664 coach jury	7706 cookie is chewy	7748 quicker wave	7790 quick pass
7665 catch huge eel	7707 cooks egg	7749 kick her up	7791 cockpit
7666 catch choo choo	7708 kicks off	7750 goggles	7792 cocoa bean
7667 cash check	7709 kick is up	7751 quickly hot	7793 kick by me
7668 catch chef	7710 cactus	7752 quick lion	7794 quick bear
7669 catch sheep	7711 kicked toe	7753 go climb	7795 weak cable
7670 weak jokes	7712 kicked in	7754 quick lawyer	7796 quick push
7671 hockey jacket	7713 kicked me	7755 quickly yell	7797 kick back
7672 go check in	7714 kick door	7756 quickly chew	7798 kick above
7673 catch a game	7715 cocktail	7757 quickly go	7799 kick puppy

287

7800 gives her away	7842 govern	7884 give fur away	7926 hockey punch
7801 OK feast	7843 give her ham	7885 give file away	7927 coping
7802 caves in	7844 gave her hair	7886 gave fish away	7928 keep knife
7803 gives me	7845 weak, frail	7887 cough off wig	7929 cabin boy
7804 gives her	7846 gave her age	7888 gave wife half	7930 keep mouse
7805 gives all	7847 weak frog	7889 give off hope	7931 keep my head
7806 gives age	7848 gave her half	7890 give pass	7932 keep money
7807 gave his OK	7849 coverup	7891 coffee pot	7933 keep Mom
7808 hockey faceoff	7850 gavels	7892 coffee bean	7934 keep more
7809 go fess up	7851 coffee lady	7893 gave poem	7935 keep mail
7810 cavities	7852 cough alone	7894 cough up hair	7936 keep my wish
7811 go feed it	7853 weak flame	7895 give up Yale	7937 keep my guy
7812 caved in	7854 cavalry	7896 cough up age	7938 keep my wife
7813 go fight him	7855 give a lily	7897 give back	7939 keep map
7814 cafeteria	7856 weak flesh	7898 give up half	7940 capers
7815 gave it all	7857 UK flag	7899 give up hope	7941 copperhead
7816 give it a wash	7858 week of love	7900 capsize	7942 cabernet
7817 cough attack	7859 go fly up	7901 capacity	7943 keep warm
7818 give it off	7860 gave chase	7902 keeps on	7944 copper wire
7819 coughed up	7861 go fish day	7903 keeps me	7945 copper wheel
7820 coffins	7862 go fishin'	7904 keeps her	7946 copper shoe
7821 go vent	7863 go fetch him	7905 capsule	7947 keep rug
7822 coffee anyone	7864 gave chair away	7906 keeps a wish	7948 keep her off
7823 cough on him	7865 give Jello away	7907 keepsake	7949 keep robe
7824 cough on her	7866 coffee, Judge	7908 keeps off	7950 cables
7825 weak vinyl	7867 coffee shake	7909 keeps up	7951 gobbled
7826 go finish	7868 cough, shave	7910 kept us	7952 goblin
7827 coughing	7869 coffee shop	7911 copped out	7953 go bloom
7828 cough on wife	7870 gave keys away	7912 captain	7954 hockey player
7829 cough on up	7871 go fake it	7913 keep time	7955 go play well
7830 weak fumes	7872 give gun away	7914 egg, butter	7956 keep leash
7831 go vomit	7873 gave game away	7915 Capitol	7957 cable guy
7832 caveman	7874 go figure	7916 keep dish	7958 cable off
7833 cough Mom	7875 gave a clue	7917 keep dog	7959 go plop
7834 give more	7876 giveaway cash	7918 captive	7960 cabbages
7835 give mail	7877 coffee cake	7919 keep it up	7961 keep jet
7836 give you a match	7878 cough, cough	7920 cabins	7962 caption
7837 coffee mug	7879 coffee cup	7921 cabinet	7963 keep chum
7838 giveaway movie	7880 gave office away	7922 egg, banana	7964 keep jury
7839 give map away	7881 gave food	7923 keep name	7965 keep shell
7840 givers	7882 give van away	7924 weak pioneer	7966 keep judge
7841 go off-road	7883 gave fame away	7925 cabin wall	7967 keep check

7968 keep chef	8010 wife sits	8052 Vaseline	8094 fuzzy bear
7969 keep job	8011 vested	8053 half slum	8095 vase, ball
7970 hockey pucks	8012 feast on	8054 face lawyer	8096 face beach
7971 Cape Cod	8013 office time	8055 fossil hole	8097 face back
7972 go back now	8014 visitor	8056 fuselage	8098 face above
7973 go back home	8015 half stale	8057 fossil egg	8099 fussy baby
7974 keep car	8016 fast wash	8058 fuzzy leaf	8100 fights us
7975 wake-up call	8017 fast guy	8059 fuzzy lip	8101 fatty acid
7976 keep the cash	8018 face TV	8060 face a choice	8102 fades in
7977 cupcake	8019 fist up	8061 ivy was shot	8103 fights me
7978 keep coffee	8020 office noise	8062 physician	8104 feet sore
7979 go back up	8021 face window	8063 face huge home	8105 fights well
7980 keep face	8022 face the nun	8064 face jury	8106 food is chewy
7981 cup of tea	8023 fasten him	8065 face jail	8107 food is weak
7982 keep phone	8024 fussy owner	8066 face judge	8108 fight's off
7983 keep fame	8025 fasten wheel	8067 voice check	8109 fights boy
7984 Cape Fear	8026 fasten shoe	8068 face chef	8110 faded house
7985 keep file	8027 facing	8069 face - chubby	8111 faded hat
7986 keep fish	8028 fasten off	8070 office keys	8112 faded in
7987 keep the fog	8029 fasten boy	8071 fussy cat	8113 feed team
7988 keep off ivy	8030 office mouse	8072 wife is gone	8114 foot odor
7989 keep VP	8031 office mate	8073 wife has gum	8115 voodoo doll
7990 keep busy	8032 office woman	8074 face car	8116 food dish
7991 cowboy boot	8033 face Mom	8075 physical	8117 feed dog
7992 keep open	8034 face him here	8076 voice coach	8118 video TV
7993 keep bomb	8035 voice mail	8077 office cake	8119 video tape
7994 egg, pepper	8036 face match	8078 fuzzy coffee	8120 video noise
7995 keep the ball	8037 face my week	8079 fuzzy cap	8121 footnote
7996 keep peach	8038 face my wife	8080 face offs	8122 fight no one
7997 keep back	8039 office map	8081 face is fat	8123 Viet Nam
7998 keep puppy off	8040 officers	8082 fuzzy phone	8124 fight - honor
7999 wake baby up	8041 voice heard	8083 face fame	8125 heavy tunnel
8000 faces us	8042 officer, no	8084 face fire	8126 food - nacho
8001 faces it	8043 face Army	8085 face full	8127 fighting
8002 faces in	8044 face her here	8086 face fish	8128 feed Navy
8003 faces me	8045 office rail	8087 face havoc	8129 heavy tune-up
8004 faces her	8046 face her shoe	8088 ivy is half off	8130 feed mouse
8005 voice is well	8047 office rug	8089 face the VP	8131 feed meat
8006 heavy seas wash	8048 office roof	8090 office boys	8132 vitamin
8007 wife is sick	8049 heavy syrup	8091 office bought	8133 feed Mom
8008 faces off	8050 fossils	8092 office open	8134 fight more
8009 faces up	8051 face lady	8093 face bomb	8135 halfway to mall

8136 fight the match	8178 wife took off	8220 often noisy	8262 finish wine
8137 food - mug	8179 photocopy	8221 van window	8263 have no shame
8138 video movie	8180 feed face	8222 funny Nun	8264 venture
8139 heavy tempo	8181 food fight	8223 funny name	8265 finish hall
8140 fighters	8182 have TV on	8224 fun owner	8266 finish show
8141 half tried	8183 fight fame	8225 funny nail	8267 funny joke
8142 veteran	8184 fight fire	8226 fun in the show	8268 finish half
8143 feed Army	8185 fight a filly	8227 wife winning	8269 finish up
8144 heavy terrier	8186 feed fish	8228 funny Navy	8270 fangs
8145 federal	8187 fought off week	8229 fun nap	8271 half naked
8146 heavy trash	8188 fought off wave	8230 funny mouse	8272 have no gun
8147 off-track	8189 feed the VP	8231 a fun mate	8273 fun game
8148 half drove	8190 feed boys	8232 funny man	8274 finger
8149 heavy trap	8191 fit body	8233 funny Mom	8275 phone call
8150 fiddles	8192 fight pain	8234 have no more	8276 fun coach
8151 fiddled	8193 fight bomb	8235 funny mail	8277 funny cookie
8152 fat - lean	8194 food buyer	8236 fun match	8278 fun coffee
8153 fat lamb	8195 football	8237 fun mug	8279 funny cap
8154 fiddler	8196 fight, push	8238 funny movie	8280 funny face
8155 feed yellow owl	8197 feedback	8239 fun, maybe	8281 funny feet
8156 foot leash	8198 feed beehive	8240 funny horse	8282 fun, fun
8157 foot, leg	8199 feed baby	8241 vineyard	8283 fun fame
8158 have to leave	8200 fences	8242 fun run	8284 fanfare
8159 photo lab	8201 have a nice day	8243 fun room	8285 fun fill
8160 feta cheese	8202 funny son	8244 funnier hair	8286 funny fish
8161 photo shoot	8203 fun is home	8245 funeral	8287 phone off hook
8162 food chain	8204 fancier	8246 funnier show	8288 fun with half off
8163 have to show me	8205 heavy nozzle	8247 funnier guy	8289 funny VP
8164 heavy teacher	8206 phone switch	8248 funnier wife	8290 funny boys
8165 feed the jail	8207 often sick	8249 funny robe	8291 funny body
8166 fat judge	8208 phone is off	8250 funnels	8292 funny bone
8167 fat check	8209 fun's up	8251 funneled	8293 have no bomb
8168 fat chef	8210 vents	8252 phone line	8294 funny bear
8169 photo shop	8211 fainted	8253 vinyl home	8295 have an apple
8170 fatigues	8212 fountain	8254 final hour	8296 fun beach
8171 feed cat	8213 phantom	8255 vinyl wall	8297 phone book
8172 Vatican	8214 find your way	8256 final show	8298 fun above
8173 video game	8215 vandal	8257 final week	8299 funny baby
8174 have to carry	8216 vintage	8258 final wave	8300 famous house
8175 half tackle	8217 fanatic	8259 funny lip	8301 have my soda
8176 fat coach	8218 funny TV	8260 finishes	8302 famous wine
8177 wife ate cake	8219 funny toupee	8261 funny shot	8303 famous home

8304 famous hair	8346 heavy march	8388 halfway move off	8430 farms
8305 famously	8347 off my rack	8389 halfway move up	8431 formed
8306 heavy massage	8348 off my roof	8390 have my pass	8432 fireman
8307 famous guy	8349 have my robe	8391 have my bat	8433 free Mom
8308 famous wife	8350 families	8392 have my pen	8434 farmer
8309 foams up	8351 family ate	8393 foamy bomb	8435 formula
8310 vomits	8352 half a million	8394 vampire	8436 very much
8311 vomited	8353 family home	8395 fumble	8437 have room key
8312 vomit honey	8354 familiar	8396 foamy peach	8438 for my wife
8313 wife, madam	8355 family law	8397 off my back	8439 off ramp
8314 vomit here	8356 family show	8398 foamy beehive	8440 free rose
8315 heavy metal	8357 family guy	8399 heavy mop up	8441 forward
8316 vomit hash	8358 have him leave	8400 freezes	8442 forewarn
8317 have my dog	8359 foamy lip	8401 frost	8443 firearm
8318 have my TV	8360 have my cheese	8402 frozen	8444 free her hair
8319 vomit up	8361 have him shot	8403 fires me	8445 free roll
8320 famines	8362 foamy, shiny	8404 freezer	8446 free reach
8321 half meant	8363 have my shame	8405 Ferris Wheel	8447 free rug
8322 have my onion	8364 have my chair	8406 frees shoe	8448 free roof
8323 have my name	8365 have my Jello	8407 fresco	8449 free ruby
8324 fame, honor	8366 foamy judge	8408 frees wife	8450 frills
8325 have no will	8367 have my check	8409 Frisbee	8451 frailty
8326 have my nacho	8368 VMI chef	8410 overdose	8452 fire lane
8327 fuming	8369 have my job	8411 freed head	8453 farewell, Ma
8328 have my knife	8370 have my keys	8412 free town	8454 frilly hair
8329 have my nap	8371 have my coat	8413 freedom	8455 farewell all
8330 have my mess	8372 have my gun	8414 ivory tower	8456 heavy relish
8331 foamy meat	8373 have my gum	8415 free toll	8457 fire log
8332 have my money	8374 have my car	8416 variety show	8458 free love
8333 have my Mom	8375 have my gal	8417 fried egg	8459 farewell, Pa
8334 have a memory	8376 have my cash	8418 afraid of	8460 free cheese
8335 have my meal	8377 have my cake	8419 fruit pie	8461 frigid
8336 foamy match	8378 foamy coffee	8420 ferns	8462 Virginia
8337 have my mug	8379 heavy make-up	8421 friend	8463 fresh ham
8338 have my move	8380 have my voice	8422 free union	8464 fresh air
8339 have Mom buy	8381 foamy feet	8423 fire on him	8465 fragile
8340 have my rose	8382 foamy phone	8424 fury owner	8466 fresh show
8341 FM radio	8383 have my fame	8425 free nail	8467 fresh guy
8342 have my run	8384 have my fur	8426 French	8468 fire chief
8343 have my room	8385 have my file	8427 firing	8469 fresh up
8344 have more hair	8386 foamy fish	8428 heavy run off	8470 franks
8345 have my roll	8387 foamy fog	8429 free nap	8471 fur coat

8472 African	8514 flatter	8556 full eyelash	8598 fly above
8473 free game	8515 flood wall	8557 fall league	8599 flyaway baby
8474 Frogger	8516 flat shoe	8558 fail love	8600 have choices
8475 freckle	8517 follow dog	8559 full lip	8601 half jest
8476 fire coach	8518 fly it off	8560 fledges	8602 have chosen
8477 free cookie	8519 fly it up	8561 flu shot	8603 half chase him
8478 free coffee	8520 violins	8562 violation	8604 fishes here
8479 free cup	8521 flint	8563 fill huge home	8605 fishes well
8480 free office	8522 flyaway nun	8564 fill chair	8606 fish switch
8481 free food	8523 flown him	8565 full jail	8607 fudges week
8482 free phone	8524 follow owner	8566 full choo choo	8608 fishes off
8483 free fame	8525 flannel	8567 fuel check	8609 fetches boy
8484 forever	8526 avalanche	8568 full shove	8610 heavy jets
8485 firefly	8527 flying	8569 fill job	8611 vegetate
8486 free fish	8528 Villanova	8570 flags	8612 fish town
8487 free heavy guy	8529 flown up	8571 Flag Day	8613 fudge time
8488 free, half off	8530 flames	8572 volcano	8614 fetch water
8489 free halfway up	8531 flamed	8573 flag him	8615 fish tale
8490 free pass	8532 full moon	8574 full car	8616 fish dish
8491 everybody	8533 follow Mom	8575 half legal	8617 fish dock
8492 free, open	8534 fly more	8576 flag show	8618 fugitive
8493 fire bomb	8535 flame wall	8577 flag week	8619 fished by
8494 free bear	8536 fill my shoe	8578 awful cough	8620 fashions
8495 free ball	8537 fill my week	8579 full cup	8621 fish net
8496 free peach	8538 fly me off	8580 Oval Office	8622 vision honey
8497 fire back	8539 volume up	8581 velvet	8623 fudge name
8498 fire above	8540 flowers	8582 awful phone	8624 visionary
8499 free puppy	8541 Florida	8583 fluff him	8625 fish on wall
8500 heavy loses	8542 fill her in	8584 flavor	8626 fashion show
8501 velocity	8543 follow her home	8585 fulfill	8627 fishing
8502 Phillies win	8544 flower hair	8586 fluffy show	8628 vision a wife
8503 follows me	8545 flower hill	8587 fluffy wig	8629 fish in bay
8504 follows her	8546 flower show	8588 fluff off	8630 have shames
8505 falsely	8547 flower week	8589 fluff up	8631 fish meat
8506 false wish	8548 flower wife	8590 flips	8632 fetch money
8507 flu, sick	8549 flower boy	8591 flipped	8633 fetch Mom
8508 philosophy	8550 fill lease	8592 fly open	8634 fish more
8509 false hope	8551 full load	8593 flip him	8635 fish meal
8510 flood house	8552 fully alone	8594 flipper	8636 fish much
8511 flooded	8553 follow lamb	8595 volleyball	8637 fudge my week
8512 fall down	8554 fly lower	8596 flip shoe	8638 fish movie
8513 full time	8555 fill oil well	8597 fall back	8639 huge, jumbo

8640 heavy chores	8682 fishy phone	8724 fake honor	8766 foggy judge
8641 heavy shirt	8683 half shove him	8725 off canal	8767 fake check
8642 heavy journey	8684 fish fry	8726 have gun show	8768 fake chef
8643 heavy germ	8685 heavy shovel	8727 viking	8769 fake job
8644 fish thrower	8686 fish, fish	8728 fake knife	8770 heavy cakes
8645 fish roll	8687 fish off walkway	8729 fake nap	8771 half cooked
8646 heavy charge	8688 fish off wave	8730 vacuums	8772 fake gun
8647 fish wreck	8689 fishy VP	8731 vacuumed	8773 fake game
8648 heavy sheriff	8690 heavy jobs	8732 fake money	8774 fake car
8649 fish robe	8691 fish bait	8733 fake mummy	8775 fake eagle
8650 officials	8692 fetch bone	8734 vacuum hair	8776 fake cash
8651 official tie	8693 fish with bomb	8735 vacuum hallway	8777 fake kick
8652 official wine	8694 fish pier	8736 fake match	8778 foggy cave
8653 official home	8695 fishbowl	8737 heavy comic	8779 fake cop
8654 official hour	8696 fish, beach	8738 vague movie	8780 heavy coughs
8655 official law	8697 fetch book	8739 fake camp	8781 fake food
8656 official show	8698 fish above	8740 figures	8782 heavy coffin
8657 official wig	8699 fetch puppy	8741 figured	8783 fake fame
8658 official wave	8700 heavy axes	8742 foghorn	8784 fake fur
8659 official pie	8701 off the coast	8743 heavy cream	8785 heavy gavel
8660 heavy judges	8702 vaccine	8744 have a career	8786 fake fish
8661 half judged	8703 fakes him	8745 heavy gorilla	8787 fake, fake
8662 fish chain	8704 fakes her	8746 heavy crash	8788 wife gave half
8663 fishy gym	8705 fakes all	8747 half groggy	8789 wife gave up
8664 fish hatchery	8706 fakes age	8748 fake roof	8790 heavy caps
8665 fishy jail	8707 fake sick	8749 fake ruby	8791 fake bat
8666 fishy judge	8708 fogs off	8750 vehicles	8792 fake pen
8667 fudge check	8709 fogs up	8751 fickled	8793 fake bomb
8668 fishy chef	8710 vacates	8752 half gallon	8794 heavy copper
8669 fish / chip	8711 vacated	8753 heavy claim	8795 heavy cable
8670 fishhooks	8712 vacate now	8754 fake lawyer	8796 foggy beach
8671 heavy jacket	8713 victim	8755 vehicle law	8797 vague book
8672 half jokin'	8714 factory	8756 fickle show	8798 off, keep off
8673 fish gum	8715 heavy cattle	8757 fake leg	8799 fake pipe
8674 fishy car	8716 fake dish	8758 fig leaf	8800 heavy voices
8675 fish kill	8717 fake dog	8759 fickle boy	8801 have a feast
8676 fishy coach	8718 fake TV	8760 fake cheese	8802 heavy fasten
8677 fish cake	8719 wave goodbye	8761 fake shot	8803 heavy, heavy sum
8678 fish cave	8720 heavy guns	8762 vacation	8804 heavy officer
8679 heavy shake-up	8721 vacant	8763 fake jam	8805 half off sale
8680 fish face	8722 heavy cannon	8764 heavy catcher	8806 half off switch
8681 fish food	8723 fake name	8765 foggy jail	8807 heavy, heavy sack

8808 half off sofa	8850 wife flies	8892 half off piano	8934 off by more
8809 half off soap	8851 wife fled	8893 if, if a bomb	8935 FBI mail
8810 half off days	8852 heavy violin	8894 heavy viper	8936 FBI match
8811 wife waved, too	8853 wife flew me	8895 half off bail	8937 FBI mug
8812 heavy, heavy twin	8854 heavy flower	8896 half of a pouch	8938 FBI movie
8813 wife fed me	8855 half of a lily	8897 halfway off bike	8939 heavy pump
8814 half off tire	8856 I have flesh	8898 half off beehive	8940 half price
8815 half off hotel	8857 heavy flag	8899 half off puppy	8941 vibrate
8816 heavy, heavy dish	8858 five alive	8900 FBI sees you	8942 VP ran
8817 heavy, heavy dog	8859 half flip	8901 heavy post	8943 heavy broom
8818 half off TV	8860 half off cheese	8902 have passion	8944 February
8819 wife fed boy	8861 half off jet	8903 VP is home	8945 halfway by rail
8820 heavy fence	8862 have a vision	8904 VP is here	8946 heavy brush
8821 have found you	8863 half off gym	8905 heavy puzzle	8947 fabric
8822 half off onion	8864 half off chair	8906 heavy passage	8948 FBI rough
8823 half off name	8865 half off Jello	8907 wife buys wig	8949 FBI rope
8824 have funny hair	8866 fife, judge	8908 VP's wife	8950 fabulous
8825 heavy vinyl	8867 half off shake	8909 VP is up	8951 heavy plate
8826 half off nacho	8868 fife, chief	8910 heavy bats	8952 heavy plane
8827 heavy fang	8869 half off a ship	8911 FBI Dad	8953 heavy plum
8828 If I have a knife	8870 half off gas	8912 heavy baton	8954 heavy player
8829 heavy, heavy nap	8871 half faked	8913 off by a dime	8955 FBI will yell
8830 half famous	8872 half off gun	8914 FBI door	8956 heavy blush
8831 half off meal	8873 half off gum	8915 heavy battle	8957 FBI log
8832 heavy, heavy man	8874 half off car	8916 FBI dish	8958 VP will wave
8833 half off my home	8875 half off call	8917 FBI dog	8959 FBI alibi
8834 half off hammer	8876 half off couch	8918 half paid off	8960 ivy bushes
8835 half off meal	8877 half off cake	8919 half paid up	8961 VIP jet
8836 half off match	8878 half off coffee	8920 heavy pianos	8962 heavy passion
8837 half off mug	8879 half off cup	8921 viewpoint	8963 FBI shame
8838 half off movie	8880 half off vase	8922 heavy banana	8964 FBI jury
8839 half off, maybe	8881 half off food	8923 VIP name	8965 FBI jail
8840 heavy furs	8882 half off phone	8924 heavy pioneer	8966 fib the judge
8841 half off road	8883 half off foam	8925 off by a nil	8967 FBI joke
8842 heavy, heavy rain	8884 half off fur	8926 heavy punch	8968 VIP chef
8843 heavy frame	8885 half of filet	8927 fibbing	8969 VIP ship
8844 heavy, heavy rear	8886 half of fish	8928 FBI, Navy	8970 heavy books
8845 half frail	8887 half off, a fake	8929 wife - a pin-up	8971 heavy bucket
8846 half fresh	8888 half off, half off	8930 heavy bombs	8972 heavy bacon
8847 heavy frog	8889 half off, half pie	8931 VP met you	8973 FBI game
8848 half off roof	8890 half of bus	8932 FBI man	8974 FBI car
8849 half off rope	8891 half off body	8933 VIP Mom	8975 heavy buckle

8976 FBI coach	9018 passed off	9060 pass the cheese	9102 bad sun
8977 FBI cookie	9019 passed up	9061 busy jet	9103 potassium
8978 FBI cave	9020 business	9062 position	9104 Budweiser
8979 heavy backup	9021 poisoned	9063 busy gym	9105 beats well
8980 FBI office	9022 busy Nun	9064 posture	9106 bad switch
8981 VIP food	9023 poison him	9065 busy jail	9107 buy desk
8982 FBI phone	9024 peace on earth	9066 busy judge	9108 paid his wife
8983 VIP fame	9025 basin wall	9067 pass check	9109 bad soup
8984 FBI fire	9026 buys new watch	9068 busy chef	9110 bad days
8985 FBI file	9027 passing	9069 busy job	9111 potato head
8986 halfway by fish	9028 poison ivy	9070 basks	9112 bite down
8987 halfway by fog	9029 buy a snap	9071 basket	9113 bedtime
8988 half up, half off	9030 boy is messy	9072 pass the gun	9114 bad odor
8989 FBI, FBI	9031 boy is mad	9073 boy's comb	9115 paid toll
8990 heavy pipes	9032 busy man	9074 buys a car	9116 bad dish
8991 FBI pad	9033 busy Mom	9075 bicycle	9117 bad dog
8992 FBI pen	9034 pays more	9076 hopscotch	9118 bad TV
8993 have baby home	9035 happy smile	9077 boys kick	9119 potato pie
8994 heavy paper	9036 pays much	9078 buys coffee	9120 buttons
8995 heavy Bible	9037 buys a hammock	9079 pass the cup	9121 buttoned
8996 VIP beach	9038 boys movie	9080 boy's face	9122 bad onion
8997 FBI bag	9039 buys map	9081 pussy foot	9123 bad name
8998 FBI above you	9040 pass her house	9082 buys van	9124 boutonniere
8999 VIP baby	9041 bus ride	9083 boy's fame	9125 bought a nail
9000 passes us	9042 boys ran	9084 pacifier	9126 bad nacho
9001 passes it	9043 boys room	9085 pass file	9127 biting
9002 passes on	9044 boys roar	9086 boys fish	9128 beat Navy
9003 passes him	9045 boys are well	9087 Pacific	9129 button up
9004 bosses her	9046 boys are huge	9088 passive wife	9130 bottoms
9005 passes law	9047 busier guy	9089 busy VP	9131 bottom out
9006 buys his watch	9048 pass her off	9090 bus pass	9132 Batman
9007 passes egg	9049 passerby	9091 busy body	9133 beat Miami
9008 passes off	9050 puzzles	9092 buys pony	9134 bought more
9009 passes up	9051 puzzled	9093 pass by him	9135 bad meal
9010 pests	9052 baseline	9094 pass by her	9136 bad match
9011 posted	9053 buys lime	9095 baseball	9137 bought hammock
9012 Boston	9054 pays lawyer	9096 pass the peach	9138 bad movie
9013 passed him	9055 buys lily	9097 pass the buck	9139 beat him up
9014 poster	9056 buys leash	9098 pass above	9140 powders
9015 postal	9057 boys league	9099 pass baby	9141 patriot
9016 upstage	9058 busy life	9100 body size	9142 patron
9017 buys a dog	9059 boys leap	9101 Pizza Hut	9143 bedroom

9144 better hair	9186 pet fish	9228 been naive	9270 banks
9145 patrol	9187 paid off guy	9229 banana pie	9271 banged
9146 better show	9188 paid off wife	9230 been messy	9272 penguin
9147 buy truck	9189 paid the FBI	9231 been mad	9273 bunk them
9148 paid her off	9190 bad boys	9232 piano man	9274 bunker
9149 batter up	9191 bad bite	9233 been a Mom	9275 bungalow
9150 beetles	9192 bought pen	9234 buy new hammer	9276 bang shoe
9151 paddled	9193 paid up Ma	9235 open mail	9277 pancake
9152 battalion	9194 bad breathe	9236 open match	9278 bank fee
9153 battle hymn	9195 beatable	9237 open hammock	9279 bang up
9154 butler	9196 body patch	9238 open movie	9280 open face
9155 paddle wheel	9197 bad back	9239 open map	9281 benefit
9156 bite leash	9198 paid PMI	9240 pioneers	9282 been funny
9157 bad leg	9199 bad puppy	9241 pony ride	9283 been foamy
9158 bad love	9200 hypnosis	9242 pony ran	9284 bonfire
9159 bite lip	9201 poinsettia	9243 piano room	9285 painful
9160 bad cheese	9202 happy in sun	9244 bony rear	9286 bon voyage
9161 bad shot	9203 pains me	9245 buy new rail	9287 pain of a week
9162 beautician	9204 bouncer	9246 been rich	9288 pain of a wave
9163 bought a gym	9205 pencil	9247 bye New York	9289 ban the FBI
9164 badger	9206 opens show	9248 buy new roof	9290 open bus
9165 bad jail	9207 been sick	9249 buy new robe	9291 open pit
9166 bad judge	9208 open safe	9250 panels	9292 open, open
9167 bad check	9209 bounce up	9251 penalty	9293 open up home
9168 bad chef	9210 pants	9252 been alone	9294 piano bar
9169 pet shop	9211 bandit	9253 been lame	9295 pineapple
9170 pay tax	9212 happy Indian	9254 been lower	9296 open pouch
9171 beat egg white	9213 bantam	9255 bye Honolulu	9297 beanbag
9172 beauty queen	9214 painter	9256 be on leash	9298 open above
9173 bad game	9215 ponytail	9257 bony leg	9299 bony baby
9174 pit crew	9216 bandage	9258 be in love	9300 bombs house
9175 bad call	9217 paint egg	9259 bony lip	9301 bombs it
9176 paid cash	9218 paint wife	9260 banjos	9302 up the Amazon
9177 patty cake	9219 open top	9261 punched	9303 bombs them
9178 bat cave	9220 bananas	9262 pension	9304 bombs her
9179 pet guppy	9221 open window	9263 punch him	9305 bombs wall
9180 about face	9222 banana, honey	9264 puncher	9306 buy a massage
9181 bad food	9223 banana, ham	9265 punch wall	9307 buy music
9182 Beethoven	9224 banana hair	9266 bunch wash	9308 bomb is off
9183 beat VMI	9225 banana oil	9267 punch a guy	9309 bombs up
9184 paid for	9226 penny in shoe	9268 bunch ivy	9310 bombed house
9185 beautiful	9227 opening	9269 bunch up	9311 bombed out

9312 buy mitten	9354 pay my lawyer	9396 Palm Beach	9438 borrow movie
9313 happy medium	9355 buy me a lily	9397 bah humbug	9439 primp
9314 palm tree	9356 buy my a leash	9398 bump off	9440 barriers
9315 bombed all	9357 bum leg	9399 pump up	9441 priority
9316 bombed show	9358 buy me love	9400 bruises	9442 poor Iran
9317 buy me a dog	9359 palm, lip	9401 priest	9443 bar room
9318 buy me a TV	9360 buy matches	9402 person	9444 bury her here
9319 bombed up	9361 buy me a jet	9403 bruise him	9445 poor rule
9320 boy - a menace	9362 pie machine	9404 appraiser	9446 bury her shoe
9321 payment	9363 bomb chime	9405 Brazil	9447 poor rug
9322 bomb no one	9364 bomb the shore	9406 power switch	9448 poor roof
9323 bomb new home	9365 bombshell	9407 brisk	9449 barrier up
9324 bomb the owner	9366 bum judge	9408 pours half	9450 burials
9325 bimonthly	9367 buy me a shake	9409 bar is up	9451 bear will hide
9326 buy me a nacho	9368 pay my wife off	9410 pirates	9452 bury lion
9327 bombing	9369 buy me a job	9411 braided	9453 apple, lime
9328 bomb Navy	9370 buy my gas	9412 baritone	9454 poor lawyer
9329 bomb the NBA	9371 buy me a cat	9413 boredom	9455 parallel
9330 bomb my house	9372 buy me a gun	9414 braid hair	9456 bear will age
9331 pay me my due	9373 bum game	9415 bridle	9457 prologue
9332 pay Mom now	9374 buy me a car	9416 Broadway show	9458 barely off
9333 pay my Mom	9375 bum call	9417 boardwalk	9459 poor leap
9334 pay me more	9376 pay me cash	9418 borrow a TV	9460 brushes
9335 buy me a meal	9377 buy me a Coke	9419 pretty boy	9461 parachute
9336 bum match	9378 buy me coffee	9420 prunes	9462 operation
9337 bomb hammock	9379 buy me a cup	9421 burnt	9463 brush him
9338 bum movie	9380 happy movies	9422 pronoun	9464 brush hair
9339 beam me up	9381 buy me food	9423 brown ham	9465 brush well
9340 bombers	9382 bomb van	9424 brown hair	9466 prejudge
9341 palm read	9383 bomb VMI	9425 perennial	9467 brush wig
9342 a bomb ran	9384 buy me fur	9426 branch	9468 brush off
9343 bomb room	9385 bomb valley	9427 pruning	9469 brush up
9344 buy mirror	9386 bomb fish	9428 prune ivy	9470 breaks
9345 buy me a roll	9387 pay me half, OK	9429 brown ape	9471 barricade
9346 happy march	9388 pay my wife off	9430 brooms	9472 broken
9347 bomb Iraq	9389 a bomb above	9431 Bermuda	9473 pro game
9348 bomb roof	9390 bumps	9432 poor man	9474 breaker
9349 buy me a ruby	9391 pumped	9433 premium	9475 broccoli
9350 boy, I'm lazy	9392 buy me a pony	9434 primer	9476 pro coach
9351 boy, I'm late	9393 pom-pom	9435 poor meal	9477 break egg
9352 buy a melon	9394 bumper	9436 pro match	9478 break off
9353 buy me lime	9395 pimple	9437 borrow mug	9479 breakup

9480 privacy	9522 plain honey	9564 bleacher	9606 bashes show
9481 approved	9523 plain ham	9565 palatial	9607 pushes guy
9482 proven	9524 planner	9566 play judge	9608 pushes off
9483 perfume	9525 plainly	9567 play joke	9609 pushes up
9484 braver	9526 buy lunch	9568 play chef	9610 beach days
9485 profile	9527 playing	9569 blue chip	9611 pushed ahead
9486 preview show	9528 plain wife	9570 blackeyes	9612 beach town
9487 preview week	9529 plain boy	9571 blackout	9613 pushed him
9488 brave wife	9530 blooms	9572 pelican	9614 PGA Tour
9489 brave boy	9531 playmate	9573 ball game	9615 beach towel
9490 props	9532 blue moon	9574 apple core	9616 push, touch
9491 burped	9533 blame me	9575 black hole	9617 poached egg
9492 bourbon	9534 bloomer	9576 black shoe	9618 pushed off
9493 prep me	9535 blue mail	9577 apple cake	9619 pushed up
9494 barber	9536 play match	9578 block wave	9620 passions
9495 propel	9537 blame guy	9579 bulk up	9621 patient
9496 prep wash	9538 blame wife	9580 bluffs	9622 push onion
9497 barbecue	9539 blue map	9581 pillow fight	9623 push name
9498 prop wife	9540 players	9582 blue van	9624 push owner
9499 prep up	9541 blue, red	9583 blue foam	9625 push nail
9500 pleases	9542 ballerina	9584 play fair	9626 happy change
9501 pool side	9543 play room	9585 playful	9627 pushing
9502 bless wine	9544 bluer hair	9586 bluefish	9628 bash with knife
9503 bless him	9545 blue rail	9587 blue fog	9629 bash the NBA
9504 blazer	9546 blue arch	9588 bluff wife	9630 bash mouse
9505 blow whistle	9547 blue rock	9589 believe boy	9631 bash meat
9506 please wash	9548 blue roof	9590 apple pies	9632 happy showman
9507 please go	9549 blue robe	9591 pulpit	9633 peachy Mom
9508 plays off	9550 blue whales	9592 play piano	9634 push more
9509 bless boy	9551 play late	9593 bleep him	9635 push the mail
9510 plates	9552 play alone	9594 blueberry	9636 push match
9511 pleated	9553 apple, lime	9595 play ball	9637 push hammock
9512 platoon	9554 pale lawyer	9596 blue patch	9638 bash movie
9513 palladium	9555 blue lily	9597 play back	9639 happy champ
9514 apple tree	9556 blue leash	9598 plop off	9640 pagers
9515 bloody wall	9557 pull leg	9599 blue baby	9641 patch road
9516 blue dish	9558 belly laugh	9600 beach houses	9642 patch worn
9517 pillow talk	9559 blue lip	9601 hope chest	9643 patch room
9518 played off	9560 apple juice	9602 pushes on	9644 patch rear
9519 blood bath	9561 blushed	9603 pushes me	9645 push her well
9520 balloons	9562 pollution	9604 pushes her	9646 happy church
9521 plant	9563 bleach them	9605 patches hole	9647 patch rug

9648 patch roof	9690 push ups	9732 Pacman	9774 pack car
9649 peach robe	9691 bash bat	9733 back home, Ma	9775 back the call
9650 bushels	9692 push open	9734 pack more	9776 pack cash
9651 happy child	9693 bash palm	9735 pack mail	9777 bake cake
9652 push alone	9694 push bear	9736 back my show	9778 pack coffee
9653 peach, lime	9695 beach ball	9737 boy comic	9779 pack a cape
9654 bachelor	9696 push, push	9738 back my wife	9780 pack office
9655 peach will yellow	9697 push back	9739 back me up	9781 back foot
9656 bash eyelash	9698 push above	9740 bikers	9782 poke fun
9657 bush league	9699 push baby	9741 backyard	9783 buck fame
9658 patch love	9700 boxes	9742 buy greenery	9784 book fair
9659 push, help	9701 back seat	9743 back room	9785 pack file
9660 happy judges	9702 backs in	9744 happy career	9786 pack fish
9661 the boy judged	9703 buxom	9745 boy / girl	9787 buck the fog
9662 beach john	9704 boxer	9746 pack her wash	9788 pick off ivy
9663 bash gym	9705 packs well	9747 bike rack	9789 pie, coffee, pie
9664 push chair	9706 packs shoe	9748 biography	9790 peek a boos
9665 bash jail	9707 back is weak	9749 pick her up	9791 pack boat
9666 push judge	9708 backs off	9750 pickels	9792 back pain
9667 push check	9709 picks up	9751 piglet	9793 pack bomb
9668 push, shove	9710 pockets	9752 back line	9794 pick berry
9669 bash job	9711 polka dot	9753 pick lime	9795 pick apple
9670 up she goes	9712 backed in	9754 pick lawyer	9796 book page
9671 bushwhacked	9713 pocket them	9755 pick lily	9797 backpack
9672 beach wagon	9714 back door	9756 backlash	9798 pick up wife
9673 beach game	9715 big deal	9757 happy go lucky	9799 bagpipe
9674 buy sugar	9716 pocket watch	9758 pick leaf	9800 above his house
9675 bash cable	9717 back deck	9759 buckle up	9801 happy feast
9676 push couch	9718 picked off	9760 packages	9802 above sun
9677 bye Chicago	9719 packed up	9761 buck shot	9803 above his home
9678 patch cave	9720 pick nose	9762 pack china	9804 buy VCR
9679 happy check up	9721 back window	9763 back gym	9805 paves well
9680 beach office	9722 buy cannon	9764 picture	9806 buffs watch
9681 beach food	9723 beckon him	9765 pack shell	9807 buff rug
9682 push van	9724 bikini wear	9766 back judge	9808 pay off his wife
9683 beach foam	9725 up the canal	9767 back check	9809 buffs up
9684 push far	9726 bygone age	9768 pick a chef	9810 happy vets
9685 push, follow	9727 picnic	9769 pick job	9811 paved it
9686 push fudge	9728 pack knife	9770 peacocks	9812 above town
9687 beach fog	9729 pack'n up	9771 back gate	9813 above dome
9688 push wife off	9730 pack my house	9772 pack gun	9814 above door
9689 a pushy VP	9731 pack meat	9773 pack comb	9815 above hotel

9816 wipe off dish	9858 above leaf	9900 happy babies	9942 pepperoni
9817 paved walkway	9859 above lip	9901 babysit	9943 baby room
9818 above TV	9860 buff shoes	9902 pops in	9944 baby rear
9819 above tub	9861 buff jet	9903 baby's home	9945 pep rally
9820 above nose	9862 wipe off chin	9904 baby's hair	9946 buy a brush
9821 above window	9863 buff, gym	9905 baby's well	9947 paprika
9822 above no one	9864 above chair	9906 baby's age	9948 baby - rough
9823 above name	9865 above the jail	9907 baby is awake	9949 baby robe
9824 buff the winner	9866 above judge	9908 pops off	9950 bubbles
9825 buff nail	9867 pave huge walk	9909 Papa's boy	9951 buy a plate
9826 happy finch	9868 above chief	9910 puppets	9952 Babylon
9827 paving	9869 above ship	9911 popped head	9953 pop limb
9828 buff knife	9870 buy fakes	9912 pipe down	9954 popular
9829 above knob	9871 above the coat	9913 wipe bottom	9955 baby lily
9830 above mouse	9872 above wagon	9914 puppeteer	9956 publish
9831 above my head	9873 above comb	9915 baby hotel	9957 public
9832 buff money	9874 happy figure	9916 puppet show	9958 puppy love
9833 above Mom	9875 above the call	9917 baby Doc	9959 bubble bath
9834 pave more	9876 above the coach	9918 popped off	9960 peep shows
9835 happy female	9877 above the cake	9919 baby top	9961 baby jet
9836 above my shoe	9878 above cave	9920 baboons	9962 baby john
9837 above hammock	9879 above cap	9921 baby net	9963 baby gym
9838 above my wife	9880 above office	9922 buy banana	9964 baby shower
9839 above the map	9881 above foot	9923 baby name	9965 buy a bushel
9840 beavers	9882 above the phone	9924 baby winner	9966 baby judge
9841 pave road	9883 above fame	9925 pop nail	9967 baby jog
9842 above the rain	9884 above fire	9926 buy a bunch	9968 baby chef
9843 buff arm	9885 above file	9927 popping	9969 baby job
9844 above rear	9886 above fish	9928 baby knife	9970 P.O. Box
9845 buff rail	9887 above fog	9929 baby nap	9971 baby, cute
9846 beverage	9888 pave half off	9930 baby mouse	9972 pop gun
9847 above rock	9889 above the FBI	9931 baby mad	9973 baby game
9848 above roof	9890 above the boss	9932 baby money	9974 baby care
9849 above rope	9891 above boat	9933 baby, Mommy	9975 baby eagle
9850 bevels	9892 pave open	9934 baby hammer	9976 baby couch
9851 beveled	9893 above palm	9935 baby meal	9977 baby cake
9852 pavilion	9894 above the bear	9936 baby match	9978 buy back half
9853 above limb	9895 above the ball	9937 baby mug	9979 baby cup
9854 buff lower	9896 above beach	9938 baby movie	9980 baby face
9855 above lily	9897 pave back	9939 pop him up	9981 baby food
9856 buff eyelash	9898 pave above	9940 papers	9982 baby phone
9857 above leg	9899 above the Pope	9941 paperweight	9983 baby fame

9984 **pop** over
9985 **pop** fly
9986 **baby** fish
9987 **pop** off, **OK**
9988 **pop** half off
9989 **baby** the **VP**
9990 **baby** wipes
9991 **baby bat**
9992 **pop** open
9993 **pipe bomb**
9994 **Papa Bear**
9995 **buy Bible**
9996 **pop, push**
9997 **baby back**
9998 **pop** above
9999 **pop pop**

Index

CPSIA information can be obtained
at www.ICGtesting.com
Printed in the USA
FFOW05n2324121015